VISUAL BASIC® 6.0
INTERNET PROGRAMMING

VISUAL BASIC® 6.0 INTERNET PROGRAMMING

Carl Franklin

WILEY COMPUTER PUBLISHING

John Wiley & Sons, Inc.
New York • Chichester • Weinheim • Brisbane • Singapore • Toronto

Publisher: Robert Ipsen
Editor: Cary Sullivan
Managing Editor: Micheline Frederick
Electronic Products, Associate Editor: Mike Sosa
Text Design & Composition: Benchmark Productions, Inc.

This book is printed on acid-free paper. ∞

This publication is designed to provide accurate and authoritative information in regard to the subject matter covered. It is sold with the understanding that the publisher is not engaged in professional services. If professional advice or other expert assistance is required, the services of a competent professional person should be sought.

Library of Congress Cataloging-in-Publication Data:
Franklin, Carl.
  Visual basic 6.0 internet programming / Carl Franklin.
        p.   cm.
  Includes index.
  ISBN 0-471-31498-6
  1. Microsoft Visual BASIC. 2. Internet programming. I. Title.
QA76.73.B3F725   1998
005.7'12768--dc21   98-33730
                                                         CIP

Printed in the United States of America.

10 9 8 7 6 5 4 3 2 1

"For my late father, John Jay Franklin. You taught me peace of mind—by example."

CONTENTS

Chapter 5   Electronic Mail   93

FOREWORD

Well, here we are again. Another version of Visual Basic (VB), a new operating system, a new family of microprocessors, and another Internet programming book and fortunately for me, there aren't that many other VB Internet programming books on the shelves, and I'm not complaining a bit.

The topic of Internet programming in Visual Basic spans many tools and technologies. Many of these tools operate at a higher level than the code in this book, while some operate at a lower level. I chose to write the example code at a low enough level so that you can understand the processes, but high enough so that you're not completely focused on code that does the arduous tasks of communications.

Winsock is a library of functions and routines that all Windows programs use when they want to access the Internet. It provides the low-level functions of sending and receiving data, as well as tools for managing connections, and everything else that has to do with basic Internet communications.

My code uses a Winsock control for communications, whereas some other books opt to access the Winsock library directly. I believe that it is neither beneficial nor necessary to do this. The real bottleneck in Internet communications is the Internet connection itself. You don't gain anything by saving a few nanoseconds, if indeed you actually can. If you really want to get the best performance, get a faster Internet connection. The benefits you gain by programming at a higher level are too numerous to ignore.

That said, there are other books that focus on higher level tools that do everything for you. You just tell a control to send an email message and it just happens. While most of the time this approach works great, there may be situations in which you need to make changes in the process due to the quirks and features of the e-mail server that you are accessing. When that happens, you need the source code. But, you need source code that is easy to follow, therefore easy to understand, therefore easy to change.

Included with this book are high-level tools that send and receive email, and access FTP and Usenet News servers (if your forehead is scrunched and your upper lip looks like Elvis' don't worry, you'll read all about these things in the book). But, you have the source code as well. Not only that, but I'll walk you through it, so you can understand the process of how these things work.

I'm not going to show you how the Winsock library works under the hood, but you don't need to know that. What I will show you is how to access the most popular services on the Internet by sending data and processing received data. And along the way, I promise it will be fun. Maybe not as fun as skydiving into a swimming pool filled with lime Jell-O, but you never know.

The last thing I'd like to tell you before you get started is that I operate a web site for issues that come up regarding this book and the example code. The URL is carl.franklins.net/vbip. Please check this out if and when you have questions about the code, or anything else related to the book. I keep a knowledge base of issues on the web site, and you can often get answers with a few mouse clicks.

THE INTERNET

Attack of the Buzzwords!

"Hey, can you show me how to surf the net?"

"Sure, let's check out the web! We can download some streaming videos!"

"Wow, I feel like a warrior of cyberspace! We're zooming down the Information Superhighway, just like those AT&T commercials!"

The Internet will go down in history as the big public discovery of the 1990s, even though it's been around for years. From the late 1960s, when the Internet was started, until the early 1990s, the Internet had been primarily the domain of Unix users, mostly at universities and research facilities around the world. Only recently has the Internet been made available to a wide array of Windows users, who've been flooding it with traffic. Once it became widely available to Windows users in early 1993, the Internet began to see a steady increase in use that grows exponentially every day.

The Internet is vast. There are millions of computers connected by it all over the world. I say connected *by* it and not *to* it because the Internet is not a computer, it's a network. It is not the computers but the *medium* by which computers communicate with each other.

There are lots of ways to access data on the Internet. The most popular way is via the World Wide Web (*the web*). The World Wide Web (WWW) is a collection of published pages that have links to each other within them. For example, there might be a page all about gardening, with pictures of flowers and trees. At the bottom of the page, there could be a list of related pages all over the world that show up as hypertext (underlined and colored) links. One click on a link, and you're instantly connected to another computer, which could be anywhere on the Internet all over the world. That page may have links to a few other pages, and you can keep going and going until you just can't take it anymore! This activity is sometimes called *surfing the net* and is the primary cause of computer widowdom all over America.

The biggest problem that users of the Internet face, and which has generated the most complaints, is that people can't find what they are looking for with any degree of ease. Sometimes, specific information cannot be found at all. The reason is the incredible diversity of user interface on Internet host computers.

As an example of this, the Library of Congress catalog is accessed by Telnet, a text-based terminal in which the user interface is custom to the program, much like a DOS program. Many universities publish papers on Gopher servers, a hierarchy of menus and documents, the design of which varies from host to host. At each potential source of information there is a learning curve, and therein lies the problem. The World Wide Web is nice because everything is graphical and mostly easy to understand, but it suffers from the same problem. There are no rules to how you present information. The WWW user interface takes less time to learn than Telnet or Gopher, but the problem still exists.

From what I have gathered, many programmers are at first slightly afraid of the Internet. You may have had some experience or heard horror stories about implementing serial communications either under DOS or Windows. I can tell you from experience it is not an easy task. The coding part is pretty much straight ahead, but there are so many low-level issues that have to be addressed with modems that it can get pretty hairy to support a serial-enabled application.

I have gotten calls from fellow programmers who are knee-deep in supporting Windows serial port applications (such as bulletin board systems, terminal programs, or custom applications that communicate through the serial port) complaining that their software doesn't work with a particular modem, or that a particular modem doesn't hang up when you try to disconnect, or whatever. The developer ends up being a liaison between the customer and the modem company, which is always a pleasant situation to be in. Kind of like a whipping boy for both parties.

The fact is that application software developers should not have to support hardware. The reason for this big mess with modems and software is because the serial port driver talks directly to the hardware, and there are no layers between them to do any kind of robust error handling. Today, most modems have error handling built right in, but some don't! What happens when a modem with error handling connects to one without it? No error handling! The result: Software developers have to do extra error handling in their application to support modems that don't handle errors during the transmission of data. It shouldn't have to be that way, and fortunately it isn't.

I am here to tell you that you can now write communications software the way you have always wanted to: That is, with the knowledge that when you receive data there is no line noise in it, and it is exactly what was sent to you. If you want to send a file, just send the data. It's easier than writing to a file. Using the tools in this book, you can write an application that can communicate with another application anywhere in the world using a modem, a network connection, wireless, or what have you. You don't even need to use the Internet to benefit from this technology. Your application is separated from the network, and will work on any machine that uses the TCP/IP protocol.

Without getting too much ahead of myself, the method by which you as a Visual Basic (VB) programmer will access the Internet is Windows Sockets (Winsock). The tools included with this book make this extremely easy. The good news is that Winsock isn't just for the Internet. You can just as easily communicate with another application on the same machine, as you can with an application on your Local Area Network (LAN), or within your domain, or anywhere in the world. A domain is simply a larger group of smaller groups of computers. You can develop both the client and the server applications on your desktop. When you move them to separate locations the only thing that changes is the Socket, or the address of the application. Add to that a robust network architecture that does error checking for you so you can concentrate on writing software. Sounds nice, doesn't it?

Given the robustness of Winsock, you may choose to use it in place of the following technologies:

1. Direct serial port modem programming.
2. Dynamic Data Exchange (DDE).
3. Network DDE.
4. Mailslots.

It is easy to see why Winsock should be used in place of direct serial port access: reliability and abstraction. By using Winsock you can support a wider market than those who only use modems can. Not only that, but you remove yourself from the hardware. There are at least two layers between your application and the hardware, and sometimes three, as you will read shortly. The new generation of operating systems utilizes the modem directly as another piece of the network architecture. If your customer has trouble with the modem, they contact the modem manufacturer, or if there is a problem with the network software, they contact Microsoft (or the network software manufacturer). You like this idea, I'm sure.

DDE programming is always frustrating. The reason for this is applications that expose functionality via DDE do not follow any kind of standards. The implementation presents a learning curve for each application that uses it. For example, manipulating data in an Excel spreadsheet is very different from sending a fax with WinFax Pro. Also, there isn't any liaison between a DDE client application and a DDE server application. This lends itself to errors beyond the scope of most VB programmers. DDE was actually a steppingstone to OLE (Object Linking and Embedding), Microsoft's inter-application communication system.

You may not have heard of Mailslots. Mailslots is a network Application Programming Interface (API) for inter-application communications on a basic send-and-receive level. You don't hear much about Mailslots. I have tried using it and it didn't live up to my expectations. Presumably for the same reason DDE doesn't always work, there isn't any abstraction between your application and another application, and there is no reliability intelligence built into Mailslots.

Picture this: You wake up in the morning, pour some coffee, rub the fruitcake out of your eyes, and sit down at the PC equipped with Windows 2000 and a satellite-based Internet connection. There is a little icon on your desktop that looks like a newspaper. You click it, and you are reading a summary of the daily news. You sip your coffee. You observe the wallpaper bitmap on the Windows desktop, a satellite weather photo taken just 15 minutes ago. You look at it, noticing a storm approaching from the east. You open the shade and see it's snowing like crazy (for those of you not familiar with snow, it's what happens when rain freezes). Realizing that the roads are closed, you resign yourself to a little chat with your electronic penpal in Barbados. You double-click an icon that says "SuperChat" on the desktop. You pick your friend's name from a list and within a few seconds you see your friend's greeting at the top of the window, "Hello there, what's up?" You type, "Not much, what are you doing?" Your friend replies, "Sitting on my porch looking at the ocean and soaking up the sun, how about you?" You type, "Sitting in my office watching the snow fall and feeling the heat from the furnace on my feet."

Well, daydream no more. After reading this book, you will be writing applications just like these, and even cooler ones.

Protocols and Data

Upon looking in *Webster's Dictionary* for the word *protocol*, I found a slew of different meanings ranging from "first sheet of a papyrus roll bearing data of manufacture" to "glue" to "record or minute" to "code." In the context of computers and networking, a protocol is a set of codes or rules; a method by which data is moved between devices.

The simplest example of a real-world protocol that I can think of is calling information for somebody's phone number. It starts with you dialing 411. The operator then answers and asks "What city please?" You reply with the name of a city. The operator then says, "Yes?" prompting you to say the name of the party whose number you are looking for. The operator looks up the number and gives it to you.

There is a set of rules that must be followed for a communication to be effective. If you do not know the rules, you might get the wrong number, or it just might take more time for you to get the right number. Can you imagine what would happen if you were following one set of rules, and the operator was following another? Actually, this premise has been used as the basis of many famous comedy routines:

OPERATOR:	"What city please?"
ME:	"Yes, I'll have a Jumbo with extra cheese, small fries, and a medium root beer."
OPERATOR:	"Excuse me?"
ME:	"Oh, I'm sorry, make that a large fry."
OPERATOR:	"What city?!"
ME:	"Oh, I see . . . make it a number 3 meal!"
OPERATOR:	"*What city?!*"
ME:	"What?"
OPERATOR:	"What city does the party live in?"
ME:	"The party's at my house in Mystic."
OPERATOR:	"And the name in Mystic?"
ME:	"Franklin, Carl Franklin. . . . Why do you want my. . ."
OPERATOR:	"The number is 555-5742."
ME:	"You mean, I have to take a *number*!? How long is the wait?"

Have you ever tried to upload a file manually to someone with a terminal program, and the other person has no idea what they're doing? You say to them, "Use the Zmodem protocol," and they pick Ymodem by accident. You both start the transfer and nothing happens. Why? Because one of you is waiting for the city name, and the other is ordering a Jumbo with extra cheese. The protocols don't match.

Using a protocol in networking isn't any different than using a protocol to transfer a file with a modem. The only difference is that network protocols are used to move all forms of data, not just files, between machines on the network, in real time.

Which brings me to the data itself. Different protocols have different names for *chunks* of data: messages, packets, streams, datagrams. These are all names for the same thing—a definable chunk of data that is passed through and processed by the network and its protocols.

You can write your own protocol if you wish. A protocol does not have to have incredibly complex algorithms. It can be as simple as one machine sending another machine a one-byte command, and the other machine sending back *n* bytes of data based on the command it received. In this book, we will be implementing popular protocols used on the Internet as Visual Basic code, which you can reuse in your own applications. These protocols are documented at the Internet Network Information Center (InterNIC) in documents called RFC documents.

RFC stands for *Request For Comments*, a collection of public documents that act both as an open forum for new ideas pertaining to the Internet, and as a source of documentation of existing protocols. RFCs are numbered. The CD-ROM that comes with this book contains all of the RFCs in their current form as of the fourth quarter of 1998.

Protocol Stacks and the OSI Model

If you are not familiar with what a protocol stack is, and are merely interested in how to write applications in Visual Basic that access the Internet, I am here to tell you that you can skip over this section with a clear conscience. Understanding the protocol stack is not crucial for successful Internet VB programming. However, knowledge of these concepts can help you understand where your Visual Basic application fits in the big picture.

The term *stack* comes from the conception of the Open Systems Interconnection (OSI) Reference Model, a conceptual framework for the design and implementation of computer networks developed in the early 1980s by the International Standards Organization (ISO). Although the Internet doesn't adhere exactly to the OSI Reference Model, the model is a useful way to understand how all networks operate.

The essence of the OSI model is a layer-cake metaphor, in which there are seven discrete layers. At each layer a function is performed by any number of protocols when data is transmitted between applications on a network. At the top is your application, at the bottom is the hardware, and everything in between supports the top and bottom layers. Think of data originating in the source application, moving down the stack to the hardware and up the stack at the destination application. Figure 1.1 shows the seven layers. From bottom to top they are: Physical, Data Link, Network, Transport, Session, Presentation, and Application. Each layer has its own responsibilities. You would not expect code at the Application layer to manipulate hardware directly. That is a no-no for proper network operation. These responsibilities will become clear shortly, unless of course you are reading in the dark.

At the Physical layer, there are cables, wires, and other electronic gadgets through which data travels. The responsibility at the Physical layer is for the circuits to be designed and implemented correctly. Data should move free of interference and noise, and the signal should be as strong as possible. You get the idea.

The Data Link layer defines the format of transmitted data relative to the Physical layer, including the logistics of how data is moved around. How are machines identified? How do you package data so that it is recognizable by other machines? The answers to these questions are different depending on the Physical

Figure 1.1 OSI model.

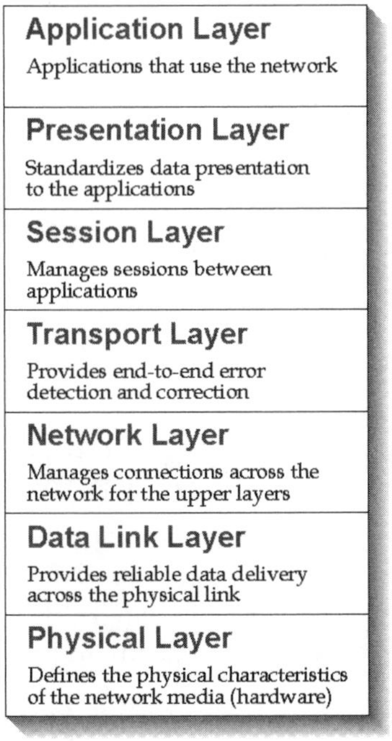

Application Layer
Applications that use the network

Presentation Layer
Standardizes data presentation to the applications

Session Layer
Manages sessions between applications

Transport Layer
Provides end-to-end error detection and correction

Network Layer
Manages connections across the network for the upper layers

Data Link Layer
Provides reliable data delivery across the physical link

Physical Layer
Defines the physical characteristics of the network media (hardware)

layer (LAN, T1 line, modem, etc.). The Data Link layer doesn't do the actual sending and receiving of data, it is just concerned with how data is packaged and interpreted from the Physical layer. You may be familiar with the word *packet*. A packet is a unit of data that is defined by the Data Link layer. It is also what you do to a suitcase.

The Network layer is responsible for moving packets of data from point A to point B. For the Internet, this is handled by routing packets through the path of least resistance, so to speak, so that they get to their final destination in the most efficient manner. The Internet Protocol (IP) handles this problem on the Internet.

The Transport layer is concerned with managing the transmission of data from point A to point B. This is where the actual delivery of data takes place. In the case of the Internet, this is accomplished by Transmission Control Protocol (TCP) or User Datagram Protocol (UDP), which we will talk about shortly.

The Physical, Data Link, Network, and Transport layers of the OSI Reference Model make up what are called the lower layers of the stack. The top three layers from bottom to top are the Session layer, the Presentation layer, and the Application layer.

The Session layer is utilized in a Local Area Network and is responsible for things such as managing when the network is accessed so that no two users attempt to access it at the exact same time, and basically providing an applications-oriented data stream to the session user.

The Presentation layer determines the format of data transmitted by applications. For example, ASCII is the most common format of transmitted data. Any data encryption such as Pretty Good Privacy (PGP) is done at the Presentation layer. Data compression and expansion is also handled at this layer.

The Application layer is where your Visual Basic application resides. Programs such as terminals, electronic mail readers, web browsers, and so forth all transmit and receive data on top of the Presentation layer of the OSI Reference Model.

TCP/IP

TCP/IP is a collection (or suite) of protocols whose name stands for two of its primary protocols, TCP (Transmission Control Protocol) and IP (Internet Protocol). Just to help avoid unnecessary embarrassment, the proper pronunciation is to spell out the letters: T-C-P-I-P, and not to say "Tick-pip" or some such nonsense. TCP resides at the Transport layer, and IP at the Network layer. What we call TCP/IP is not limited to these two protocols, but instead describes the entire suite of protocols used with the Internet.

Names and Addresses

IP uses a special addressing scheme to identify a connection. I use the word *connection* because although we identify computers by IP address, the address actually defines the connection between the computer and the network. Don't let it throw you, though. For all intents and purposes we can identify each computer on the network by its IP address.

An IP address is made up of four 8-bit numbers (from 0 to 255) separated by periods. For example, the IP address of the machine running Carl & Gary's Visual Basic Home Page is 206.210.64.181.

Because it is more difficult to remember numbers than it is to remember names, every IP address can have a name. The name of Carl & Gary's server is www.cgvb.com. The rightmost word in the name is called the *top-level domain*. Inside the United States, the top-level domain defines the type of organization. For example, gov = government, com = commercial organization, edu = educational institution, net = network, org = noncategorized organization, and so on. Outside the United States, though, the top-level domain usually identifies the country or continent. For example, jp = Japan, uk = United Kingdom, and so forth.

IP addresses and names of domains are issued by the Internet Network Information Center (InterNIC). For a nominal fee you can apply to register a domain name, which can then have several machines, the exact number of which is defined by the class of domain you register. Without spending too much time on this, different classes of IP addresses exist for accommodating a small or large group of computers in a given domain. For more information you can connect to the InterNIC's web site at www.internic.net.

Ports

An IP address identifies a machine or other device on the Internet. An IP port identifies an application running on an Internet host machine. Unlike serial communications, where you may have four ports, there is no functional limit to the number of IP ports you can have. This is because a port is just a number. If you were to count the number of applications running on your machine right now (or whenever you are at your machine), and assign each application a number, you have grasped the concept of an IP port. It simply identifies an application.

There are some applications that will always have the same port number, and you will see why in a minute. To access an application on an Internet host machine you need to know the machine name (or IP address), and you need to know the port number. If you have those two pieces of information, you can communicate with that host application.

For example, all World Wide Web servers communicate on port 80. This makes it easy for clients like Netscape and MS Internet Explorer to jump from web server to web server in an instant. The port is a given—80. The only piece of information needed to connect to a web server is the machine name or IP address. Once connected you can use the Hypertext Transfer Protocol (HTTP) to communicate with the web server, retrieving documents, graphics, music, video, or whatever is available.

There are quite a few reserved ports when using TCP/IP. Here is a list of some of the more popular Internet applications and the ports they use:

1. HTTP (WWW)   80
2. FTP   20 and 21
3. Gopher   70
4. SMTP (e-mail)   25
5. POP3 (e-mail)   110
6. Telnet   23
7. Whois   43
8. Finger   79

Name Resolution

As previously stated, any connection that has an IP address can also have a name. Names are not required but they do make it easier for people to access machines on the network. The network doesn't understand names, though. It understands IP addresses.

There are two methods for resolving names into addresses. The old method, still in use, is to store all names and addresses in a text file called HOSTS. In Unix, this table is accessible in a shared directory. In Windows95 this file exists in the \WINDOWS directory of each machine on the network. In Windows NT it resides in the \WINNT\System32\Drivers\etc directory. It is up to the user (usually) to edit this file if need be.

The file format is incredibly simple. On each line, specify an IP address followed by at least one space, and then one or more names separated by at least one space. For example, you might have an entry for Carl & Gary's VB Home Page:

206.210.64.181   www.cgvb.com

The disadvantage of this system is pretty obvious. Name resolution is a global issue; it is not local to your machine. If everyone in the world used a HOSTS file for name resolution, you'd have to give everybody your IP address and machine name, and they would have to make an entry before they even connected to you. If your IP address changes, everyone's HOSTS file needs to be updated. The advantage of using the HOSTS file system is primarily for systems that do not use the Internet, but use TCP/IP on a local network. It serves as a quick solution to name resolution when there is no other option.

The currently used method for resolving names is using a system called the Domain Name System (DNS). DNS is a distributed database that contains IP addresses for all registered Internet hosts.

Sockets

A socket is simply the combination of an IP address and port. It can be said, therefore, that a socket identifies an application running anywhere on the Internet. This idea originates from the Berkeley Software Distribution system, created at the University of California at Berkeley. In this system, there lives an API called Berkeley Sockets, which is widely used in the world of Unix programming for Internet communications.

When you hear the word *socket*, it may mean several things. First and foremost, it refers to the combination of an IP address and port, as in the earlier definition. However, it can also refer to Berkeley Sockets, a set of functions for Unix programmers that provides Internet access. There is one other definition of sockets, though, and that is Windows Sockets, a similar set of functions for Windows programmers that provides Internet access. The Windows Sockets 1.1 API (or Winsock) is consistent with release 4.3 of the Berkeley Software Distribution, and also provides Windows-specific routines to aid in the process of writing Windows applications that communicate via the Internet. When I refer to a socket, I mean a Winsock socket connection, consisting of an IP address and a port.

The reason Winsock is so cool is because of its high-level accessibility. There are only 44 functions in Winsock 1.1, so implementation is fairly straight ahead in a C/C++ environment.

But what about Visual Basic? As you would expect, there are a few people (including Microsoft) trying to make Winsock programming even easier by creating programming tools that simplify access to the API. As of this writing there are a handful of commercial ActiveX controls, and a couple of shareware controls. Microsoft also has a Winsock control. I can tell you from experience that the best one I've seen so far is a shareware ActiveX control called DSSOCK, from Dolphin Systems in Toronto, Canada. It supports all versions of Visual Basic (as well as other platforms), and they even have a .VBX for you Visual Basic 3.0 enthusiasts. The latest version of DSSOCK is included with this book, and all of the sample code uses them.

The TCP/IP Model

Although TCP/IP's implementation closely resembles the OSI Reference Model, the most widely accepted description of the TCP/IP model (although there are many) has four layers: Application, Host to Host Transport, Internet, and Network Access (see Figure 1.2). At each layer, a special header is tacked onto each packet as it passes down the stack. When data comes up the stack at the receiving application, the header information is stripped off at each layer. This process is called *encapsulation*.

At the lowest level in the TCP/IP model is the Network Access layer. It provides the functionality of the Physical, Data Link, and Network layers of the OSI model. Its functions include mapping IP addresses to physical network addresses, and encapsulating IP datagrams (packets) into data that the local network understands. Because TCP/IP works with many different types of networks, the Physical layer of the Internet is not handled by TCP/IP. In the case of Windows, TCP/IP's Network Access layer is in the form of a network driver.

The Internet layer sits right above the Network Access layer, and is really the heart of TCP/IP. The Internet Protocol, or IP, does most of the work at this layer.

Figure 1.2 TCP model.

Application Layer
Applications and processes that use the network
Host To Host Transport Layer
Provides end-to-end data delivery services
Internet Layer
Defines the datagram and handles the routing of data
Network Access Layer
Consists of routines for accessing physical networks

IP provides the framework for the delivery of data from point A to point B. IP is a connectionless protocol, meaning that it does not have to have an acknowledgment of connection (or handshake) from the other side to begin sending data. IP instead relies upon other protocols (namely TCP) to handle this important function. IP also does not do any error handling. Again, this task is left to other protocols.

Let's say you have a Visual Basic command called TCP_Print that sends a string of data to the host you are currently connected to via TCP/IP. Let's say we call this command with a 1024-byte string. The task is to send 1024 bytes from your application to your host application, which for the sake of argument, let's say, is a simple data terminal running on a Windows NT machine in the back office of a brewery in Munich (hey, this is my fantasy). IP breaks the data into several datagrams, each with a header containing, among other things, the IP address and port of the terminal application in Germany. The IP sends each datagram to a gateway that is connected to both the local network and an Internet Access Provider's network. The term *gateway* can mean any machine that passes on received datagrams, but in this case I am talking specifically about an IP router, which is an intelligent device whose sole purpose is to move datagrams to and from other connections. IP looks at the destination address and decides where to send the datagram so that it will arrive at its destination the fastest. This ability to determine the path of least resistance is what makes IP and the Internet extremely efficient and reliable. If a router goes down, IP just finds a new route. This characteristic was extremely important to the designers of TCP/IP. The network must be able to adapt to the prospect of numerous gateways being shut down (or blown up) in the event of nuclear war. As you can see, they did it right.

I know, I know, this book is about Visual Basic. You don't really need to know how TCP/IP works in order to write applications that use it, but bear with me. When you understand how rich this protocol is, it may change the way you approach writing VB applications, as you will see shortly.

The layer of the TCP/IP model directly above the Network layer is called the Host-to-Host Transport layer. The two most important protocols used here are TCP and UDP. TCP provides reliable data transmission and error correction for moving data from source to destination. UDP is a connectionless datagram delivery protocol that does not perform reliability checking or error correction; it simply moves data blindly from point A to point B.

You might be wondering "What good is UDP if it's not reliable?" Plenty, actually: Since UDP does not do any special handling of data, it is faster than TCP. Also, UDP is useful for sending small blurbs of the same piece of data over and over again, like the timeserver protocol on port 37. When you connect to a timeserver on port 37 you receive a string containing the time of day (GMT) over and over again. It does not matter if one of those time packets did not make it to your application; you'll get the next one.

TCP, on the other hand, is a connection-based error-handling protocol, and is widely used throughout the Internet for moving data around. TCP verifies that data was sent across the network and that it is received in the proper sequence. When datagrams are sent across the network, they may arrive at the destination in random order. If there are five datagrams in a transmission, the destination may receive number three first, then number four and five, followed by two and then one. This is not uncommon because, if you remember, IP routes datagrams according to the path of least resistance at the time of transmission. This is the really amazing part of TCP/IP. Fifty percent of your datagrams may have arrived by way of New Zealand, 25 percent by way of the United Kingdom, and 25 percent by way of Australia. To me, that's just incredible.

The Application layer of the TCP/IP model is the same as in the OSI model, except that it performs all functions above the OSI model Transport layer, which include the Presentation layer (how data is formatted and recognized) and the Session layer (synchronizing access to the network, etc.). Among the most widely known application protocols at this layer are Hypertext Transport Protocol (HTTP), the language of the World Wide Web; File Transfer Protocol (FTP), the most common way of accessing files through the Internet; Simple Mail Transfer Protocol (SMTP), which deals with moving e-mail messages around; and Network News Transfer Protocol (NNTP), which is used by Usenet News clients and servers.

For more information on the inner workings of TCP/IP, I suggest the following book: *TCP/IP Network Administration*, by Craig Hunt (O'Reilly & Associates, ISBN: 0-937175-82-X).

Hey, wake up! Class dismissed.

WINSOCK PROGRAMMING

Introduction

In this chapter, you will learn about dsSocket, the Winsock ActiveX control included with this book. You will learn how to create both client and server applications quickly and easily.

dsSocket was first released as a shareware VBX for VB 3.0. The implementation is the best I've ever seen, but you should be aware that unregistered copies exhibit a quite annoying splash screen when loaded into memory. It will cost you a fee for the registered version, which does not have a splash screen. In my opinion, it is well worth it. If you are just going to mess around with Winsock and the Internet, you may be willing to live with the splash screen, but it is not wise to ship a commercial application that displays someone else's logo when it starts up. If you wish to purchase a registered copy of dsSocket, you can call, write, or e-mail Dolphin Systems at:

Dolphin Systems
20132 Shaws Creek Rd.
Alton, Ontario L0N 1A0
Phone: (519) 942-0344
Fax: (519) 942-8111
E-mail: stephenc@dophinsys.com

I should point out that Microsoft does ship a Winsock control with Visual Basic. The reason that I don't recommend it is because it is not complete enough to use in a real-world situation. dsSocket, on the other hand, has been used in the real world by its designers, is bug-free, and has been well-supported since version 1.0.

Why Not Use the Winsock API?

This is a good question. Ambitious programmers may want to use the Winsock API directly from Visual Basic, but it requires more work. However, if you want to maintain the ultimate level of control, I recommend using Spyworks from Desaware, Inc. It comes with Winsock objects written in VB, so you always have source code to refer back to. However, you don't gain *any* real technical advantage by using the Winsock API in VB, and you certainly don't gain speed. All you gain is an increase in your learning curve as well as in your development time. I like working at the level of a Winsock control. That is, higher than the Winsock API, with substantial control over everything you're doing.

Installing the Software

Your CD-ROM disc comes with sample code, as well as an unregistered version of Dolphin Systems' dsSocket ActiveX control for Winsock programming. Installing is easy. Simply load the disc into your CD-ROM reader and wait for 30 seconds. If the install program does not pop right up, simply run SETUP.EXE from the root of the CD-ROM drive. Follow the instructions in the setup program and reboot your machine. That's all there is to it.

Loading DSSOCK32.OCX into Visual Basic

Before you can load dsSocket into VB, you must register it. This is done from Visual Basic's Components window (see Figure 2.1). Pop up the box by either pressing Ctrl-T or selecting Components from the Project menu. For VB 4.0 users, select Custom Controls from the Tools menu.

The Components window pops up and displays a list of all registered ActiveX controls. To add dsSocket to the list, click the Browse button. Navigate to your System directory and select DSSOCK32.OCX by either double-clicking on it, or single-clicking on it and then clicking the Open button (see Figure 2.2). Make sure that the entry "Dolphin Systems dsSocket TCP/IP Control" is checked off in the list, and click the OK button. dsSocket is now registered on your machine as an OLE server. If you have not installed the CD-ROM software, do so before attempting to register dsSocket.

Next, you must register the dsSocket Type Library (.TLB), which lets you access the control without using a form. As you will see, this is what all of my sample code is based upon, and I feel it is the best way to use the control in VB.

To register the Type library, select References from the Projects menu. Click the Browse button, and select DSSOCK32.TLB from your system directory. Just as

Figure 2.1   Components window.

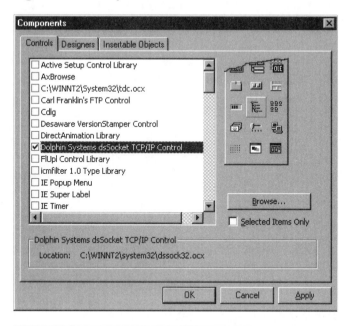

Figure 2.2   Add Custom Controls.

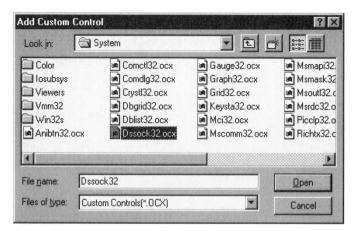

you did with the OCX, double-click on the filename or press the Open button, and verify that "Dolphin Systems dsSocket TCP/IP Control" is checked off in the list, and press the OK button.

DSSOCK.BAS

DSSOCK.BAS is a module containing global constants, types, variables, arrays, and a few simple utility functions that are always coming in handy.

SocketConnect

The SocketConnect function is a nice synchronous wrapper for everything that needs to happen when you connect to a host machine. Here is the calling syntax:

```
Dim ErrCode As Integer

ErrCode = SocketConnect(dsSocket1, Port, HostAddress, Timeout)
```

where `dsSocket1` is the dsSocket control, `Port` is the port number of the host application, `HostAddress` is a string containing either a host name such as www.cgvb.com or a DOT address such as 206.210.64.181, and `Timeout` is the number of seconds you want it to wait for a connection before it gives up. If no Timeout value is specified, it will wait forever and your program will be hooped (that's Latin for really messed up).

SocketConnect returns zero if you've connected; otherwise, it returns an error code.

IsDotAddress

IsDotAddress is another useful function. You pass it a string and it tells you whether or not it's a valid IP address. A valid IP address must have four numbers ranging from 0 to 255 separated by periods. The following strings will cause IsDotAddress to return false:

```
Invalid IP address:    Reason:
this.is.not.legal      characters are not allowed
100.2A.11.33           contains the letter A
100.14.7               only three numbers specified
199.22..3              missing the third number
80.-2.40.8             contains a negative number
256.120.20.13          contains a number greater than 255
```

ParseString

The ParseString function returns a section of a string given a delimiter and a section number. This is useful when walking through received data looking for specific pieces of information. Here is the calling syntax:

```
Dim SubString As String

SubString = ParseString(Data, Delimiter, SegmentNumber)
```

where Data is the string you're examining, Delimiter is the delimiter, or the string that separates the segments of the Data string, and SegmentNumber is the segment that you want to return. Here is an example:

```
SubString = ParseString("The quick brown fox", " ", 3)
```

In this example, SubString would be "brown."

Getting Started with dsSocket

Place a dsSocket control on Form1. You can do this by selecting Form1, and then double-clicking the dsSocket Toolbox icon, or single-clicking the dsSocket Toolbox icon and drawing the control on Form1. If the Toolbox is not visible (on the left-hand side of the screen), you can make it visible by selecting Toolbox from the View menu.

Let's start out by looking at two properties: LocalDotAddr and LocalName. *Note: although these properties exist, they do not show up in the Properties window or the list of properties that drops down in the editor.* LocalDotAddr contains the IP address (sometimes called the Dot Address) of the local machine, and LocalName contains the machine name. As a first exercise, add the following code to Form1's Form_Load event to display the IP address and machine name:

```
Private Sub Form_Load

    Caption = dsSocket1.LocalDotAddr & " - " & dsSocket1.LocalName

End Sub
```

Run the application by pressing F5, clicking the Run button, or selecting Start from the Run menu. This program simply displays the local IP address and machine name in the caption. The LocalDotAddr and LocalName properties are both string properties (see Figure 2.3).

Figure 2.3   Local IP address.

Making a Sockets Connection

This book comes with a starter project called WINSOCK.VBP, located in the Winsock directory, which contains a form with a dsSocket control on it. Load the WINSOCK project now, and save it as a new project.

Place a second dsSocket control on Form1. Next, add a new form to the project (Form2) and place a dsSocket control on it. Add a command button to both Form1 (name = btnEnd, caption = "End") and Form2 (name = btnAction, caption = "Connect"). Size the forms so they appear as they do in Figure 2.4. If you have not already done so, set the startup form to Form1. The task here is for Form1 to open up a server socket on an arbitrary port and have a client socket connect to it from Form2. Before I discuss what is really happening here, let's implement and run the code.

The code required for Form1 is shown in Figure 2.5. The code required for Form2 is shown in Figure 2.6. You can type it all in if you like, or if you prefer to load the source code from disk, the name of the project is SAMPLE1.VBP in the Winsock directory on the CD-ROM.

Figure 2.4 Two dsSocket controls.

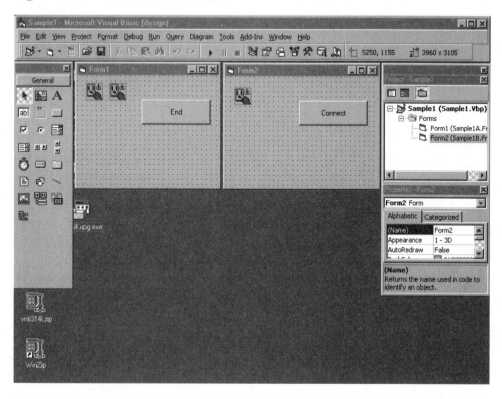

Figure 2.5 Code for Form1 in the Sample1 application.

```
Option Explicit

Private Sub Form_Load()

    '-- Show the client form
    Form2.Show

    '-- Set the local port number to 2700 (arbitrary)
    dsSocket1.LocalPort = 2700

    '-- Open a server socket to Listen to port 2700
    On Error Resume Next     '-- Trap errors
```

Continues

Figure 2.5   Code for Form1 in the Sample1 application. *(Continued)*

```
    dsSocket1.Listen

    If Err Then
        '-- An Error occurred, display the error
        MsgBox Error, vbExclamation, "Listen Error"
    End If

    '-- If there was no error, the dsSocket1_Listen event
    '   should fire, indicating that dsSocket1 is listening
    '   to port 2700.

End Sub

Private Sub dsSocket1_Listen()

    '-- We are now monitoring port 2700 on this machine.
    '   When a client connects, the dsSocket1_Accept event will fire.

    Caption = "Listening to port 2700"
End Sub

Private Sub dsSocket1_Accept(SocketID As Integer)

    '-- A client is attempting to connect. We must complete
    '   the connection by setting the Socket property of
    '   *any* dsSocket control to SocketID. In this case, we
    '   will use the second dsSocket control.

    On Error Resume Next    '-- Trap errors
    dsSocket2.Socket = SocketID

    If Err Then
        '-- An Error occurred, display the error
        MsgBox Error, vbExclamation, "Accept Error"
    Else
        '-- No errors. We are connected!
        Caption = "Connected!"
    End If

End Sub

Private Sub dsSocket2_Close(ErrorCode As Integer, ErrorDesc As String)

    '-- The client closed the connection.
    Caption = "Listening to Port 2700"
```

Figure 2.5 *Continued.*

```
End Sub

Private Sub btnEnd_Click()

    '-- When the "End" button is pressed, unload the client
    '   form, which closes the connection, and then unload this
    '   form, which closes all connections and sockets and ends.
    Unload Form2
    Unload Me

End Sub

Private Sub Form_Unload(Cancel As Integer)

    '-- Make sure the socket is closed
    On Error Resume Next     '-- Trap errors
    dsSocket1.Close

    End

End Sub
```

Figure 2.6   Code for Form2 in the Sample1 application.

```
Option Explicit

Private Sub Form_Load()

    '-- Tell everyone we are not connected to anything.
    Caption = "Not Connected"

End Sub

Private Sub btnAction_Click()

    If btnAction.Caption = "Connect" Then

        '-- Set the port of the server socket
        dsSocket1.RemotePort = 2700
        '-- Set the address of the server computer.
        '   In this case it is the same as the client.
```

Continues

Figure 2.6   Code for Form2 in the Sample1 application. *(Continued)*

```
            dsSocket1.RemoteDotAddr = dsSocket1.LocalDotAddr
            '-- Try and connect.
            On Error Resume Next      '-- Trap error
            dsSocket1.Connect

            If Err Then
                '-- An Error occurred, display the error
                MsgBox Error, vbExclamation, "Connect Error"
            End If

            '-- If there was no error, than the
            '    dsSocket1_Connect event will fire, indicating
            '    that we've connected to the server.
        Else
            '-- Close the connection (if there is one)
            On Error Resume Next
            dsSocket1.Close

            '-- Reset the button and form captions
            btnAction.Caption = "Connect"
            Me.Caption = "Not Connected"

        End If

End Sub

Private Sub dsSocket1_Connect()

    '-- We have connected to the server!
    Caption = "Connected!"

    '-- Reset the functionality of the command
    '    button to closing the port.
    btnAction.Caption = "Close"

End Sub

Private Sub Form_Unload(Cancel As Integer)

    '-- Make sure the socket is closed
    On Error Resume Next      '-- Trap errors
    dsSocket1.Close

End Sub
```

Run the program. The two forms appear, with Form1's caption reading "Listening to port 2700" and Form2's caption reading "Not Connected." Press the Connect button on Form2. If everything works, you should see the word "Connected" in both the client and the server application, and the Connect button should now read "Close." Press the Close button and the program should look exactly as it did at startup, with Form1's caption reading "Listening to port 2700" and Form2's caption reading "Not Connected."

Repeat the process as many times as you like, connecting and disconnecting the socket. When you are satisfied that it's actually working, click the End button on Form1 to exit the program. Do not click VB's Stop button to end the program. You will see why in a minute.

What's Going On Here?

The two controls on the server form serve two different purposes. The first control acts as an *answering* socket. Its job is to answer the port, if you will. The second control is the data socket. The data socket takes over the connection, leaving the answering socket ready to answer the next connection request. All socket activity between client and server occurs with the data socket.

Take a look at the Form_Load event of Form1 in Figure 2.5. The first thing that happens is that Form2 is displayed, after which a socket is opened on port 2700. 2700 is an arbitrary number, and you can change it to whatever you like, as long as there isn't already an application using it. Port numbers are 16-bit, so they can be as high as 32767 in Visual Basic (actually you can use negative numbers for values greater than 32767). If you plan on using an arbitrary port number for an application, use a number above 1024. The reason for this is that many reserved ports fall below 1024, so it just makes good sense to use higher numbers.

The socket is set to port 2700 via the LocalPort property. Then, dsSocket is told to listen to that port, or become a server when Listen method is invoked. By using On Error Resume Next, we can trap any error that occurs. In this case, the typical error is that the local port is already being used. This can happen if you do not close the connection before the program is exited.

The Form_Unload event procedure, which is run right before the form is unloaded from memory, closes the connection. Again, by using On Error Resume Next, we can discard any error, such as "Socket not connected," that might occur. You should not end the program by clicking Visual Basic's Stop button because doing so does not allow the Unload event procedure of each form a chance to run. The Form_Unload event is where open sockets are usually closed. If you do not close any open listening sockets, they will remain open until you reload Visual Basic. In the words of NOMAD, "Error!, sterilize!"

If there is no error when you attempt to listen, then the dsSocket1_Listen event will fire, indicating that a server socket has been opened on port 2700. Check out the dsSocket1_Listen event procedure. In this procedure, we set the form's caption to "Listening to port 2700." If you do not see this in the caption when you run this program, then the socket was not opened properly. But, if this were the case, you would get an error message, so the fact that the form comes up without an error means that it is listening on port 2700.

Now, let's jump over to Figure 2.6 to the btnAction_Click event. When you click this button, an attempt to connect to the server on port 2700 is made.

To connect a client to a server, you must set the RemotePort property and either the RemoteDotAddr or RemoteName property. If you specify the RemoteName property and the name exists outside of your domain, your Domain Name System (DNS) service will kick in and resolve the IP address (see Chapter 1). If you specify the IP address, the connection will be made without the need for resolving a name. In this case, the server machine is the same as the client machine, so we just specify the RemoteDotAddr property to be the LocalDotAddr property, our IP address.

If an error occurs here, it will most likely be that either the connection is already open or the connection failed because the server is either not running or out of connections. There is no predefined limit to the number of connections a server application can handle. Basically, you must decide on a limit based on performance. For example, if your server application is file intensive and running on an Intel P-60 or lower, you may want to limit the number of active connections to 30 or 40. Only your observations can determine how many connections to allow. I will talk more about handling multiple connections later, but I wanted to bring it up here in context for your benefit.

SocketID and the Socket Property

At this point, the client (Form2) has attempted to connect to the server (Form1). Let's jump back to Figure 2.5, the server application, to the dsSocket1_Accept event procedure. This occurs on the server when a connection attempt is made. The argument SocketID is passed to the Accept event. This is the Socket Identifier number. Think of it as a token, or a handle, that identifies one side of a socket connection. You are free to assign this connection to any dsSocket control. Typically this is done by loading a new instance of an array of dsSocket controls, and assigning the SocketID to the new instance, which keeps the listening control (in this case dsSocket1) open to accept more connections.

I will show you how to handle multiple connections shortly, but for our example, we are going to accept only one connection. The second dsSocket control on Form1, called dsSocket2, is used in the communication. dsSocket1 is used to accept only incoming connections. This is typical of TCP/IP server applications. In our example, we pass the connection to dsSocket2 by setting its Socket property to the SocketID. If no error occurs, the caption displays the word "Connected."

At this point Form2.dsSocket1 is connected to Form1.dsSocket2. If these two forms were inside of two applications anywhere in the world, they could send data back and forth to each other, the speed of the transmission limited only by the speed of one's Internet connection, which can range from a slow modem connection to a lightning-fast direct connection. Think of it, there is some extremely cool software to be written here!

Closing the Connection

When you click the btnAction button at this point, as the caption "Close" indicates, the client will close the connection. Take a look again at Figure 2.6 at the btnAction_Click event procedure. If the caption of the button is "Close," then the second piece of code in this procedure is executed. The Close method is invoked, inside a local error handler of course, and the button and form captions are reset.

The server detects that the connection was closed and fires the dsSocket2_Close event (shown in Figure 2.5). In this event, the server form's caption is reset to "Listening to port 2700" and the whole process is ready to happen again.

The Close event occurs only when the other side closes the connection. It does not fire when you close the connection by invoking the Close method.

Two properties, Timeout and Linger, determine what happens when you close a connection yourself. When the Linger property is True and the Timeout is greater than zero, then when you close the connection the connection isn't closed until either all data in the send buffer is sent, or Timeout number of seconds have elapsed.

If Linger is True and Timeout is false, dsSocket closes immediately without waiting for data to be sent. If Linger is false, and Timeout is greater than zero, then dsSocket waits Timeout number of seconds before closing, and does not close prematurely even if all data has been sent.

The only thing left to talk about for this example is what happens when the End button is clicked. What happens is important. Instead of just executing a

Visual Basic End statement, the forms are unloaded. In each form's Unload event, any and all socket controls on that form are told to close their connections, whether or not there are any connections. Using On Error Resume Next prevents any "The connection is already closed" errors from rearing their ugly heads. In the main form's Unload event procedure, after all the other forms are unloaded, an End statement can safely end the program.

Visual Basic's End statement, like the Stop button, does not allow forms' Unload event to fire, which means that data can be lost and connections stranded. Can you imagine if you were running a web server, which absolutely *must* listen and respond to connections on port 80, and an error brought the application down? You would have to reboot. Oops!

Handling Multiple Connections on the Server Side

This sample we've been looking at is fine for demonstration purposes, but you and I both know that in the real world a *server* has to handle multiple connections at the same time. Fortunately, with a little smart code you can handle as many connections as your server can handle.

The main idea behind multiple connections is that one instance of a dsSocket control equals one connection. So, for every incoming connection you must have an available dsSocket control loaded in memory to act as a data socket. Therefore, you must have at least one socket control as a control array (Index Property set to 0) so that new instances can be loaded as needed. You still use only one listen control to act as an answer agent.

Assuming that dssData is a control array, here is how you would load a new instance:

```
Load dssData(Index)
```

where `Index` is the control index that you want to load. You must keep track of this index. Every time you load a new instance, you have to keep track of its instance. For example:

```
Private NumSockets As Integer

NumSockets = NumSockets + 1

Load dssData(NumSockets)
```

Since NumSockets keeps track of how many Socket controls are being used, the index will always be correct. If dssData(1) is not loaded, you can load dssData(3); but if you have already loaded dssData(3) and you try and load it again, you will get an error.

Right now you might be thinking that you could just keep loading new instances of the dsSocket control for each new connection. Although this will work up to the point where you run out of memory, it is not a good idea. Every time you get a connection you have to first look at each of the loaded controls and use the first one that is not already in use.

The source code to the project \Winsock\Server\SERVERTEST.VBP is shown in Figure 2.7. This project demonstrates the smallest amount of code required to handle multiple connections effectively. ServerTest makes use of a user-defined Type array (Socket) that holds information about the sockets used in the project. Every time a new dsSocket control is loaded, the Socket array grows so that the new control's index is the same as the highest index in the Socket array. Therefore, for a given index the following is always true: Socket(Index) holds information about DSSock1(Index).

Figure 2.7 SERVERTEST handles multiple connections.

```
Option Explicit

Private Type SockStatusType
    Connected As Integer    '-- Is the socket connected?
    SendReady As Integer    '-- Is the socket ready to send data?
End Type

Private Socket() As SockStatusType

Private NumSockets  As Integer

Private Sub dssAnswer_Accept(SocketID As Integer)
'-- Assign a dsSocket control instance to this connection.

    Dim Index As Integer

    Debug.Print "New connection at " & Now

    For Index = 1 To NumSockets
        If Socket(Index).Connected = False Then
```

Continues

Figure 2.7   SERVERTEST handles multiple connections. *(Continued)*

```
            '-- This socket control is not in use. Use it.
            Socket(Index).Connected = True
            dsSocket1(Index).Socket = SocketID
            Exit Sub
        End If
    Next

    '-- All loaded socket controls are in use. Load a new one.
    NumSockets = NumSockets + 1
    Load dsSocket1(NumSockets)

    '-- Grow the Socket array
    ReDim Preserve Socket(1 To NumSockets) As SockStatusType
    Socket(NumSockets).Connected = True

    '-- Assign the socket connection
    dsSocket1(NumSockets).Socket = SocketID

    Caption = "Controls used:" & Str$(NumSockets)

End Sub


Private Sub dsSocket1_Close(Index As Integer, ErrorCode As Integer, _
ErrorDesc As String)

    '-- Default SendReady to False
    Socket(Index).Connected = False

    Debug.Print "Connection closed at " & Now

End Sub


Private Sub dsSocket1_Exception(Index As Integer, ErrorCode As Integer, _
ErrorDesc As String)

    '-- Default SendReady to False
    Socket(Index).Connected = False

    Debug.Print "Connection Error at " & Now

End Sub
```

Figure 2.7   Continued.

```
Private Sub Form_Unload(Cancel As Integer)

    Dim i    As Integer

    On Error Resume Next
    dssAnswer.Close
    For i = 1 To NumSockets
        dsSocket1(i).Close
    Next

End Sub
```

dsSocket has a property called State. It is used to determine whether or not the socket is connected. I choose not to use it because the documentation states that if an exception has occurred, the State property may not be accurate. Instead, my code sets the Socket(Index)Connected array member to True when the socket is initially connected, and to False if and when either the Close event is fired or the Exception event with a close error is fired.

You can test ServerTest with the Windows Telnet client from a command window. Open a command window (\Start Menu\Programs\Command Prompt), and at the prompt enter:

```
TELNET <MyIPAddress> 200
```

where <MyIPAddress> is the IP address of your machine. You can determine this with the first sample program in this chapter. Telnet will connect to your server on port 200. Closing the Telnet client will cause the close event to fire.

When a new connection attempt is made in the Accept event, the code walks through the Socket array looking to see if one of the controls already loaded is available. It does this by checking the Socket(Index).Connected value. If one is available, the SocketID is assigned to it, and its corresponding Connected value is set True.

If the loop completes indicating that no free socket controls were found, a new one is loaded, NumSockets, the number of sockets variable is incremented by one, the SocketID is assigned, and its corresponding Connected value is set to True. Using this technique, there are only as many controls in memory as the highest number of simultaneous connections.

Sending Data

What could be easier than sending data? dsSocket1.Send = <string>. Well, yes, it is that easy, but a problem can occur that you should be aware of. If you send data to Winsock faster than it can send it down the stack, it will return an error. The error is Winsock 1.1 error 21035, or "Operation Would Block." This occurs when the underlying network is busy sending other data, and cannot send your data right away. *Blocking* is what happens when an application goes into a tight loop waiting for the availability of some other process, and in doing so it locks up the system.

DSSOCK.BAS includes a routine called SendData, which accepts a string of data and makes sure it is sent to the server if a Would Block error occurs. Let's look at how SendData works.

```
Sub SendData(dsSocket As Control, Data As String)

    Do
        m_SendReady = False        '-- Initialize this flag to False
        On Error Resume Next       '-- Catch errors
        dsSocket.Send = Data       '-- Send the data
        If Err = SOCK_ERR_OPERATIONWOULDBLOCK Then   '-- Error?
            dsSocket.RecvBlock = True    '-- Before calling DoEvents,
                                         '   turn RecvBlock on to prevent
                                         '   receive events from firing.

            Do                           '-- Wait for the SendReady event
                                         '   to fire, which sets the
                                         '   m_SendReady flag to True.
                DoEvents
            Loop Until m_SendReady = True

            dsSocket.RecvBlock = False   '-- Turn Receive events back on.

            '-- At this point the SendReady event
            '   has fired, loop back and try again.
        Else
            '-- No errors. Exit.
            Exit Do
        End If
    Loop

End Sub
```

In this routine, if a Would Block error occurs when trying to send the data (Data), the code goes into a loose loop (for lack of a better word), calling DoEvents

---

so the system doesn't lock up. The loop is broken when the m_SendReady global variable is set to True, which occurs only when dsSocket's SendReady event is fired after a Would Block error is resolved.

The only other gotcha in the SendData routine is that you must turn off receive events before you go into the DoEvents loop. When DoEvents is called, your program is allowing other code to execute. If a Receive event occurs, and then your code executes in the Receive event, sending data with the SendData method, you could overflow the stack due to a recursion error. At the very least, it could upset the flow of data through your application, which could result in bad data.

Receiving Data

The smooth operation of your Winsock program depends almost entirely on how you handle received data. There are many different ways to do this, and you will have to make the final decision as to how you are going to approach it.

The dsSocket Winsock custom control fires a Receive event when data is received:

```
Private Sub dsSocket1_Receive (ReceiveData As String)

End Sub
```

Anytime data is received by dsSocket, this event fires. The Receive event will not fire if your code is in a tight loop, or a loop in which DoEvents is not called. *If the Receive event does not fire when it has to, you will lose your data, unless the RecvBlock property is set to True.*

LineMode, EOLChar, and DataSize

There are two ways to tell dsSocket to receive data, in line mode or binary mode. When dsSocket is in line mode then the Receive event is fired for every line of text received. A line of text usually ends with a line feed (ASCII 10) but you can tell dsSocket which character to recognize as an *end-of-line* character with the EOLChar property. When dsSocket is in binary mode (the default), the Receive event is fired after every block of data is received by Winsock.

To set dsSocket into line mode, set the LineMode property to True. Define the end-of-line character by setting the EOLChar property to the ASCII value of the character. The default value is 10 (line feed).

Figure 2.8   Simple example of handling received data.

```
Private Sub dsSocket1_Receive (ReceiveData As String)

  '-- A one-line command was received from the server.

    Dim Cmd as String

    '-- The leftmost two characters define the command.
    Cmd = Left$(ReceiveData, 2)

    '-- Everything from the third character on is data.
    ReceiveData = Mid$(ReceiveData, 3)

    '-- What does the server want us to do?
    Select Case Cmd

        Case "GD"   '-- GetDate command.
            Call GetDate(ReceiveData)

        Case "SD"   '-- SetDate command.
            Call SetDate(ReceiveData)

    End Select

End Sub
```

When LineMode is False, indicating binary mode, the DataSize property defines the maximum size of the ReceiveData variable, or the largest amount of data dsSocket will receive before firing the Receive event.

The Simple Approach

The first and easiest method for handling received data is to write the data processing code right in the Receive event itself. For example, let's say you connect to a server application, and the server application sends you one line command to which you must respond. It would be very easy to write it like the code shown in Figure 2.8.

A New Twist

Since dsSocket is in line mode, and every line consists of a command and data, you can parse the data easily with a Select Case statement. What if the server sent two lines per command, the first line being the command and the second line being data? How would you discern the command from the data? Is the command a fixed length? If so, then you can test the length of ReceiveData to determine whether you are receiving a command or data. The code in Figure 2.9 shows how to handle this scenario.

If the data received is four bytes (characters) long, then we have received a command. The Static keyword tells VB to preserve the value of this variable. When a command is received, it is saved into the Cmd string variable, and saved for the next time the Receive event is fired. When that happens, if ReceiveData is not a command, then the last command received is processed, the data associated with the command being the current ReceiveData variable. The only problem with this approach occurs when the data is exactly four bytes, the same size as a command.

Figure 2.9　A slightly more sophisticated example of handling received data.

```
Private Sub dsSocket1_Receive (ReceiveData As String)

    '-- Save the value of Cmd between events.
    Static Cmd as String

    '-- Is this a command?
    If Len(ReceiveData) = 4 Then
        '-- Yes. The leftmost two characters define the command.
        Cmd = Left$(ReceiveData, 2)
    Else
        '-- What was the last command we received?
        Select Case Cmd

            Case "GD"   '-- GetDate command.
                Call GetDate(ReceiveData)

            Case "SD"   '-- SetDate command.
                Call SetDate(ReceiveData)

        End Select

        '-- Reset the command to an empty string because
        '    we are done with it.
        Cmd = ""

    End If

End Sub
```

Splitting Up the Process with Flags

Sometimes your program executes a series of commands, each of which must be handled differently. Many times, the data cannot be identified simply by its length or its content. It is for this reason I like to use flags. A flag is a variable that is set in one part of the program and read in another part of the program to help your program communicate with itself across its functions and subroutines.

Many people have a dislike for flags because they can be easily abused and you feel you have lost control. I disagree. Ever since the days of assembler programming, flags have played an important part in determining states of code and data. If you are careless in how you use flag variables they can make your life miserable. However, the problem isn't the use of flags, but simply knowing when, and when not, to use them.

Consider the following scenario. You are requesting to download a file from a server, but first you need to know how many files there are. The protocol dictates that first you must send a DIR command to get a list of files. The server then sends one filename per line followed by a period on a line by itself to indicate the end of the list. Let's also say that you want to write a routine to handle the whole process. The routine sends the DIR command to the server. How is your routine going to know when the list of files has been completely received? Consider the code in Figure 2.10.

Figure 2.10   Receiving data with flags—example 1.

```
Option Explicit

Dim NumLinesReceived As Integer   '-- Number of lines received.
Dim Complete As Integer    '-- Flag set True when data has
          '          been completely received.
Dim Data() As String       '-- String array that holds
          '          received data.

Private Sub dsSocket1_Receive (ReceiveData As String)

    '-- A new line has been received. Up the count
    NumLinesReceived = NumLinesReceived + 1

    '-- Grow the szData array by one element
    Redim Preserve Data(NumLinesReceived) As String

    '-- Set the data into the new array element

    Data(NumLinesReceived) = ReceiveData
```

Figure 2.10 *Continued.*

```
'-- Is this data a period on a line by itself?
If ReceiveData = "." & vbCrLf Then
    '-- Yes. Tell the app we've received all the data.
    Complete = True
End If

End Sub

Private Sub Command1_Click ()
    '-- We are assuming the dsSocket1 control
    '     already connected to the server.

    Dim Index As Integer

    '-- Initialize
    Command1.Enabled = False
    Complete = False
    Redim szData(0) As String
    NumLinesReceived = 0

    '-- Send the command to get the list of files.
    dsSocket1.Send = "DIR" & vbCrLf

    '-- Wait for flag to clear
    Do Until Complete
        DoEvents
    Loop

    '-- Fill a list box with the file names.

    ListBox1.Clear '-- clear the contents first.

    '-- Indexes 1 through NumLinesReceived - 1 hold
    '    the list of files. The last line is the period.
    For Index = 1 To NumLinesReceived - 1
        ListBox1.AddItem Data(Index)
    Next

    Command1.Enabled = True

End Sub
```

This code shows the interaction between an initiating process (Command1_Click) and the Receive event where data is received. The code assumes that you have a list box and a dsSocket control on the form, and that the dsSocket control is already connected to its host. Also, it is assumed that the dsSocket control's LineMode property is set to True, and that the EOLChar property is set to 10 (line-feed). The goal is to receive an array of filenames from the server by issuing a DIR command. The server responds by sending a list of files, one per line, ending with a period on a line by itself.

The NumLinesReceived variable, Complete variable, and the Data string array are shared between all subs and functions in the form because they are defined in the form's General Declarations section. Every time a new line is received, the NumLinesReceived integer is incremented by one, a new element is added to the Data array, and the received data is copied to the new array element. If the received data is a period on a line by itself, then the Complete flag is set to True.

In Command1_Click, the DIR command is sent to the server, which prompts the server to send the list of filenames. After the command is sent, the code waits in a DoEvents loop until the Complete flag is set, indicating that all the filenames have been received. It is imperative that you use DoEvents in this loop; otherwise your application will appear to hang as it executes the loop over and over again without allowing other processes to occur. People will begin to think you are a terrible programmer. You'll be fired, and you'll lose all your friends. You think I'm kidding?

A Slight Variation

OK, what if your commands elicit short, one- or two-line responses from the server, with no period on a line by itself to indicate the end of the server's responses? What if all you have to go by is the number of lines that should be received? Simple: Just wait in your loop until x number of lines have been received. Skip the Complete flag altogether. Consider the code in Figure 2.11, a modification to Command_Click in Figure 2.10. The difference is that instead of waiting for a period to be received signifying the end of transmission, simply wait until the appropriate number of lines have been received. If the server is supposed to send back two lines of text, wait until two lines are received. Also, in the Receive event, increment the NumLinesReceived variable last so that the loop will not exit until the routine has completed.

Figure 2.11   A slight modification to the code in Figure 2.10.

```
Private Sub Command1_Click ()
    '-- We are assuming the dsSocket1 control
    '       already connected to the server.

    '-- Initialize
    Command1.Enabled = False
    Redim Data(0) As String
    NumLinesReceived = 0

    '-- Send some command that elicits a two-line response
    dsSocket1.Send = "FOO"

    '-- Wait to receive two lines
    Do
        DoEvents
    Loop Until NumLinesReceived >= 2

        '-- At this point the data has been received. Process it here.

    Command1.Enabled = True

End Sub
```

Event Driven = No Loops

What if you don't want to use DoEvents in your code? You've heard that excessive use of DoEvents can cause recursion (see recursion). This is both true and not true. It could cause problems in this case only if the user could press the Command button again while your loop is executing. Fortunately, though, setting the Enabled property of the button to False at the top of the code and re-enabling it at the bottom of the code prevents this from happening, so you are safe.

It does bring up a good point, however. What if you don't want to sit in a loop for any particular reason? You could instead have the Receive event call a particular routine when it has completely received the data. Imagine now that the server responds to two commands: DIR and GET. DIR is the same as before, but a new command, GET, tells the server to send a file. In your client application you want to let the user pick a filename from the list box we filled in Figure 2.10, and then once the file has been received you want it to show up on the Windows95 desktop.

The code in Figure 2.12 does this by introducing CommandNumber, a new variable that will identify the last command sent to the server. Clicking the command button sets CommandNumber to COMMAND_DIR, or 1, sends the DIR command, and exits. No loops are necessary in this case.

Figure 2.12   Receiving data with flags—example 2.

```
Option Explicit

Dim NumLinesReceived As Integer   '-- Number of lines received.
Dim Data() As String      '-- String array that holds
      '          received data.
Dim CommandNumber As Integer       '-- Holds the command last issued.

Const COMMAND_DIR = 1     '-- Command number constants.
Const COMMAND_GET = 2

Private Declare Function GetWindowsDirectory Lib "kernel32" Alias _
    "GetWindowsDirectoryA" (ByVal lpBuffer As String, _
    ByVal nSize As Long) As Long

Private Sub dsSocket1_Receive (ReceiveData As String)

    '-- A new line has been received. Up the count
    NumLinesReceived = NumLinesReceived + 1

    '-- Grow the szData array by one element
    Redim Preserve Data(NumLinesReceived) As String

    '-- Set the data into the new array element
    Data(NumLinesReceived) = ReceiveData

    '-- Is this data a period on a line by itself?
    If ReceiveData = "." & vbCrLf Then
        '-- Yes. Call the appropriate procedure
        Select Case CommandNumber
            Case COMMAND_DIR
                Call FillListBox
            Case COMMAND_GET
                Call SaveFileToDesktop
        End Select
    End If
```

Figure 2.12   Continued.

```
End Sub

Private Sub Command1_Click ()
    '-- We are assuming the dsSocket1 control
    '       already connected to the server.

    '-- Initialize
    Command1.Enabled = False
    Redim Data(0) As String
    NumLinesReceived = 0

    '-- Set the nCommandNumber
    CommandNumber = COMMAND_DIR

    '-- Send the command to get the list of files.
    dsSocket1.Send = "DIR" & vbCrLf

    Command1.Enabled = True

End Sub

Private Sub ListBox1_Click ()
    '-- We are assuming the dsSocket1 control
    '       already connected to the server.

    '-- Initialize
    Command1.Enabled = False
    Redim Data(0) As String
    NumLinesReceived = 0

    '-- Set the nCommandNumber
    CommandNumber = COMMAND_GET

    '-- Send the command to receive the currently selected file.
    dsSocket1.Send = "GET " & ListBox1.List(ListBox1.ListIndex) & vbCrLf

    Command1.Enabled = True

End Sub

Private Sub FillListBox ()

    Dim Index As Integer
```

Continues

Figure 2.12   Receiving data with flags—example 2. *(Continued)*

```
    '-- Fill a list box with the file names.

    ListBox1.Clear '-- clear the contents first.

    '-- Indexes 1 through NumLinesReceived - 1 hold
    '   the list of files. The last line is the period.
    For Index = 1 To NumLinesReceived - 1
        ListBox1.AddItem Data(Index)
    Next

End Sub

Private Sub SaveFileToDesktop ()

    Dim FileNum As Integer
    Dim Index As Integer
    Dim Buffer As String
    Dim LenBuffer As Long
    Dim WindowsDir as String

    '-- Get the Windows directory name
    Buffer = Space$(255)
    LenBuffer = GetWindowsDirectory(Buffer, Len(Buffer))
    WindowsDir = Left$(Buffer, LenBuffer)

    FileNum = FreeFile

    '-- Index 1 holds the name of the file.
    Open WindowsDir & "\DESKTOP\" & Data(1) For Output As FileNum
    '-- Indexes 2 through NumLinesReceived - 1 hold
    '   the file data. The last line is the period.
    For Index = 1 To NumLinesReceived - 1
        Print #FileNum, Data(Index);
    Next

    Close FileNum

End Sub
```

The Receive event receives all the data, and just like in Figure 2.10, determines if the data is complete by looking for a period on a line by itself. When complete, it calls the appropriate routine, based on the value of CommandNumber. In the case of COMMAND_DIR, the FillListBox routine is called, which fills the list box with the names of the files, just as in Figure 2.10.

When the user clicks on a filename in the list box, CommandNumber is set to COMMAND_GET, or 2, the GET command is sent to the server, and the routine exits. Again, no looping is necessary. Let's assume that the server will send the name of the file on the first line, then the file data itself line by line, and ending, of course, with a period on a line by itself. Once the file has been completely received in the Receive event the SaveFileToDesktop routine is called, which gets the desktop directory name and saves the file right on the Windows95 desktop. The user sees the file just *appear*. This approach to receiving data makes the most sense in an event-driven language, such as Visual Basic, because the code is never polling or sitting in a loop waiting for something.

Which Approach Is Better?

Use whatever is appropriate for the task at hand. If you are processing only a few commands, and you know the requirements will not grow, then you are extremely naive. No! You should use whatever approach fits the requirements. There is no best approach for all situations across the board. If you are going to have lots of different types of transactions that all require different processing then use the event-driven method. If there is lots of conversation between the client and server for a particular transaction, use the polling method, where you wait in a loop until x number of lines have been received. As long as you know what options are available to you, you can use the best method for the job.

Error Handling

Error handling is an essential part of communications programming. Communications applications are among the hardest to debug because they happen in real time. It is absolutely vital that you implement some method of error handling. In this section I'll show you a few techniques that you can use to help you write the perfect application.

Winsock Errors

dsSocket catches all of the Winsock errors and reports them via the Exception event. Figure 2.13 shows a list of all the possible Winsock errors. If you are confused about what they mean, don't worry. There are only two people on the planet who actually do. If it sounds like I'm brushing off an opportunity for some extended research, you're right. I am doing exactly that. The fact is that you are an applications programmer and you don't care why your Winsock isn't working. All you need to know is that it doesn't work. There are plenty of diagnostic tools available for network administrators that help pinpoint problems with the network. Besides, your users don't want to see seven consecutive dialog boxes that say stuff like "Address family not supported by protocol family" or some other wacky message. When I write Winsock applications, I usually just throw up a dialog box saying that the connection has been broken when it breaks because of an error. The only time I will attempt to reconnect is if the application is in the middle of transferring a file or some other valuable information.

Figure 2.13 Winsock error codes and descriptions.

Error Variable	Number	Explanation
WSAEINTR	21004	Interrupted system call
WSAEBADF	21009	Bad file number
WSAEACCES	21013	Permission denied
WSAEFAULT	21014	Bad address
WSAEINVAL	21022	Invalid argument
WSAEMFILE	21024	Too many open files
WSAEWOULDBLOCK	21035	Operation would block
WSAEINPROGRESS	21036	Operation now in progress
WSAEALREADY	21037	Operation already in progress
WSAENOTSOCK	21038	Socket operation on non-socket
WSAEDESTADDRREQ	21039	Destination address required
WSAEMSGSIZE	21040	Message too long
WSAEPROTOTYPE	21041	Protocol wrong type for socket
WSAENOPROTOOPT	21042	Bad protocol option
WSAEPROTONOSUPPORT	21043	Protocol not supported
WSAESOCKTNOSUPPORT	21044	Socket type not supported
WSAEOPNOTSUPP	21045	Operation not supported on socket
WSAEPFNOSUPPORT	21046	Protocol family not supported
WSAEAFNOSUPPORT	21047	Address family not supported by protocol family
WSAEADDRINUSE	21048	Address already in use
WSAEADDRNOTAVAIL	21049	Can't assign requested address
WSAENETDOWN	21050	Network is down
WSAENETUNREACH	21051	Network is unreachable

Figure 2.13 *Continued.*

WSAENETRESET	21052	Net dropped connection or reset
WSAECONNABORTED	21053	Software caused connection abort
WSAECONNRESET	21054	Connection reset by peer
WSAENOBUFS	21055	No buffer space available
WSAEISCONN	21056	Socket is already connected
WSAENOTCONN	21057	Socket is not connected
WSAESHUTDOWN	21058	Can't send after socket shutdown
WSAETOOMANYREFS	21059	Too many references, can't splice
WSAETIMEDOUT	21060	Connection timed out
WSAECONNREFUSED	21061	Connection refused
WSAELOOP	21062	Too many levels of symbolic links
WSAENAMETOOLONG	21063	File name too long
WSAEHOSTDOWN	21064	Host is down
WSAEHOSTUNREACH	21065	No Route to Host
WSAENOTEMPTY	21066	Directory not empty
WSAEPROCLIM	21067	Too many processes
WSAEUSERS	21068	Too many users
WSAEDQUOT	21069	Disc Quota Exceeded
WSAESTALE	21070	Stale NFS file handle
WSAEREMOTE	21071	Too many levels of remote in path
WSASYSNOTREADY	21091	Network SubSystem is unavailable
WSAVERNOTSUPPORTED	21092	WINSOCK DLL Version out of range
WSANOTINITIALISED	21093	Successful WSASTARTUP not yet performed
WSAHOST_NOT_FOUND	22001	Host not found
WSATRY_AGAIN	22002	Non-Authoritative Host not found
WSANO_RECOVERY	22003	Non-Recoverable errors: FORMERR, REFUSED, NOTIMP
WSANO_DATA	22004	Valid name, no data record of requested type

Even though you should shield the user from these errors when they occur, you should monitor them while you are writing and debugging your code. There are times when you go to open a socket and it's already open because you stopped the program in the middle somewhere before it had a chance to close.

For the final version the only exception you need to be concerned with (other than Operation Would Block) is the close error SOCK_ERR_CLOSED. If the connection is lost due to an error, you have a decision to make. Do you attempt to reconnect, do you do nothing, or do you ask the users if they want to attempt to reconnect? It totally depends on the design of your application.

Error-Handling Techniques

I have a few general error-handling techniques up my sleeve that lend themselves very nicely to communications programming, and let me tell you, they itch! The most valuable technique for debugging is using error-handling options, which can be controlled by the user via the command line. I like to give my applications a command line switch that tells me whether or not to catch errors and whether or not to display them.

Visual Basic's Command$ function returns the entire command line, or everything after the executable name that is used to launch your program. For example, say that your application's name is NETZAP.EXE and the command used to start it is defined like so:

C:\NETZAP\NETZAP.EXE /D

In this case, Command returns /D. Anywhere in your program you can use the Command$ function as a string variable that contains /D, or whatever the command line consists of.

You might want to establish a command line option /D that stands for *debug mode*. Immediately following the /D the user enters a number to indicate the mode; for example, /D1, /D2, and so on.

Minimal Error Trapping

When your application is not in debug mode, that is, no command line switch, it is best to present only those errors that the user can do something about. For example, if your Winsock connection is unexpectedly broken because of a network error you will first get an Exception event indicating the network error, then you will get another Exception event with the close error, indicating that the connection is closed.

Don't just pop up a MsgBox in the Exception event. Ignore the first error. When the close error (via the Exception event) occurs, inform the user that the connection was unexpectedly broken and that he or she might want to wait a few minutes before reconnecting in case there is a problem at the other end. You might want to explain that this kind of thing happens from time to time and that he or she can still save her data, or whatever. The more you make the user feel at ease, the more enjoyable the experience of using your software. I can't tell you how invaluable that advice has proven itself to be in my part of the world.

Every time an error occurs, you could save the description, date, and time in module-level variables. If an error causes the connection to be lost, display a message box with the last error that occurred and when it occurred, if at all. This is a nice level of error handling to give the user. You might also want to display any helpful tips at this time to restore the user's confidence.

Debug.Print Error Trapping

The Visual Basic Debug window is a nice way to monitor your application during development. You can display any string with the Debug.Print method like so:

```
Debug.Print "This is what I'm displaying in the debug window"
```

Since you can print any string, you can comprise your own error and status messages from variables that you wish to monitor. For example, let's say you want to monitor the number of lines of text received. With LineMode set to True, you could use the following code in the Receive event:

```
Sub dsSocket1_Receive(ReceiveData As String)

    Static LineCount As Integer

    LineCount = LineCount + 1
    Debug.Print Str$(LineCount) & " lines received"

    '-- Process data here

End Sub
```

Message Dialog Reporting

This is the most widely used and abused method of reporting errors. Most programmers don't realize that reporting errors during development and reporting errors to the user are *two totally different globs of petroleum*. When you are developing you want errors to be short and to the point. The user, however, is probably not a developer and has not spent half as much time using the program as you have developing it. Therefore, it is absolutely vital that you clean up error messages for the user before you ship your product. Did I mention that this was important?

Error Log Reporting

This is my favorite method of debugging. You can write errors and data to a log file in real time as you are sending and receiving data. A little extra code is required to implement this, but when you need it, it will save your behind (see Figure 2.14).

Figure 2.14   Intelligent error handling.

```
Sub dsSocket1_Exception(ErrorCode As Integer, ErrorDesc As String)

    Static LastError As String
    Static LastTime As String
    Dim Msg As String
    Dim ErrorMsg As String

    ErrorMsg = "Error" & Str$(ErrorCode) & " " & ErrorDesc

    Select Case m_DebugMode
        Case DEBUG_MODE_MINIMAL
            If ErrorCode = SOCK_ERR_CLOSED Then
                Msg = "The connection has been unexpectedly broken."
                If Len(LastTime) Then
                    Msg = Msg & vbCrLf & _
                        "The Last error to occur was " & _
                        Chr$(34) & LastError & Chr$(34) & _
                        " which occurred at " & LastTime
                End If
                MsgBox Msg, vbInformation
            End If
        Case DEBUG_MODE_DESIGNTIME
            Debug.Print ErrorMsg
        Case DEBUG_MODE_DIALOG
            MsgBox ErrorMsg
        Case DEBUG_MODE_WRITELOG
            WriteLogFile ErrorMsg
    End Select

    LastError = ErrorMsg
    LastTime = Now

End Sub
```

UDP—User Datagram Protocol

UDP, or User Datagram Protocol, is a Transport layer protocol like TCP that can be used to move data. Since UDP is part of the TCP/IP protocol suite, it is readily available. In fact, dsSocket is among the available Winsock controls that support UDP in addition to TCP.

The main difference with UDP is that it is connectionless and unreliable. Connectionless means that a handshake is not required before data can be sent, and unreliable means that no error checking is performed on the data to insure that it arrived intact at its destination.

Since UDP does not have to do so much work to send data, it is faster than TCP. Since there is no error checking, however, UDP is not always used over TCP. Remember my motto, "Use the right tool for the job." Sometimes UDP is the right tool for the job and sometimes TCP is. You might not be able to think of a situation in which reliability is not an issue; however there are many different situations where UDP is very desirable.

One such situation is the broadcasting of digital audio and/or video over the Internet. Many of the high-tech Internet audio and video systems on the market today use UDP over TCP because it is fast and error checking is not necessary. What happens if you are listening to digital audio in real time and you miss a few bytes? Considering that you are probably listening to eight thousand or more bytes per second, you won't even notice it. CU-SeeMe is a very popular Internet video-conferencing program that uses UDP. For more information on CU-SeeMe, check out the Yahoo! database list of CU-SeeMe links at the following URL:

http://www.yahoo.com/Computers_and_Internet/Multimedia/Videoconferencing/CU_seeme/

Another good application of UDP is the U.S. Naval Observatory's Time server, which gives you an accurate time of day via UDP by connecting to their server. For more information on the U.S. Naval Observatory's Network Time Services, check out their home page at the following URL:

http://tycho.usno.navy.mil/ntp.html

Because of the lack of error handling there are risks that go along with using UDP. One risk is that you may receive packets out of sequence. One of the things TCP does very well is the resequencing of packets. Every TCP packet is numbered, and TCP guarantees that the packets are moved up the stack at the destination in the correct order. UDP does not employ such a method. UDP does no processing at all to the data except to tack a source address and a destination address onto each packet. If a router between the source and destination went down in mid-transmission of your packets, and then came back on again before the transmission was complete, you might receive your packets out of order. This can be helpful, however, if the application using UDP wishes to handle packet sequencing itself and doesn't want the added overhead of TCP. Because of the sequencing issue, UDP is used mostly when sending either small and complete pieces of data or broadcasting streams of data, the idea being that if one packet misses the boat there are plenty more chances for successful transmission.

Another risk is that the data may not get to the destination at all. If a TCP packet fails to reach the destination, TCP re-attempts to send the data until it is received. UDP packets are not so lucky. Therefore, UDP is well suited for query-response systems in which a response is required for each transmission. If a response is not received, then another query is sent until a response is delivered.

Yet another risk associated with UDP is that some routers filter out UDP packets entirely. The Network File System (NFS) is a file-sharing system that allows users to mount drives, like the way Windows95 Explorer or Windows 3.1 File Manager allows you to *attach* or *connect* other users' drives and directories to your machine. Well, NFS uses UDP. Therefore, many firewalls block UDP packets so outsiders can't mount local directories and access the network unlawfully (as if there are actual laws to protect us from such crimes).

Since UDP is fast, it is desirable to use as an interprocess communication system on a local area network. Use it like you would use NetDDE (*gasp*) to send messages between applications on a network. Notify all the clients attached to the same server database that you've just changed the data they are viewing, and to refresh their display, and so on. dsSocket has a property called SocketType. When set to 0 (default), Winsock is used. When set to 1, however, dsSocket uses UDP if it is available. Since no connection is necessary, simply set the RemotePort and RemoteDotAddr properties, and send data with the send property.

Terminal—A Winsock Terminal Program

The Terminal program that comes with this book (TERMINAL.VBP) will help you determine the input and output requirements of any Winsock application you write. Terminal simply lets you connect to any machine on any port, lets you send data, and displays received data in a window.

Figure 2.15 shows the main screen of Terminal. You can open a connection by either clicking the Open button, or selecting Open from the Connection menu. Doing so displays the dialog box shown in Figure 2.16.

Enter the address and port number you wish to connect to. The Host Name can be either a name or IP address. If you check off the Line Mode Character option, the ASCII value given will be interpreted as the end of a line. If Line Mode is not checked off, the ASCII value given will not be used. Clicking the Cancel button cancels the operation of connecting.

Figure 2.15   Main terminal screen.

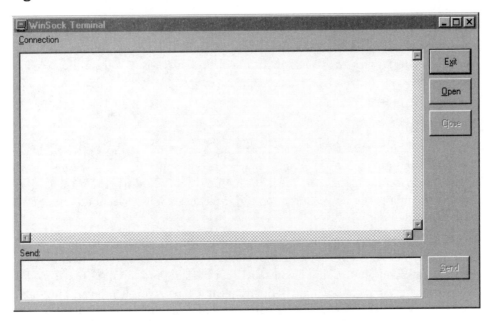

Once connected, you will see received data displayed in the window as it is received. Sending data requires a bit more explanation, however. Typically when talking to servers on the Internet, you will be required to send single-line commands and parameters. Enter the text you want to send in the *send window* below the display window. To send, either press Enter or click the Send button. You can optionally append the text you send with a carriage return, a linefeed, or both.

Figure 2.16   Connection dialog box.

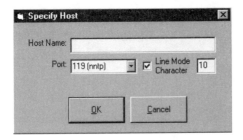

Typically a server will require a carriage return/linefeed (CR/LF) pair at the end of each line. This is not always the case, however; hence the option.

I originally wrote Terminal to help me visualize how the protocols I write about in this book work. It's a lot of fun to connect to an NNTP server, for example, and browse Usenet articles with the raw protocol. It really gives you an idea of how things work.

Epilogue

By now you should have a good understanding of some of the most efficient techniques for communications programming, and you should have a working knowledge of the dsSocket custom control. The chapters that follow use these techniques to access the more popular resources on the Internet: Gopher, Usenet, e-mail, FTP, and the World Wide Web.

I feel it is wise to keep your protocols in Visual Basic so that they may be changed or updated easily and quickly as changes in technology advance. It is not necessary to spend a lot of money on tools that basically manipulate text through a high-level network connection. By using Visual Basic, you are leveraging VB's greatest strength, short development time, and at the same time keeping the size and requirements of your application to a minimum.

As you read these next chapters, try to think of ways that you can integrate the protocols into your own real-world problems and opportunities. The time is now for the creative spark to redefine completely how computers are used in the twenty-first century and beyond.

SIMPLE PROTOCOLS

Introduction

In this chapter you'll cut your teeth on Internet programming by writing a few very simple protocols: NTP, WHOIS, and FINGER. These are very simple protocols that simply make a connection on a specified port, send a command, and receive an answer.

NTP (Network Time Protocol)

NTP is a very simple protocol that returns the current time (in Universal Time) from a time server. A Winsock client connects on port 13 to a time server, and the server immediately sends back the current time in the following format:

```
DDD MMM DD HH:NN:SS UTC YYYY <CRLF>
```

For example:

```
Mon Jul 27 14:55:52 UTC 1998
```

After sending this string, the server closes the connection. That's it!

OK, let's write a simple NTP client application. Create a new project in Visual Basic. Press Ctrl-T to bring up the components window. Check off Dolphin Systems dsSocket TCP/IP Control and click OK. Add a dsSocket control to the form. Double-click on the form, and enter the following line in the Form_Load event:

```
Private Sub Form_Load ()
    dsSocket1.LineMode = True
End Sub
```

This code sets the LineMode property to True, which tells dsSocket to fire the Receive event after receiving a line feed. Next, add a new button, name it btnGetTime, and enter the following lines of code in the btnGetTime_Click event:

```
Private Sub btnGetTime_Click()

    dsSocket1.RemoteHost = "tycho.usno.navy.mil"
    dsSocket1.RemotePort = 13
    dsSocket1.Connect

End Sub
```

This code connects to a machine named tycho.usno.navy.mil, on port 13. It does not do any error handling, in the event that the control cannot connect, but that's OK for our purposes. Next, add the following code in the dsSocket1_Receive event:

```
Private Sub dsSocket1_Receive(ReceiveData As String)

    MsgBox ReceiveData

End Sub
```

This code simply displays the date/time string that is sent by the time server machine. Now, go ahead and run the program. Click the button. In a few seconds, the current date and time will pop up. Figure 3.1 shows the NTP sample program. Remember, this is in Universal time. If you want to convert it to your time zone, check out the following web page:

sandbox.xerox.com/stewart/tzconvert.cgi

I can't think of a simpler example of writing an Internet client than accessing a Time server. The next two examples are similar, but a bit more involved in that they require sending a string after connecting.

Figure 3.1   NTP example program.

WHOIS

WHOIS was originally developed as a central database that held information about everyone on the Internet. Well, we all know what happened. The Internet grew so quickly that the original goals proved to be pointless if not impossible. WHOIS is now used by network administrators who want to publish information about their network and its users.

Using the WHOIS protocol is just as easy as NTP, except that after connecting, the client sends a string. Then the server sends a response and closes the connection. When you use WHOIS, you connect on port 43 and send the name of the user or machine (or whatever) you are inquiring about.

Let's create a very simple WHOIS client that returns information about domains registered on the Internet with the InterNIC. This application will return information about who owns a given domain name, such as microsoft.com.

Create a new project with dsSocket just as we did with NTP, including setting the LineMode property to True in the Form_Load event.

Add a button to the form and name it btnInquire. Double-click on the button and enter the following code:

```
Private Sub btnInquire_Click()

    dsSocket1.RemoteHost = "rs.internic.net"
    dsSocket1.RemotePort = 43
    dsSocket1.Connect

End Sub
```

This code connects to an InterNIC domain database machine on port 43. Next, add the following code to the dsSocket1_Connect event:

```
Private Sub dsSocket1_Connect()

    dsSocket1.Send = "microsoft.com" & vbCrLf

End Sub
```

This code sends the domain name microsoft.com to the WHOIS server. Substitute any domain you wish for microsoft.com. This is only an example. You can leave it as is, if you like, however. The point is, you can enter any domain name, even if it does not exist. In fact, this application is most useful in determining whether or not a given domain name is already registered.

Next, enter the following code in the dsSocket1.Receive event.

```
Private Sub dsSocket1_Receive(ReceiveData As String)

    Debug.Print ReceiveData;

End Sub
```

This code prints the information that the WHOIS server sends back into the debug window. Press Ctrl-G to make sure the debug window is visible when you run this program.

Figure 3.2 shows the output of the WHOIS sample. This is just a quick example of how the protocol works. There is a more complete WHOIS and FINGER application in the Finger directory of the sample code.

FINGER

FINGER, like WHOIS, is a protocol that was designed when the Internet was in its infancy. FINGER was designed to provide nonspecific information about a user or a device. It was simply designed as a way to ask a machine a question and get a response.

Figure 3.2   WHOIS example program.

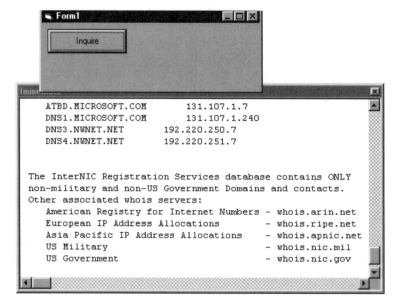

In the mid-seventies, computer science students at Carnegie-Mellon University found a now infamous use for the FINGER protocol. They installed a small serial device connected by FINGER in a Coke machine in the CS department that would report the different kinds of soda in the machine, as well as which button would yield the coldest drink. Since it was accessible by FINGER, the entire Internet could constantly check the status of the now famous Coke machine.

Even though that original machine is not online anymore, you can still use FINGER today to check the status of numerous other copycat Coke machines, including the Pepsi machine at Columbia University. Let's write a program to check the status of this machine.

Create a new application project in exactly the same manner as we did in both of the previous examples in this chapter, including setting the LineMode property to True in the Form_Load event.

Add a button to this form named btnFinger, and enter the following code in the btnFinger_Click event:

```
Private Sub btnFinger_Click()

    dsSocket1.RemoteHost = "www.cc.columbia.edu"
    dsSocket1.RemotePort = 79
    dsSocket1.Connect

End Sub
```

This code connects to the Internet Coke machine on the FINGER port (79). Next, add the following code to the dsSocket1_Connect event:

```
Private Sub dsSocket1_Connect()

    dsSocket1.Send = "/w pepsi" & vbCrLf

End Sub
```

This code sends the name of the user or machine to query, in this case "coke." You do not always need to use the /w query, but in this case you do. Next, add the following code to the dsSocket1_Connect event:

```
Private Sub dsSocket1_Receive(ReceiveData As String)

    Debug.Print ReceiveData

End Sub
```

Figure 3.3   FINGER example program.

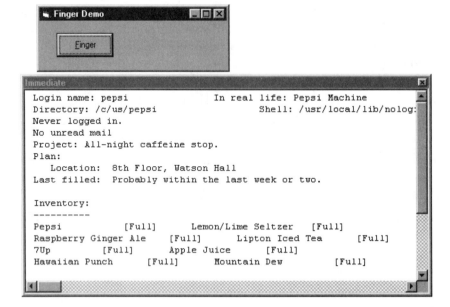

This code prints the information that the FINGER server sends back into the debug window. Press Ctrl-G to make sure the debug window is visible when you run this program.

Figure 3.3 shows the output of the FINGER sample. This is just a quick example of how the protocol works. There is a more complete WHOIS and FINGER application in the FINGER directory of the sample code.

SetTime Application

And now the moment you've been waiting for, your first *real* Internet application. This application will get the current time from the NTP server at the University of Manchester, in Manchester, England. It converts the time to your time zone, and sets your clock accordingly.

Start with the NTP sample you wrote at the beginning of this chapter, but change the address from tycho.usno.navy.mil to ntp2a.mcc.ac.uk. Enter the code in Figure 3.4 in the Receive event. This code looks complex, but all it does is convert the time string into a format that VB can recognize as a valid date.

You will also need to enter the declare statements and type definitions in Figure 3.5 into the declaration section of the program.

Figure 3.4   SetTime Application Receive event.

```
Private Sub dsSocket1_Receive(ReceiveData As String)

    Dim Pos         As Long
    Dim TZI         As TIME_ZONE_INFORMATION
    Dim ThisTime    As SYSTEMTIME
    Dim Adjusted    As Date

    If GetTimeZoneInformation(TZI) Then
        Mins = TZI.Bias

        'Examples: Mon Jul 27 14:55:52 UTC 1998
        '          Thu Jul 30 14:40:53 1998

        '-- Remove CR & LF characters
        Pos = InStr(ReceiveData, vbLf)
        If Pos Then
            ReceiveData = Left$(ReceiveData, Pos - 1)
        End If
        Pos = InStr(ReceiveData, vbCr)
        If Pos Then
            ReceiveData = Left$(ReceiveData, Pos - 1)
        End If

        '-- Is UTC in this string?
        Pos = InStr(ReceiveData, "UTC")
        If Pos = 0 Then
            '-- No. Take the Year off the end.
            Yr = Right$(ReceiveData, 4)
            ReceiveData = Left$(ReceiveData, _
                Len(ReceiveData) - 5)
        Else
            '-- Yes. Parse out the Year
            Yr = Mid$(ReceiveData, Pos + 4)
            ReceiveData = Left$(ReceiveData, Pos - 2)
        End If

        '-- Take the day of week off the left
            'hand side of the string.
```

Continues

Figure 3.4   SetTime Application Receive event. *(Continued)*

```
        Pos = InStr(ReceiveData, " ")
        If Pos Then
            ReceiveData = Mid$(ReceiveData, Pos + 1)

            '-- Take the month off the left.
            Pos = InStr(ReceiveData, " ")
            If Pos Then
                Mon = Left$(ReceiveData, Pos - 1)
                ReceiveData = _
                    Mid$(ReceiveData, Pos + 1)

                '-- Day the day off the left.
                Pos = InStr(ReceiveData, " ")
                If Pos Then
                    Dy = Left$(ReceiveData, Pos - 1)
                    ReceiveData = _
                        Mid$(ReceiveData, Pos + 1)

                    '-- Create the date.
                    Date = Mon & " " & Dy & " " & Yr

                    '-- The time is what's left.
                    Time = ReceiveData

                    '-- Adjust for our time zone.
                    Adjusted = DateAdd("n", _
                        -TZI.Bias, Date & " " & Time)

                    '-- Set the date and time.
                    Date = Adjusted
                    Time = Adjusted

                    '-- That's it. Play the
                    '   default beep.
                    Beep
                End If
            End If
        End If
    End If

End Sub
```

Figure 3.5 SetTime Declaration section.

```
Private Type SYSTEMTIME
    wYear As Integer
    wMonth As Integer
    wDayOfWeek As Integer
    wDay As Integer
    wHour As Integer
    wMinute As Integer
    wSecond As Integer
    wMilliseconds As Integer
End Type

Private Type TIME_ZONE_INFORMATION
    Bias As Long
    StandardName(32) As Integer
    StandardDate As SYSTEMTIME
    StandardBias As Long
    DaylightName(32) As Integer
    DaylightDate As SYSTEMTIME
    DaylightBias As Long
End Type

Private Declare Function GetTimeZoneInformation _
    Lib "kernel32" (lpTimeZoneInformation _
    As TIME_ZONE_INFORMATION) As Long
```

The Bias portion of the TIME_ZONE_INFORMATION type specifies the current bias (or offset), in minutes, for local time translation on this computer. The bias is the difference, in minutes, between Coordinated Universal Time (UTC) and local time. All translations between UTC and local time are based on the following formula:

UTC = local time + bias

   OR

local time = UTC − bias

As I said earlier, almost all of the code in this routine is just to parse the date and time information so that it can be processed by VB. Although this particular string algorithm works for this server, there is no guarantee that it will work for another server. You always have to tweak stuff like this because it is tied to the format of the received data.

The DateAdd function is used to subtract bias number of minutes from the UTC time. This new date, Adjusted, is the current date and time. Using the Date and Time statements, the code resets the date and time on the local machine. Once you hear the beep your machine's date and time has been correctly updated.

Epilogue

In this chapter you've successfully programmed three simple protocols that use the Internet. All of the other protocols in this book work in the exact same way, except more information is sent back and forth. In the next chapter, you will see how easy it is to post articles to and read articles from a Usenet News server. Stick around, and HEY! Don't ever change.

USENET NEWS

Introduction

Next to electronic mail and the World Wide Web, Usenet news is the most widely utilized service on the Internet. The ARPANET and Internet communities have always been big on the idea of news. In the beginnings of the Internet, scientists and researchers needed a way to distribute memos throughout the Internet to keep everyone up to date on research and other projects. Usenet provides a way for news messages (called articles) to spread throughout the Internet community at a fair speed.

Usenet is a network of news servers within the Internet that propagate messages spanning a huge number of discussion groups (called *newsgroups*). There are thousands of newsgroups with topics ranging from software bug fixes to recipes to fan clubs to diaper fetishes (I'm not making this up). If you are familiar with messaging on electronic Bulletin Board Systems (BBS) you may be familiar with FIDONet, a network similar to Usenet that operates within the BBS community. Usenet is similar except that the messages are propagated throughout the entire Internet. Your Internet access provider should offer Usenet service via an NNTP server at their network site.

The first Usenet software used UUCP (Unix-to-Unix Copy Protocol) as a data transport mechanism. UUCP is a somewhat outdated protocol for moving data, being replaced by TCP/IP. However, it is still used in some places for dialup access to Usenet.

Usenet actually preceded the Internet, starting in 1979 at Duke University and the University of North Carolina, Chapel Hill. Graduate students from both universities created the Usenet rules and wrote the first programs to handle the flow of news articles. They had over 50 sites signed up after the first year. Once TCP/IP hit the streets, Usenet news took the Internet by storm.

News articles bounce around from news server to news server via the NNTP (Network News Transfer Protocol), a text-based protocol that you will have no trouble utilizing in Visual Basic. Like most mainstream Internet protocols, NNTP is line-based, employing a command and response system that we have come to know and love.

Once you learn how to use NNTP in Visual Basic you can do many powerful things. How would you like to write a program that monitors your favorite Usenet newsgroups, searches for several key words, and based on the existence of those words, e-mails the articles to you or archives them in a database? Looking for a job? Monitor the bc.jobs or the biz.jobs.offered newsgroup. Be quick to respond to posted articles thanks to your special program that's constantly scanning the news-groups for you. Interested in a specific topic? Start archiving articles in a database. When you have a question that people in the newsgroup might have an answer to, search your database. There are hundreds of vertical applications waiting to be written that involve Usenet news.

In this chapter I'll show you how to log onto an NNTP server, get lists of arti-cles (new and old), retrieve specific articles, and post new articles. You won't believe how easy it really is.

NNTP

NNTP is a text-based protocol used to send and receive Usenet news articles between a newsreader client and an NNTP server, and also between two NNTP servers. If your Internet Access Provider gives you the ability to read Usenet news, then it probably has an NNTP server on site. Request For Comments (RFC) 977 states that "NNTP specifies a protocol for the distribution, inquiry, retrieval, and posting of news articles using a reliable stream-based transmission of news among the ARPA-Internet community. NNTP is designed so that news articles are stored in a central database allowing a subscriber to select only those items he wishes to read. Indexing, cross-referencing, and expiration of aged messages are also provided."

Although it sounds like all the news is in one central repository, this is not true. Unlike popular online services such as CompuServe, America Online, or the Microsoft Network, Usenet news articles are instantly replicated throughout the Internet by connected servers. Servers must subscribe to specific newsgroups in order to be able to send and receive articles on a given topic.

NNTP servers maintain 24-hour socket-connections to each other. Any one server may be connected to three or four (or many more) other servers. There are commands that ask questions such as "Do you have message number 11233 in alt.winsock.programming?" to which the other side says yea or nay. This should give you some idea of the intricate network that is Usenet.

NNTP servers accept connections on port 119, which are maintained throughout the entire session until either the client or server closes it. If you wish you can use the Winsock Terminal included with this book to connect to an NNTP server and actually navigate through newsgroups and articles by using NNTP manually as you are reading and learning about NNTP.

MessageIDs vs. Message Numbers

First of all, a message number is a number and a MessageID is a combination of alphanumeric characters. Here is a typical MessageID:

```
<1995Nov1.133231@apexsc.com>
```

A message number is relative to the server, and a MessageID is relative to the Internet. A message number is simply a number that identifies an article on a server. Think of a newsgroup as a table in a database, and each article in that newsgroup is a separate record. The MessageID is the primary key of the table. It's a means for local identification.

A MessageID is a string that identifies a single Usenet article throughout the entire Internet. For this reason, servers have to make sure to assign MessageIDs carefully, so that there is no chance of creating a duplicate. Typically, a MessageID consists of some extraction of the system time, an @ sign, and the domain that assigned it.

Some of the NNTP commands accept both message numbers and MessageIDs as ways to specify a particular article. You can't go wrong if you follow this rule: If you are a news client use message numbers. If you are a server, use MessageIDs.

NNTP Versions

As with all public protocols, NNTP is constantly changing. At the time of this writing, the current NNTP standard is defined by RFC 977 by Brian Kantor (U.C. San Diego) and Phil Lapsley (U.C. Berkeley), dated February 1986.

Although this is the most current RFC regarding NNTP, today's NNTP servers support extended NNTP commands that are not defined in RFC 977.

These commands were derived from an Internet Draft Document called draft-bar-ber-nntp-imp-01.txt, which was released June 26, 1995. Internet Drafts have a life span of six months and are not meant to be reference material, but since almost all of Usenet operates with the commands set forth in this document I am choosing to ignore this. After all, why let a little thing like reality spoil our fun?

To learn the current status of any Internet Draft, you can download the file, lid-abstracts.txt listing contained in the Internet Drafts Shadow Directory on the following FTP servers:

ftp.is.co.za (Africa)

nic.nordu.net (Europe)

munnari.oz.au (Pacific Rim)

ds.internic.net (US East Coast)

ftp.isi.edu (US West Coast)

This file contains the current filenames and versions of all Internet Drafts.

NNTP Commands

NNTP is a text protocol. All commands are single words, some of which require parameters. Parameters are always separated by a space Chr$(32) or a tab Chr$(9). Commands are always terminated with a carriage return and a linefeed (vbCrLf).

For example, the GROUP command selects a Usenet Newsgroup. Here are two examples of an assembled GROUP command string ready to be sent to the NNTP server:

```
Cmd$ = "GROUP alt.winsock.programming" & vbCrLf
```

or

```
Cmd$ = "GROUP rec.audio.pro" & vbCrLf
```

Sample Conversation

Figure 4.1 shows a typical conversation between a newsreader and an NNTP server. <T> stands for the Tab character (ASCII 9). Note that the header and body are separated by a period. Lines starting with an apostrophe are comments.

Figure 4.1 A typical conversation between an NNTP client and server.

```
[CONNECT]

'-- This line is the first thing received. It identifies the server and
'    indicates whether or not posting is allowed.
[RECV] 200 joes.net InterNetNews NNRP server INN 1.4 22-Dec-93 ready
(posting ok).

'-- The LIST command returns a detailed list of newsgroups available on the
'    server. The first field is the name of the newsgroup. Second is the
'    first known article number. Third is the last known article number.
'    The last field is y or n to indicate whether the article is currently
'    available.
[SEND] LIST<CRLF>

'-- The first line should be 215 to indicate that the server is sending
'    the list.
[RECV] 215 list of newsgroups follows<CRLF>
'-- The server then sends a listing of newsgroups followed by a period on a
'    line by itself.
alt.1d 0000001252 000000459 y<CRLF>
alt.0d 0000001257 000000364 y<CRLF>
alt.2600 0000024553 000001183 y<CRLF>
. <CRLF>

'-- The GROUP command selects a newsgroup
[SEND] GROUP comp.lang.basic.visual.misc<CRLF>

'-- The server sends back a 211 reply indicating the number of articles,
'    first article number, last article number, and the name of the newsgroup.
[RECV] 211 61 14614 14674 comp.lang.basic.visual.misc<CRLF>

'-- The XOVER command receives the Subject, From address, Date, ArticleID,
'    Byte Size, and number of lines for each article in the specified range.
[SEND] XOVER 14614-14616<CRLF>

'-- The server sends a 224 reply to indicate that the list of messages follows.
[RECV] 224 data follows<CRLF>

'-- The server then sends the selected header information for each article
'    followed by a period on a line by itself
14614 <Subj><T><From><T><Date><T><ArticleID><T><Size><T><Lines><CRLF>
14615 <Subj><T><From><T><Date><T><ArticleID><T><Size><T><Lines><CRLF>
14616 <Subj><T><From><T><Date><T><ArticleID><T><Size><T><Lines><CRLF>
```

Continues

```
.

'-- The ARTICLE command tells the server to send the header and message body
'   of a specified article (by article number or ID)
[SEND] ARTICLE 14615<CRLF>
'-- The server sends a 220 reply indicating that it is sending the article.
'   Also included in this line is the poster's email address.
[RECV] 220 14615 <From Address> article<CRLF>
'-- The server then sends the header followed by a period on a line by
'   itself. This is immediately followed by the article body ending with a
'   period on a line by itself.
<HEADER TEXT>
.

<BODY TEXT>
.


'-- The quit command ends a session
[SEND] QUIT<CRLF>

'-- The server acknowledges the QUIT command by sending a 205 reply, and
'   drops the connection.
[RECV] 205<CRLF>


[SERVER DISCONNECTS]
```

The WILDMAT Format

WILDMAT is a format for specifying a search pattern. Some NNTP commands use the Wildmat format for text arguments such as a newsgroup pattern like comp.lang.basic.visual.* Here is a definition of this format taken from the Internet Draft file draft-barber-nntp-imp-01.txt by S. Barber, June 1995:

> *The WILDMAT format was first developed by Rich Salz to provide a uniform mechanism for matching patterns in the same manner that the UNIX shell matches filenames. There are five pattern matching operations other than a strict one-to-one match between the pattern and the source to be checked for a match. The first is an asterisk (*) to match any sequence of zero or more characters. The second is a question mark (?) to match any single character. The third specifies a specific set of characters. The set is specified as a list of characters, or as a range of characters where the beginning*

and end of the range are separated by a minus (or dash) character, or as any combination of lists and ranges. The dash can also be included in the range as a character if it is the beginning or end of the range. This set is enclosed in square brackets. The close square bracket (]) may be used in a range if it is the first character in the set. The fourth operation is the same as the logical not of the third operation and is specified the same way as the third with the addition of a caret character (^) at the beginning of the test string just inside the open square bracket. The final operation uses the backslash character to invalidate the special meaning of the open square bracket ([), the asterisk, or the question mark.

Examples

[^]-]	Matches any character other than a close square bracket or a minus sign/dash.
*bdc	Matches any string that ends with the string bdc including the string bdc (without quotes).
bdc	Matches any string that contains the string bdc including the string bdc (without quotes).
[0-9a-zA-Z]	Matches any alphanumeric string.
a??d	Matches any four-character string that begins with a and ends with d.

Server Responses

Server responses consist of a three-digit number and a space Chr$(32), usually followed by one or more parameters (also separated by spaces), and ending with a carriage return and a linefeed (vbCrLf).

For example, the appropriate positive response from the aforementioned GROUP command is the number 201 followed by the number of messages in the newsgroup, the first article number, the last article number, and then a message indicating the group is selected:

```
"201 112 43211 43323 alt.winsock.programming group selected" & vbCrLf
```

This response from the GROUP command indicates that the alt.winsock.programming group has been selected, that there are 112 articles available, and that the first article number is 43211 and the last is 43323. "Being selected" means that any ARTICLE or HEAD commands (or any other commands that refer to article numbers) are to be acted upon within the selected newsgroup.

Figure 4.2   The response code's first two digits classifies it according to these general rules.

```
The first digit indicates broad success or failure:
1xx - Informative message. You can generally ignore these.
2xx - Command OK.
3xx - Command OK so far, send the rest of it.
4xx - Command was correct, but couldn't be performed for some reason.
5xx - Command unimplemented, or incorrect, or a serious program error occurred.
The second digit indicates the response's category:
x0x - Connection, setup, and miscellaneous messages
x1x - Newsgroup selection
x2x - Article selection
x3x - Distribution functions
x4x - Posting
x8x - Nonstandard (private implementation) extensions
x9x - Debugging output
```

I know this is not really the place to discuss the 201 response, but you cannot always count on the first argument (number of articles) to be accurate. Sometimes the value may be zero, sometimes it may be incorrect. You also cannot count on getting the number of articles by subtracting the first article number from the last. Don't ask me why, it's just the way it is. My feeling is that you should check both, and when in doubt go with the second method (subtracting the first number from the last number). Besides, who cares if the number is off by a couple messages? The point is that you should never assume anything in your application, except that the user has not paid for his or her copy of your software.

Figure 4.2 shows what each digit of the response code represents, and Figure 4.3 shows a summary of NNTP server responses. The first number identifies the message to your program, and the text describes the reply.

Figure 4.3   Summary of NNTP server responses.

```
100 help text follows
190-199 debug output

200 server ready - posting allowed
201 server ready - no posting allowed
202 slave status noted
205 closing connection - goodbye!
211 n f l s group selected
```

Figure 4.3 *Continued.*

```
         n = estimated number of articles in group,
         f = first article number in the group,
         l = last article number in the group,
         s = name of the group.
215 list of newsgroups follows
220 <article number> <message-id> article retrieved - head and body follow
221 <article number> <message-id> article retrieved - head follows
222 <article number> <message-id> article retrieved - body follows
223 <article number> <message-id> article retrieved - request text separately
230 list of new articles by message-id follows
235 article transferred ok
240 article posted ok
282 XOVER data follows.
335 send article to be transferred.  End with <CR-LF>.<CR-LF>
340 send article to be posted. End with <CR-LF>.<CR-LF>

400 service discontinued
411 no such news group
412 no newsgroup has been selected
420 no current article has been selected
421 no next article in this group
422 no previous article in this group
423 no such article number in this group
430 no such article found
435 article not wanted - do not send it
436 transfer failed - try again later
437 article rejected - do not try again
440 posting not allowed
441 posting failed
480 Transfer permission denied

500 command not recognized
501 command syntax error
502 access restriction or permission denied
503 program fault - command not performed
```

Usenet Article Format

A Usenet article is comprised of a header and the text body. Figure 4.4 shows a sample of a Usenet article header. The article format is essentially the widely accepted ARPANET mail message format with a few extensions required by

Figure 4.4   Sample Usenet article headers.

```
Path: mindport.net!newsfeed.internetmci.com!news
From: mnguyen@clark.net (CDSI)
Newsgroups: alt.winsock.programming
Subject: Q : winsock programming server
Date: 4 Sep 1995 13:58:32 GMT
Organization: Clark Internet Services, Inc., Ellicott City, MD USA
Lines: 14
Message-ID: <42f0m8$9ho@clarknet.clark.net>
NNTP-Posting-Host: clark.net
Mime-Version: 1.0
Content-Type: TEXT/PLAIN; charset=ISO-8859-1
Content-Transfer-Encoding: 8bit
X-Newsreader: TIN [UNIX 1.3 950726BETA PL0]

Relay-Version: version B 2.10 2/13/83; site cbosgd.UUCP
Posting-Version: version B 2.10 2/13/83; site eagle.UUCP
Path: cbosgd!mhuxj!mhuxt!eagle!jerry
From: jerry@eagle.uucp (Jerry Schwarz)
Newsgroups: net.general
Subject: Usenet Etiquette -- Please Read
Message-ID: <642@eagle.UUCP>
Date: Friday, 19-Nov-82 16:14:55 EST
Followup-To: net.news
Expires: Saturday, 1-Jan-83 00:00:00 EST
Date-Received: Friday, 19-Nov-82 16:59:30 EST
Organization: Bell Labs, Murray Hill
```

Usenet. For a complete description of the Usenet message format, see RFC 850 entitled "Standard for Interchange of USENET Messages," by Mark R. Horton.

Sometimes an article header can have the following older format:

```
From: cbosgd!mhuxj!mhuxt!eagle!jerry (Jerry Schwarz)
Newsgroups: net.general
Title: Usenet Etiquette -- Please Read
Article-I.D.: eagle.642
Posted: Fri Nov 19 16:14:55 1982
Received: Fri Nov 19 16:59:30 1982
Expires: Mon Jan  1 00:00:00 1990
```

Either way, you will be able to retrieve specific header lines with NNTP, so if there is no Subject header, you can get the Title header instead.

VB Programming Technique

I have found that the best way to write for this type of protocol is by writing a response handler in the Receive event or within the event or subroutine that receives incoming data. You must use LineMode with dsSocket. If you are using another tool, make sure it fires a Receive event for each line of text it receives. Chapter 2 covers programming with dsSocket, and you should refer to it if you have any questions specific to dsSocket as you read the rest of this chapter.

Fortunately, I have already done the dirty work of writing an NNTP class in Visual Basic (cfNNTP.cls) that you can drop right into your application, or simply reference as a DLL. I have put comments in the code for each of the responses so you can step through the handler code for each response and modify it if need be. See Chapter 9 for more information on using cfNNTP object.

NNTP commands can be sent anywhere from within your program, such as from a command button, menu option, or list box double-click. Unlike some of the other code in this book, it is not necessary to wait for a response in a loop after sending a command. The client code is state-oriented, meaning a command is sent and a state is entered, the state of waiting for a response. Once the response has been received, the state changes back to idle. The response handling code operates on the response codes differently depending on the state when the code was received. This will become more obvious when we start looking at the code.

Take a look at the sample code in Figure 4.5, which simply sends the server a GROUP command to specify the alt.winsock.programming newsgroup, and retrieves the number of articles and their number range. This code clip assumes that you are already connected to the NNTP server on port 119 using a dsSocket control. When the Command1 button is clicked, the GROUP command is sent, which tells the server to select the alt.winsock.programming newsgroup. The application is at that time waiting for a response from the server, which could be either a 211 indicating success, or a 411 indicating that there is no such newsgroup.

Figure 4.5   This code sends the server a GROUP command to specify the alt.winsock.programming newsgroup, and retrieves the number of articles and their number range.

```
Sub Command1_Click ()
    SendData dsSocket1, "GROUP alt.winsock.programming" & vbCrLf
End Sub
```
Continues

Figure 4.5   This code sends the server a GROUP command to specify the alt.winsock.programming newsgroup, and retrieves the number of articles and their number range. *(Continued)*

```
Sub dsSocket1_Receive(ReceiveData As String)

    Dim nPos As Integer
    Dim nCode As Integer

    Dim lNumArticles As Long
    Dim lFirstArticle As Long
    Dim lLastArticle As Long

    If Len(ReceiveData) > 3 Then

        '-- Determine the reply code
        nCode = Val(Left$(ReceiveData, 3))
        Select Case nCode

            Case 211 '-- Article information for selected newsgroup

                '-- Trim the reply code off the left of the string
                nPos = InStr(ReceiveData, " ")
                ReceiveData = Mid$(ReceiveData, nPos + 1)

                '-- Get the number of articles
                nPos = InStr(ReceiveData, " ")
                lNumArticles = Val(Left$(ReceiveData, nPos - 1))
                ReceiveData = Mid$(ReceiveData, nPos + 1)

                '-- Get the first article number
                nPos = InStr(ReceiveData, " ")
                lFirstArticle = Val(Left$(ReceiveData, nPos - 1))
                ReceiveData = Mid$(ReceiveData, nPos + 1)

                '-- Get the last article number
                nPos = InStr(ReceiveData, " ")
                lLastArticle = Val(Left$(ReceiveData, nPos - 1))

            Case 411

                MsgBox "No Such Newsgroup Exists"

        End Select
End Sub
```

If the 211 reply string is received via the Receive event then the number of articles, the first article number, and the last article number are parsed out of the reply string. If the 411 reply string is received, a message box pops up to tell the user that the specified newsgroup does not exist on the server.

String Parsing

The string parsing code is fairly common for this type of programming. Let me explain the first four lines of code following the "Case 211" line. These four lines (actually the first, third, and fourth lines) are all you need to parse values from a string.

Step 1 is to identify the position of the next space within the string. The Instr function returns the position of one string within another string:

```
'-- Suppose ReceiveData = "211 100 1200 1300"
nPos = InStr(ReceiveData, " ")
'-- nPos equals 4 because the space after "211" is the fourth character.
```

Step 2 is to trim the 211 and the space from the left of the string. The Mid$ function returns the portion of the string (first argument) starting with the character position (second argument):

```
'-- ReceiveData = "211 100 1200 1300" and nPos = 4
ReceiveData = Mid$(ReceiveData, nPos + 1)
'-- ReceiveData now equals "100 1200 1300"
```

Step 3 is a repeat of Step 1, which returns the position of the next space within ReceiveData using the Instr function:

```
'-- Suppose ReceiveData = "100 1200 1300"
nPos = InStr(ReceiveData, " ")
'-- nPos equals 4 because the space after "100" is the fourth character.
```

Step 4 is to retrieve the value of the string up to but not including the space. The Left$ function returns the leftmost number of characters (second parameter) of the string (first parameter). The Val function returns the value of the string returned by the Left$ function:

```
'-- ReceiveData = "100 1200 1300" and nPos = 4
lNumArticles = Val(Left$(ReceiveData, nPos - 1))

'-- lNumArticles = 100
```

The szParseString Function

Although it is important to understand how to parse strings using VB, it is not always desirable to do it manually. That's why I wrote the szParseString function for returning portions of a string. szParseString is a function in DSSOCK.BAS that will return a portion of a string given the string, a delimiter character, and the segment number. For example, say we have the following string:

```
szText = "The Quick Brown Fox"
```

The following code will return "The":

```
Debug.Print szParseString(szText, " ", 1)
```

The following code will return "Brown":

```
Debug.Print szParseString(szText, " ", 3)
```

Sample Program—NNTP.VBP

Figure 4.6 shows NNTP, a simple newsreader application. You can use it to browse and view news in any newsgroup and post new articles (if posting is allowed). The code snippets discussed here are all taken from this sample application.

Enter the news server name or address in the NNTP Server Name text box and click the Connect button. The client connects to the NNTP server on port 119.

Figure 4.6   The NNTP sample newsreader program.

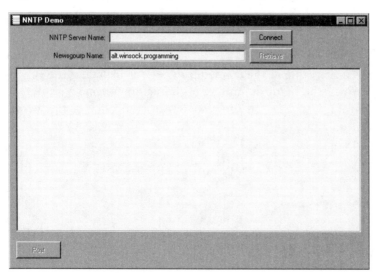

After a successful connection, you can view a newsgroup by entering its name in the Newsgroup Name text box and pressing the Retrieve button. The client then logs onto the specified newsgroup and sends you a list of articles, as shown in Figure 4.7. You can view any article by double-clicking on it. The client downloads the article and displays it, as in Figure 4.8.

If you want to post to any newsgroup, hit the Post button. The post form, shown in Figure 4.9, pops up. Fill in the newsgroup, your e-mail address, the subject, and the article text, and hit the Post button to post the message. When the client receives a positive reply it shows a confirmation dialog box, shown in Figure 4.10.

Connecting to an NNTP Server

Connect to your NNTP server the same way you'd connect to any Internet server. NNTP listens to port 119. Therefore, the following syntax will do nicely:

```
If SocketConnect(dsSocket, 119, "your.nntp.server", 30) Then
    MsgBox "Error Connecting to server", vbInformation
Else
    MsgBox "Connected!"
End If
```

Figure 4.7   NNTP displays a list of articles when you enter a newsgroup name and press the Retrieve button.

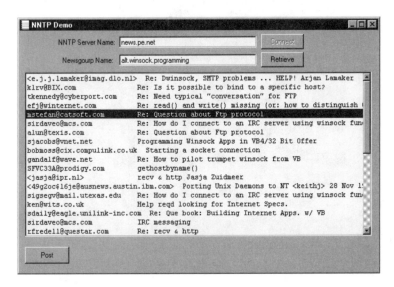

Figure 4.8   View an article by double-clicking on it in the list.

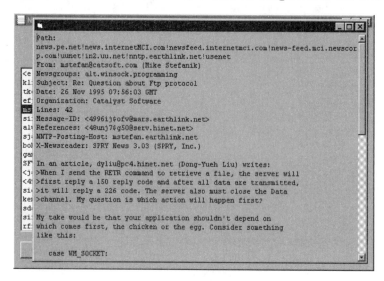

Figure 4.9   Click the Post button to pop up the Post form. Enter a message and press the Post button on the Post form.

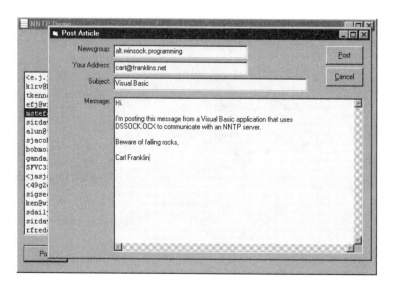

Figure 4.10   The client gives you confirmation following a successful post.

Upon connection you will receive either a 200 or a 201 reply and a welcome line that might look like the following:

```
200 mindport.net InterNetNews NNRP server INN 1.4 22-Dec-93 ready (posting ok).
```

The 200 reply indicates that posting is allowed, and a 201 reply indicates that it isn't. The reply number is followed by the domain name, the version of NNTP software, and sometimes a textual indication of posting being allowed or not. After receiving this line, you should send the command, "MODE READER" to tell the server that you are a newsreader. The server sends back another 200 reply. At this point you are ready to converse with the server.

Retrieving an Article Header

Now that you know how it works, let's add some complexity to the above example. When the number of articles and first and last article numbers are received, the code should send the HEAD command to retrieve the header for the first article in the newsgroup, and display the date, subject, and sender's name in the debug window.

Now there must be two states, or *modes* if you will. State 1 is when we are receiving reply strings, and state 2 is when we are receiving text (the article's header).

The header is sent as individual lines of text terminated by a period on a line by itself (with a CR/LF on either side of it). The HEAD command is fairly simple. The format is "HEAD" followed by a space and the article number, and terminated with a CR/LF.

The example in Figure 4.11 adds onto the Receive event from the previous example with code to return and parse the header of the first article in the archive. There are some fundamental differences between this example and the first one. Besides using szParseString to return the different portions of ReceiveData, the nCode variable is among several variables declared Static. Static variables hold their values for the life of the program. When the subroutine runs, the Static variables will be whatever their values were when the subroutine was previously exited. nCode is Static so that the last reply code received is always available.

Figure 4.11   This code logs into a newsgroup, then returns and parses the header of the first article.

```
Sub dsSocket1_Receive(ReceiveData As String)

    Dim nPos As Integer   '-- Used with Instr
    Const chrSpace = " " '-- Used with Instr"
    Const szPeriod = "." '-- Used to determine the end of x-mission.

    Static lNumArticles As Long   '-- Number of articles in group
    Static lFirstArticle As Long  '-- First Article Number
    Static lLastArticle As Long   '-- Last Article Number

    Static szSubject As String    '-- Article Subject
    Static szDate As String       '-- Creation Date
    Static szSender As String     '-- Who posted the article
    Static szArticleText As String

    Static nTextMode As Integer   '-- When True, we are receiving data
        '   When False, reply codes.
    Static nCode As Integer       '-- The last reply code received.
'---------------------------------------------------------------------------

    If nTextMode = False Then
        '-- Receiving reply codes

        nCode = Val(Left$(ReceiveData, 3))

        Select Case nCode
            Case 211 '-- Article information for selected newsgroup

                '-- Get the number of articles
                lNumArticles = Val(szParseString(ReceiveData, chrSpace, 2))

                '-- Get the first article number
                lFirstArticle = Val(szParseString(ReceiveData, chrSpace, 3))

                '-- Get the first article number
                lLastArticle = Val(szParseString(ReceiveData, chrSpace, 4))
```

Figure 4.11 *Continued.*

```
            '-- Retrieve the Header for the first article

SendData dsSocket1, "HEAD" & Str$(lFirstArticle) & vbCrLf

        Case 220, 221, 222
            '-- 220 Header and Body follows
            '-- 221 Header follows
            '-- 222 Body follows

            '-- Prepare to receive data
            nTextMode = True

        Case Is > 399   '-- An error occurred
            MsgBox szParseString(ReceiveData, 2), vbInformation

    End Select
Else
    '-- Transmission complete?
    If SuperTrim$(ReceiveData) = szPeriod & vbCrLf Then
        '-- What was the last code received?
        Select Case nCode
            Case 220 '-- Header and body follows
                '-- szArticleText holds the complete article text.
                Debug.Print szArticleText
            Case 221 '-- Header follows
                Debug.Print szSubject
                Debug.Print szDate
                Debug.Print szSender
        End Select
        '-- Done receiving text. Ready for another code.
        nTextMode = False
    Else
        '-- What was the last code received?
        Select Case nCode
            Case 220 '-- Header and body follow
                szArticleText = szArticleText & ReceiveData & vbCrLf
            Case 221 '-- Header follows
                If Left$(UCase$(ReceiveData), 8) = "SUBJECT:" Then
                    szSubject = ReceiveData
                ElseIf Left$(UCase$(ReceiveData), 5) = "DATE:" Then
                    szDate = ReceiveData
                ElseIf Left$(UCase$(ReceiveData), 5) = "FROM:" Then
                    szSender = ReceiveData
```

Continues

```
                    End If
            End Select
        End If
    End If

End Sub
```

Also static are string variables szSubject, szDate, and szSender. These will hold the values extracted from the article header until the header has been completely received, at which point they are displayed in a message box.

nCommandMode is a flag that indicates whether we are receiving reply strings or header data. If nCommandMode is False (the default value) then we are receiving reply strings. When nCommandMode is True, then we are receiving header text.

After sending the HEAD command you should receive a 221 message indicating that the header is being sent to you. The next several lines will be the text of the header ending with a period on a line by itself. Remember that every line ends with a CR/LF.

If the code received is 221, then nCommandMode is set to True. When a line of header data is received, then the nCode value is tested, indicating the last reply code received. If this code is 221, then ReceiveData is a line of header text.

Retrieving a Complete Article

With just a slight modification of the preceding code, we can tell the NNTP server to send us a specific article. The code is exactly the same, except that you send the ARTICLE command instead of the HEAD command. Where HEAD retrieves the header for an article, ARTICLE retrieves the entire article. To return just the body text of the article, send the BODY command.

Instead of this:

```
'-- Retrieve the Header for the first article
SendData dsSocket1, "HEAD" & Str$(lFirstArticle) & vbCrlf
```

specify this command:

```
'-- Retrieve the whole article
SendData dsSocket1, "ARTICLE" & Str$(lFirstArticle) & vbCrlf
```

Retrieving Article Information

When you use a newsreader program, such as Netscape, Microsoft Internet News, or Outlook Express application, to browse a newsgroup you are usually presented with a one-line description of each article. This line may include the date, subject, sender's e-mail address, number of lines, and so on. Where does this information come from? The answer is the XOVER command. Here is the syntax for this command:

```
XOVER <article number range. ex: 200-400> <CRLF>
```

See the XOVER command definition at the end of this chapter for range options.

XOVER returns the following information on a line for each article in the specified range, ending with a CR/LF on a line by itself:

```
<Article Number> <Subject> <Date> <Article ID> <Size in bytes> <Number of Lines>
```

Example: Displaying Article Descriptions in a List Box

The following example shows how to ask for a list of all articles in a newsgroup using the XOVER command, and displays the result in a list box (it is assumed that you are already connected).

```
'-- Send the XOVER command to retrieve all messages.
SendData dsSocket1, "XOVER 1-" & vbCrLf
```

The server sends back a 211 reply, indicating the number of messages in the group, and the first and last MessageIDs. At that point the XOVER command is sent to retrieve the descriptions of all messages in the entire group.

The server then sends back a 224 reply, indicating that the list is about to be sent. At that point a flag is set to indicate that we are receiving the list. Each line received after that is parsed and the data displayed in a list box. At the end of the list, the server sends a period on a line by itself. When this is received, the connection is closed.

Posting an Article

Before you can post an article, you must have received the words "posting ok" in the first line received when you connect to the server. If you don't receive this string there's a good chance the server is not accepting posts.

To initiate a posting, send the POST command like so:

```
SendData dsSocket1, = "POST" & vbCrLf
```

You will receive back either a 340 reply indicating that you can go ahead and send the article, or a 440 reply indicating that posting is not allowed. If you get a 340, you can immediately start sending the article text.

To post a message, you need to create at least a minimal header. In NNTP land the following fields are considered required:

From. Name and e-mail address of the sender having the following format:

```
Carl Franklin <carl@franklins.net>
```

Newsgroups. List of groups to post to separated by comma

Subject. Subject of your message

Here is a perfect example of a header that you will create when posting a new article:

```
From: Carl Franklin <carl@franklins.net>
Newsgroups: test.newsgroup
Subject: This is a test post
```

The NNTP server fills in all the detail header fields, such as the Message-ID, Date, and so on.

The message body follows the header, from which it is separated by a blank line. The body ends with a period on a line by itself. Figure 4.12 shows an example of a complete article ready to be posted. All lines are terminated with a CR/LF.

Figure 4.12   A complete Usenet article ready to be posted.

```
From: Carl Franklin <carl@franklins.net>
Newsgroups: test.newsgroup
Subject: This is a test post

This is a test post from a Visual Basic Application.

Carl Franklin
```

Figure 4.13   Example: Posting an article.

```
SendData dsSocket1, "From: Carl Franklin <carl@franklins.net>" & vbCrlf
SendData dsSocket1, "Newsgroups: test.newsgroup" & vbCrlf
SendData dsSocket1, "Subject: This is a test post" & vbCrlf
SendData dsSocket1, vbCrlf
SendData dsSocket1, "This is a test post from a Visual Basic Application!" & vbCrlf
SendData dsSocket1, vbCrlf
SendData dsSocket1, "Carl Franklin" & vbCrlf
SendData dsSocket1, "." & vbCrlf
```

After sending the POST command and receiving a 340 reply, you can execute the sample code shown in Figure 4.13 to post a message. Of course, you would want to let your user specify the actual article data, but this is a good example from a programmer's perspective.

After executing this code, you will either receive a 240 indicating success, or a 4xx series error, indicating a wide variety of errors all meaning that the post was rejected for one reason or another. Figure 4.14 shows the actual errors you could receive.

TIP   It is not efficient to send your text one line at a time; I wrote the example this way to bring attention to the different lines that make up the sent text. It would be better to concatenate the entire message together into one string, and then send that string.

Figure 4.14   Possible errors resulting from posting an article.

```
400 service discontinued
435 article not wanted - do not send it
437 article rejected - do not try again
440 posting not allowed
441 posting failed

500 command not recognized
501 command syntax error
502 access restriction or permission denied
503 program fault - command not performed
```

```
Path: mindport.net!news
From: Carl Franklin <carl@franklins.net>
Newsgroups: test.newsgroup
Subject: This is yet another test post
Date: 30 Oct 1995 14:39:07 GMT
Organization: Mindport Internet Services
Lines: 3
Message-ID: <472o2b$98c@draco.mindport.net>
NNTP-Posting-Host: 199.35.240.135

This is a test post from a Visual Basic Application.

Carl Franklin
```

Assuming that you receive a 240 reply back from the server, you can immediately retrieve the article with the ARTICLE command, although you will need to get the article number. There is a good chance that it will be the last article posted to the group, although this is not 100 percent guaranteed because someone else could be posting at the exact same moment as you. It's best to do an XOVER on the last 10 or so articles to find your article number. Figure 4.15 shows what the article might look like when read with a newsreader.

Posting a Reply to a Previous Message

When posting a reply, you need to fill in just one other header, the Reply-To header. For example, Figure 4.16 shows the same message posted as a reply to an article posted by Jon Smith. The original message is enclosed in quotes, as is the common practice when replying to an article.

Figure 4.16   Posting a reply to a previous message.

```
SendData dsSocket1, "From: Carl Franklin <carl@franklins.net>" & vbCrlf
SendData dsSocket1, "Newsgroups: rec.audio.pro" & vbCrlf
SendData dsSocket1, "Subject: Re: Why should I get a sampler?" & vbCrlf
SendData dsSocket1, "Reply-To: Jon Smith <jons@somewhere.net>" & vbCrlf
SendData dsSocket1, vbCrlf
SendData dsSocket1, "> Why would one buy a sampler?" & vbCrlf
SendData dsSocket1, "> What is a sampler, anyway?" & vbCrlf
```

Figure 4.16   Continued.

```
SendData dsSocket1, "> Just Curious," & vbCrlf
SendData dsSocket1, "> " & vbCrlf
SendData dsSocket1, "> Jon Smith" & vbCrlf
SendData dsSocket1, vbCrlf
SendData dsSocket1, "Jon," & vbCrlf
SendData dsSocket1, "A sampler lets you record small digital clips" & vbCrlf
SendData dsSocket1, "of your favorite instruments and them reproduce them" & vbCrlf
SendData dsSocket1, "with a MIDI controller. They are great for drums." & vbCrlf
SendData dsSocket1, vbCrlf
SendData dsSocket1, "Carl Franklin" & vbCrlf
SendData dsSocket1, "." & vbCrlf
```

Retrieving a List of Newsgroups

The LIST command retrieves a list of newsgroups from the server. By sending the LIST command you are really asking for trouble in that the server will return the monster list of all newsgroups. The server sends a 215 reply followed by each newsgroup's information on separate lines and ending with a period on a line by itself. Each line has the following format:

```
<newsgroup> <last article number> <first article number> <posting allowed (y or n)>
```

For example, the following command:

```
SendData dsSocket1, "LIST" & vbCrLf
```

would return the following:

```
215 List Follows
alt.barney.dinosaur.die.die.die 1100 1000 y
alt.barney.dinosaur.why.why.why 320 297 y
<and so on>
```

If you are writing a newsreader, it would be best to save the output of the list command to a database or some other file and give the user the option of retrieving it every time.

LIST ACTIVE Returns Selective Newsgroups

LIST ACTIVE returns a listing of active newsgroups, and perhaps more importantly, lets you limit the range of groups for which information is returned. The server returns a 215 reply followed by a list of newsgroups. For example, the following command:

```
SendData dsSocket1, "LIST ACTIVE comp.lang.basic.visual.*" & vbCrLf
could return the following data:
215 list follows
comp.lang.basic.visual.3rdparty 2200 1923 y
comp.lang.basic.visual.announce 240 237 y
comp.lang.basic.visual.database 11293 11245 y
comp.lang.basic.visual.misc 23098 22432 y
.
```

 TIP   It has been my experience that LIST ACTIVE does not always accept an argument, and will only return a complete list of active newsgroups.

XGTITLE Returns Newsgroup Descriptions

The XGTITLE command returns a list of newsgroups that fit the specified WILD-MAT search mask. The server returns a 282 reply followed by a list of newsgroups. On each line is returned the name of the newsgroup and a short description. For example:

```
SendData dsSocket1, "XGTITLE comp.lang.basic.visual.*" & vbCrLf
```

would return the following:

```
282 list follows
comp.lang.basic.visual.3rdparty  Add-ins for Visual Basic.
comp.lang.basic.visual.announce  Official information on Visual Basic. (Moderated)
comp.lang.basic.visual.database  Database aspects of Visual Basic.
comp.lang.basic.visual.misc      Visual Basic in general.
.
```

You could return the description of just one newsgroup by specifying it without any wildcards. For example:

```
SendData dsSocket1, "XGTITLE comp.lang.basic.visual.misc" & vbCrLf
```

would return this:

```
282 list follows
comp.lang.basic.visual.misc      Visual Basic in general.
.
```

LIST NEWSGROUPS also Returns Newsgroup Descriptions

The LIST NEWSGROUPS command does essentially the same thing as XGTITLE, but it returns a 215 result code. For example, this command:

```
SendData dsSocket1, "LIST NEWSGROUPS comp.lang.basic.visual.*" & vbCrLf
```

would return the following:

```
215 Descriptions in form "group description".
comp.lang.basic.visual.3rdparty  Add-ins for Visual Basic.
comp.lang.basic.visual.announce  Official information on Visual Basic. (Moderated)
comp.lang.basic.visual.database  Database aspects of Visual Basic.
comp.lang.basic.visual.misc      Visual Basic in general.
```

 It has been my experience that LIST NEWSGROUPS does not always accept an argument, and will only return a complete list of newsgroups.

Retrieving a List of Article Numbers

You can retrieve a list of just the valid article numbers for a newsgroup with the LISTGROUP command. LISTGROUP takes as an argument the name of a newsgroup. Here is the syntax:

```
LISTGROUP <newsgroup name> <CRLF>
```

After receiving a LISTGROUP command the server sends a 211 reply followed by a list of article numbers, each on a line by itself and ending with a period. For example, the following command:

```
SendData dsSocket1,  "LISTGROUP comp.lang.basic.visual.announce" & vbCrLf
```

would return the following output:

```
211 List follows
11143
11145
11146
.
```

Retrieving a Specific Header Field

The XHDR command lets you retrieve a specific header field for a given article. Here is the command syntax:

```
XHDR <Field Name> <Article Number> <CRLF>
```

The server returns a 221 reply followed by a line containing the article number and header information and a period on a line by itself. For example, the following command:

```
SendData dsSocket1, "XHDR Subject 14619" & vbCrLf
```

could return the following server output:

```
221 Subject fields follow
14619 Re:VB Decompiler
.
```

This is very handy when you want only specific pieces of the header. For example, if you were to write an application that routes certain newsgroup articles by e-mail, you would not need all the distribution headers, and whatnot. You just want the sender's name, e-mail address, and the date and subject of the message.

Searching for Articles by Header

The XPAT command is used to search for Usenet articles. XPAT retrieves a list of articles in the current newsgroup given a range of articles, a header field, and a match pattern. XPAT returns the article number and the specified header field for all articles where the header field matches the pattern. Here is the syntax:

```
XPAT <Header> <Range|Message-ID> <Wildmat String> [<Wildmat String>] <CRLF>
```

Here is some example code that searches for all articles where "VB6" appears in the subject for the comp.lang.basic.visual.misc newsgroup:

```
SendData dsSocket1, "XPAT Subject 1- *VB6*" & vbCrLf
```

Here is an example that returns all messages posted by Carl Franklin:

```
SendData dsSocket1, "XPAT From 1- *carl@franklins.net*" & vbCrLf
The server returns a 221 reply followed by a list of articles ending with a period
on a line by itself. For example, consider the output of XPAT From 1-
*carl@franklins.net*:
221 From matches follow.
10894 Carl Franklin <carl@franklins.net>
.
```

There are many great practical uses for this type of search. Are you having trouble finding someone who you know is active on Usenet? Pick out a list of newsgroups that he or she frequents and search them on a daily basis for any articles with your friend's name in the From header field.

Is someone you know looking for a job? Search biz.jobs.offered headers for keywords like "Engineer" or "Sacramento." Just for kicks, e-mail all the desired articles to yourself, or throw them into an Access database.

You see, programming the Internet is not just about accessing the Internet, it's about disseminating the information available for real-world practical reasons.

Server-to-Server Communication

NNTP is much more than a protocol for news clients, it's also how NNTP servers communicate with each other. An NNTP server will have at least one other server connected to it at all times, although it is not uncommon for it to be linked to three or four other servers. Whenever your site receives a post from a local user it is quickly passed on to the other servers using the IHAVE command. Your server is constantly receiving news from the other servers with the IHAVE command also. IHAVE is the way news is replicated throughout the Internet.

Here is a conversation that takes place between two servers to successfully replicate an article:

```
RECV: IHAVE <krwaosRREdf3.342@netcom.com> <CRLF>
SEND: 335 send article to be transferred.  End with <CR-LF>.<CR-LF>
RECV:  [Server sends the article ending with a period on a line by itself]
SEND: 235 article transferred OK <CR-LF>
```

Here is a conversation that takes place between two servers when the receiver already has the article:

```
RECV: IHAVE <krwaosRREdf3.342@netcom.com> <CRLF>
SEND: 435 article not wanted - do not send it <CR-LF
```

Using the cfNNTP Object

Now that you know how NNTP works you can use the cfNNTP object in your own projects without having to cut and paste my sample code into your project. Chapter 9 shows you how to drop this object into your own projects with just a few lines of code.

Epilogue

NNTP may seem at first like it wouldn't fit well into an existing framework. However, you can use NNTP to supplement an information system by tapping the largest source of subject-oriented material the Internet can offer.

One practical (and profitable) use of Usenet is archiving. Write an application to archive news articles for one or more newsgroups and then provide search capabilities either on the subject line or on the articles themselves. I know that on Carl & Gary's Visual Basic Home Page our news archive database is a real crowd-pleaser. We receive a steady stream of compliments on it. Although it was originally written with Perl scripts in Unix, the same thing could easily be written in Visual Basic. You can store the articles in any database format from Access to MS SQL Server.

ELECTRONIC MAIL

Introduction

Electronic mail, or e-mail, is the most widely used resource on the Internet. Many modern companies, large and small, rely on e-mail as their primary source of communication. The world of electronic mail seems mysterious when you first approach it. There are all these computers whizzing your messages around the world at the speed of light. How do they work? What happens when you send mail? What's the difference between e-mail and CompuServe or America Online mail messages?

After reading this chapter, you'll understand how e-mail systems work, and you will know how to use the SMTP and POP3 protocols to send and receive e-mail messages and files using Visual Basic.

Electronic mail is a kind of catch-all phrase that describes any transfer of textual (and binary) data from one computer user to another via some sort of communications network. For me, as for many of us, my first encounter with electronic mail was CompuServe. I went nuts when I saw CompuServe for the first time. I could send mail to people. I could get into the CB simulator and talk in real time (almost) with other people all over the world.

CompuServe uses its internal network and software to move messages around from mailbox to mailbox. This includes pieces of the Internet at certain points of transmission, but the whole process is managed by CompuServe. America Online, Prodigy, and the Microsoft Network are other examples of commercial networks that offer electronic mail.

But there is another type of electronic mail that is much broader in scope and definition. Its roots are in the academic institutions of the world. Internet mail can be set up and accessed by anyone, not just a CompuServe or an AOL. In fact, there are many new Internet Service Providers (ISPs) that offer connectivity to the Internet including e-mail for a monthly fee, using a local access phone number. These ISPs are increasing daily all over America, and are really representative of the open architecture of Internet protocols. Most all ISPs have a mail server that speaks SMTP and POP3. You can access e-mail from this server with one of many shareware or commercial e-mail applications like Pegasus, Eudora, or Microsoft Outlook Express, which do exactly what the sample code in this chapter does.

If you couldn't wait and have already looked at the sample code for this chapter, you may be struck by how simple it is. The truth is that these and other Internet protocols are so easy that a big marketing focus of the large commercial networks is convincing the masses that using their system is better than using just the public Internet systems, which in reality are some of the biggest reasons for the Internet's incredible popularity. In most cases commercial online services add a layer between you and the mail gateway.

I'm not saying that commercial networks are not excellent sources of information and Internet services, I'm merely trying to help you understand that there is a difference between CompuServe mail and Internet mail. This difference really becomes apparent when you try to write programs to access e-mail on a commercial network versus an Internet server. To access e-mail on CompuServe you need either a high-level system such as Microsoft Exchange or you need to write a serial communications program to access CompuServe with a modem, coding your way to the e-mail section and sending the right strings to send or get your mail. Each commercial network has a different protocol (or set of rules) for sending and receiving mail. Some networks may not even offer a way for you to write code to get your mail, instead making you use their own applications. This is why it's very important that there be some sort of standard protocol for sending and receiving mail with a mail server. Enter SMTP (for sending) and POP3 (for receiving).

If you access the Internet through an ISP, you need to know the name of your mail server. Call them up and ask them if they have an SMTP/POP3 mail server, and if you could please have the address. This information is usually supplied with your sign-up package that you should have received from the ISP. With only the address of the server and your name and password, you are ready to use some very simple Visual Basic code to send and receive e-mail.

The SMTP Protocol

The Simple Mail Transport Protocol (SMTP) is used to send mail messages. SMTP uses port 25. That is, to send a message to a mail server with SMTP you must first connect to that server on port 25. Once connected, there is an exchange of commands and responses back and forth between you (the client) and the mail server. Every line you send must end with a carriage return/linefeed pair.

Take a look at the sample session in Figure 5.1, which sends an e-mail message to an SMTP server taken from RFC 821. The letter S stands for Send and the letter R for Receive.

The first line sent tells the server who the mail is from, to which the server responds with a 250 OK reply. The number 250 is a code that means OK. Other numbers mean other things, but we'll get to that in a minute.

The next line sent to the server identifies the receiver. The server responds with OK. This can be repeated for as many recipients as required. The third line sent in

---

Figure 5.1 Sample session between an SMTP client and server.

S: MAIL FROM:<me@myhouse.com>

R: 250 OK

S: RCPT TO:<you@yourhouse.com>

R: 250 OK

S: RCPT TO:<someone@somewhere.com>

R: 550 No such user here

S: RCPT TO:<anotherone@somewhere_else.com>

R: 250 OK

S: DATA

R: 354 Start mail input; end with <CRLF>.<CRLF>

S: Blah blah blah...

S: ...etc. etc. etc.

S: <CRLF>.<CRLF>

R: 250 OK

---

this example shows what happens if the specified receiver does not exist at the domain. The server will send back the number 550 followed by an error message.

Jumping down to the fourth block, this is where the message itself is sent. If the server accepts the DATA command indicating it is ready to receive data, it will send back the number 354, at which point the client sends the message followed by carriage return/linefeed pair, a period, and another carriage return/linefeed. If the message was sent successfully the server sends back 250 OK.

SMTP Commands

SMTP uses a series of simple four-character commands such as MAIL and QUIT that perform the various tasks required to send an e-mail message. These commands are listed in the SMTP Reference Appendix at the back of this book. SMTP commands are always followed with a CR/LF pair.

Server Responses

After sending an SMTP command, you will receive a reply that consists of a three-digit number followed by a space and a text message. Figure 5.2 shows a list of reply codes in numeric order. The full descriptions of these codes can be found in RFC 821.

Reply Code Categories

Each digit of the reply code has a specific meaning. There are five values for the first digit of the reply code: 1 is not used in SMTP, 2 indicates a positive reply, 3 indicates a positive intermediate reply in which case the server is waiting for more information, 4 indicates that the command was not accepted and the requested action did not occur yet the condition is temporary, and 5 indicates absolute failure.

The second digit indicates the category of the reply: 0 indicates a syntax error, 1 indicates informational content, 2 indicates a message concerning the transmission channel, 3 and 4 are not used, and 5 indicates a message concerning the status of the mail system. The third digit merely specifies the level of granularity of messages in a particular category.

Figure 5.3 shows a quick summary of how to interpret SMTP reply codes. You should consult RFC 821 for a complete discussion of these.

Figure 5.2   SMTP reply codes.

211 System status, or system help reply

214 Help message

[Information on how to use the receiver or the meaning of a particular nonstandard command; this reply is useful only to the human user]

220 <domain> Service ready

221 <domain> Service closing transmission channel

250 Requested mail action okay, completed

251 User not local; will forward to <forward-path>

354 Start mail input; end with <CRLF>.<CRLF>

421 <domain> Service not available, closing transmission channel

[This may be a reply to any command if the service knows it must shut down]

450 Requested mail action not taken: mailbox unavailable

[E.g., mailbox busy]

451 Requested action aborted: error in processing

452 Requested action not taken: insufficient system storage

500 Syntax error, command unrecognized

[This may include errors such as command line too long]

501 Syntax error in parameters or arguments

502 Command not implemented

503 Bad sequence of commands

504 Command parameter not implemented

550 Requested action not taken: mailbox unavailable[E.g., mailbox not found, no access]

551 User not local; please try <forward-path>

552 Requested mail action aborted: exceeded storage allocation

553 Requested action not taken: mailbox name not allowed

[E.g., mailbox syntax incorrect]

554 Transaction failed

Figure 5.3   How to interpret SMTP reply codes.

2xx   Positive Reply

3xx   Positive Intermediate Reply

4xx   Transitive Negative Completion Reply

5xx   Permanent Negative Completion Reply

x0x   Syntax Error

x1x   Information

x2x   Connections

x3x   Unspecified as yet

x4x   Unspecified as yet

x5x   Mail system

VB Programming Technique

SMTP is a command/reply protocol. That is, for every SMTP command, the server will respond with one or more reply codes. In Visual Basic, this is all handled in the Receive event of dsSocket.

Brain-Dead SMTP

Don't laugh, it works most of the time. I'm talking about Brain-Dead SMTP, or sending blind without listening to the server. You can just ignore all the servers responses if you are so sure of yourself, but I don't recommend shipping product with Brain-Dead SMTP. Still, it's good for demonstration purposes, so here's how to do it.

Figure 5.4 shows the Visual Basic routine, SendBrainDead, which accepts a dsSocket control connected to a mail server on port 25, a "from" string, a "to" string, a subject string, and a string containing the message, and sends it blindly, in true brain-dead fashion.

The szCompleteMsg string is made up of a header, which is simply the date, from address, to address, and the subject on four lines, and the message itself, with a blank line in between the header and the message. Notice that every line ends with a carriage return/linefeed pair and that the whole message ends with a period on a blank line by itself.

Do you want to try it? Go ahead: Load the project called BRAINDED from the SMTP subdirectory. BRAINDED uses this routine to send a mail message.

Figure 5.4   SendBrainDead sends an e-mail message with no error checking.

```
Sub SendBrainDead(dsSock As Control, szFrom As String, szTo As String, _
    szSubject As String, szMsg As String)
    Dim szCompleteMsg As String
    szCompleteMsg = "HELO " & szFrom & vbCrlf _
        & "MAIL FROM: <" & szFrom & ">" & vbCrlf _
        & "RCPT TO: <" & szTo & ">" & vbCrlf _
        & "DATA" & vbCrlf _
        & "DATE: " & Format$(Now, "dd mmm yy ttttt") & vbCrlf _
        & "FROM: " & szFrom & vbCrlf _
        & "TO: " & szTo & vbCrlf _
        & "SUBJECT: " & szSubject & vbCrlf & vbCrlf _
        & szMsg & vbCrlf & "." & vbCrlf

    dsSock.Send = szCompleteMsg

End Sub
```

True SMTP

The cool thing about Brain-Dead SMTP is that you can write it quickly and use it right away. The obvious downside is that there is no error handling. What happens if the recipient doesn't exist? Your program should know if it sends mail with a bad recipient address so the user can fix it. The server sends reply codes after every command it receives. For example, if you specify a bad recipient address the server will send a 550 reply code, which means "mailbox not available."

To have a true SMTP service, you must interact with the other machine on a command/reply basis. The basic idea behind command/reply programming is that you set up a reply code handler in the Receive event and take action based on the reply code that you've received as well as on the last command that you issued. You must react to reply codes accordingly. Fortunately, SMTP is fairly simple.

Connecting and Disconnecting

When you connect to an SMTP server you will receive a 220 reply, at which time you should send a HELO command with the following format:

```
HELO <SP> <domain> <CRLF>
```

where <domain> is the domain portion of your e-mail address. For example, if your e-mail address is santa@northpole.com, your domain is northpole.com.

When disconnecting, send the QUIT command. It is considered rude to simply disconnect the socket, although it is perfectly acceptable in most cases because SMTP servers are fairly thick-skinned and do not insult easily. Anyway, here is the format of the QUIT command:

```
QUIT <CRLF>
```

After sending the QUIT command, you will receive a 221 reply and then the socket will disconnect. When using dsSocket, the lose event will fire.

Sample Application: SMTP.VBP

Figure 5.5 s(ows the main screen of the SMTP sample application and Figure 5.6 shows the code. It is important that you keep track of the last command you sent the server so that you will know how to interpret the reply codes you receive. The SendSMTP Command procedure sends a specified command string, and assigns the command portion to a global string (gszCommand). At any time you can determine the last command sent by looking at gszCommand.

Figure 5.5   SMTP Main screen.

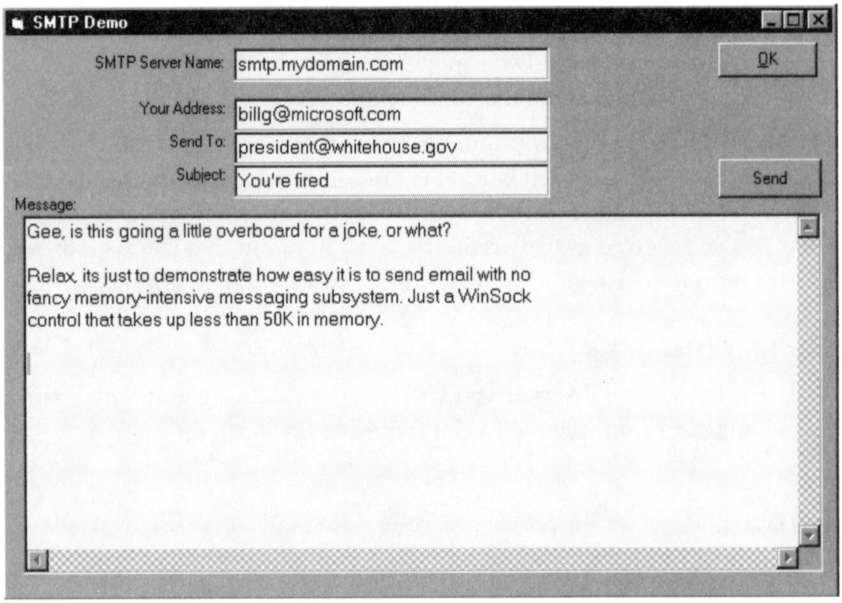

Figure 5.6   SMTP listings.

```
SMTP.BAS Listing
Option Explicit

'-- Holds the last command issued
Global gszCommand   As String

'-- These variables hold fields of the
'   message to be sent.
Global gszTo        As String
Global gszFrom      As String
Global gszSubject   As String
Global gszMsg       As String

Sub SendSMTPCommand(DSSock As Control, szCmd As String)

    '-- Save the last command sent
    gszCommand = szParseString(szCmd, " ", 1)

    '-- Send the command
    SendData DSSock, szCmd & vbCrlf

End Sub

SMTP.FRM Listing
Option Explicit

Sub CheckFields()

    '-- Enables the send button only
    '   if all the fields are filled in.
    If Len(txtHost) Then
        If Len(txtFrom) Then
            If Len(txtTo) Then
                If Len(txtSubject) Then
                    If Len(txtMsg) Then
                        btnSend.Enabled = True
                        Exit Sub
                    End If
                End If
            End If
        End If
    End If
```

Continues

Figure 5.6   SMTP listings. (Continued)

```
btnSend.Enabled = False

End Sub

Private Sub btnOK_Click()

    Unload Me

End Sub

Sub btnSend_Click()
'-- Send an Email message. All we have to do here is `
'    fill in the global strings that make up the message
'    from the text controls, and connect. The protocol does
'    the rest.

    '-- Disable the buttons
    btnSend.Enabled = False
    btnOK.Enabled = False
    Screen.MousePointer = vbHourglass

    '-- Fill in the global strings
    gszFrom = txtFrom
    gszTo = txtTo
    gszSubject = txtSubject
    gszMsg = txtMsg

    '-- Connect to the host
    If SocketConnect(dsSocket1, 25, (txtHost), 30) Then
        '-- An error occurred.
        MsgBox "Could not connect", vbInformation, "SMTP Client"
        btnSend.Enabled = True
        btnOK.Enabled = True
        Screen.MousePointer = vbNormal
    End If

    '-- The protocol takes over from here (dsSocket1_Receive)

End Sub

Sub dsSocket1_Close(ErrorCode As Integer, ErrorDesc As String)

    gnConnected = False
```

Figure 5.6 *Continued.*

```
End Sub

Private Sub dsSocket1_Connect()

    gnConnected = True

End Sub


Sub dsSocket1_Receive(ReceiveData As String)
'-- SMTP Client Protocol in action!
    Dim nPos        As Integer       '-- Used with Instr

    Dim nIndex      As Integer
    Dim szFullMsg   As String

    Const chrSpace = " "        '-- Used with Instr
    Const szPeriod = "."        '-- Used to determine the end of x-mission.

    Static nTextMode As Integer '-- When True, we are receiving data
                                '   When False, reply codes.
    Static nCode As Integer     '-- The last reply code received.

    Static bReceived220 As Integer       '-- Set true after receiving the first
                                         '   220, indicating a connection.


'-------------------------------------------------------------------------

    '-- Grab the reply code.
    nCode = Val(Left$(ReceiveData, 3))

    '-- What is it?
    Select Case nCode

        Case 220    '-- Connect and/or Command OK.
            '-- Is this the first 220?
            If Not bReceived220 Then
                '-- Yep. Flip the flag.
                bReceived220 = True

                '-- This means we're connected. At this
                '   point SocketConnect will exit.
```

Continues

Figure 5.6   SMTP listings. (*Continued*)

```
'-- Send the MAIL command to initiate the send
'    process.
SendSMTPCommand dsSocket1, "HELO <" & _
    Mid$(gszFrom, Instr(gszFrom, "@")) & ">"
gnConnected = True

End If

Case 250    '-- Command OK
    '-- What was the last command?
    Select Case gszCommand$
        Case "HELO"
            '-- Send the MAIL command to initiate the send
            '    process.
            SendSMTPCommand dsSocket1, "MAIL FROM: <" & gszFrom & ">"
        Case "MAIL"
            '-- After MAIL, send the RCPT command to
            '    establish the final destination
            SendSMTPCommand dsSocket1, "RCPT TO: <" & gszTo & ">"
        Case "RCPT"
            '-- After RCPT, send the DATA command
            '    to request permission to send the mail message.
            '    This should yield a 354 reply.
            SendSMTPCommand dsSocket1, "DATA"
        Case "DATA"
            '-- This is the second time we get 250... after the
            '    mail has been sent. We actually get a 354
            '    after sending the DATA command (see below)

            '-- Confirmation that the message was delivered.
            MsgBox "Message Delivered", vbInformation, "SMTP Client"
            btnSend.Enabled = True
            btnOK.Enabled = True
            Screen.MousePointer = vbNormal
            bReceived220 = False

    End Select

Case 354
    '-- There should only be one command... DATA
    Select Case gszCommand$
        Case "DATA"
            '-- Now we have permission to send the message.
```

Figure 5.6   Continued.

```
                            '    Compose the complete message. Note the date format.
                            '    This is very important.
                     szFullMsg = "DATE: " & Format$(Now, "dd mmm yy ttttt") & vbCrlf _
                            & "FROM: " & gszFrom & vbCrlf _
                            & "TO: " & gszTo & vbCrlf _
                            & "SUBJECT: " & gszSubject & vbCrlf & vbCrlf _
                            & gszMsg & vbCrlf & "." & vbCrlf

                            '-- Don't use SendSMTP command, so the
                            '    last command will still be "DATA"
                            SendData dsSocket1, szFullMsg

                  End Select

            Case Is >= 400

                  '-- An error of some sort occurred. Display to the user and
                  '    reset everything.

                  MsgBox Mid$(ReceiveData, 4), vbInformation, "Error From Server"
                  btnSend.Enabled = True
                  btnOK.Enabled = True
                  Screen.MousePointer = vbNormal
                  bReceived220 = False

            Case Else
                  '-- Something we weren't expecting
                  Debug.Print ReceiveData

      End Select

End Sub

Sub dsSocket1_SendReady()

      gnSendReady = True

End Sub

Sub Form_Load()

      dsSocket1.LineMode = True
```

Continues

Figure 5.6   SMTP listings. *(Continued)*

```
End Sub


Sub Form_Unload(Cancel As Integer)

    SocketDisconnect dsSocket1
    End

End Sub
Private Sub txtFrom_Change()
    CheckFields

End Sub


Private Sub txtHost_Change()

    CheckFields

End Sub

Private Sub txtMsg_Change()

    CheckFields

End Sub


Private Sub txtSubject_Change()

    CheckFields

End Sub


Private Sub txtTo_Change()

    CheckFields

End Sub
```

Check out the dsSocket1_Receive event procedure. The first thing that happens is the reply code is determined. Since this code is always the first three digits of a received string, we can simply use the Left$ function to return the three leftmost characters, and convert this to an integer with the Val function like so:

```
nCode = Val(Left$(ReceiveData, 3))
```

Next, a Select Case structure defines the reply handler. The first code you will receive after connecting is a 220 (Connect OK or Command OK). Receiving this code is the true indication that you've successfully connected to the SMTP server. Therefore, the sample code sets the gnConnected variable to True upon receiving this code, rather than in the Connect event.

Sending Mail

After receiving a 220 code for the first time the SMTP project code initiates a transaction by sending a MAIL command. At this point you could substitute SEND, SAML, or SOML for the MAIL command depending on how you want the message to be delivered. More on this shortly.

You will receive a 220 code more than once, so in order to send at the appropriate time you must set a flag after receiving 220 the first time. Then, simply check to see that the flag is not set before sending the MAIL command. The bReceived220 variable is used for this purpose. Figure 5.7 shows how this static variable is used.

The MAIL command specifies the sender's e-mail address. The correct syntax is as follows:

```
MAIL FROM: <email_address>
```

After receiving the MAIL command the server will send back a 250 reply if it can accept e-mail. If you do not get a 250 then you cannot send mail. Figure 5.8 shows how the code handles a 250 reply. The code response will depend on the last command sent. In this case, the last command was "MAIL" so the RCPT command is sent:

```
'-- After MAIL, send the RCPT command to
'    establish the final destination
SendSMTPCommand dsSocket1, "RCPT TO: <" & gszTo & ">"
```

RCPT tells the SMTP server who the recipient is. The correct syntax for RCPT is as follows:

```
RCPT TO: <email_address>
```

Figure 5.7   Using static variables.

```
'-- What is it?
Select Case nCode

    Case 220    '-- Connect and/or Command OK.
        '-- Is this the first 220?
        If Not bReceived220 Then
            '-- Yep. Flip the flag.
            bReceived220 = True

            '-- This means we're connected. At this
            '   point SocketConnect will exit.
            gnConnected = True

            '— Send the MAIL command to initiate the send
            '   process.
            SendSMTPCommand dsSocket1, "MAIL FROM: <" & gszFrom & ">"
        End If
```

If the SMTP server has no problem with the RCPT command, you will again get a 250 reply. When a 250 is received after sending a RCPT command, the DATA command is issued:

```
Case "RCPT"
    '-- After RCPT, send the DATA command
    '   to request permission to send the mail message.
    '   This should yield a 354 reply.
    SendSMTPCommand dsSocket1, "DATA"
```

Figure 5.8   Handling a 250 reply.

```
    Case 250, 251    '-- Command OK

    '-- What was the last command?
    Select Case gszCommand$
        Case "MAIL"
            '-- After MAIL, send the RCPT command to
            '   establish the final destination
            SendSMTPCommand dsSocket1, "RCPT TO: <" & gszTo & ">"
        Case "RCPT"
            '-- After RCPT, send the DATA command
            '   to request permission to send the mail message.
```

Figure 5.8 *Continued.*

```
            '    This should yield a 354 reply.
            SendSMTPCommand dsSocket1, "DATA"
        Case "DATA"
            '-- This occurs after successfully sending an
            '    email message.

            '-- Confirmation that the message was delivered.
            MsgBox "Message Delivered", vbInformation, "SMTP Client"

            btnSend.Enabled = True
            btnOK.Enabled = True
            Screen.MousePointer = vbNormal
            bReceived220 = False
    End Select
```

DATA is just sent as is. This tells the server that you are about to send the message header and body. When the server is ready for you to send the message it sends a 354 reply, which means "go ahead and send your message." When you send the message you are not sending a command, you are sending data. Therefore, you should just use the SendData routine and not SendSMTP Command.

What happens here is a little tricky to code. After receiving the 354 you send the message and then you receive a 250 when the server has successfully received it. Using our current programming technique, after receiving the 250 the last command sent will be DATA. Figure 5.9 shows the code for handling the 354 reply. The format of the message is the most important factor here. If it's not perfect it will be refused. Figure 5.10 shows a sample message. Assume that every line ends with a CR/LF.

OK, now you've sent the message. You will now receive a 250 from the server. Here is what happens when you receive this:

```
Case "DATA"
    '-- This occurs after successfully sending an
    '    email message.
    '-- Confirmation that the message was delivered.
    MsgBox "Message Delivered", vbInformation, "SMTP Client"
    btnSend.Enabled = True
    btnOK.Enabled = True
    Screen.MousePointer = vbNormal
    bReceived220 = False
```

Figure 5.9   Handling a 354 reply.

```
'-- What is it?
Select Case nCode

    Case 354
        '-- There should only be one command... DATA
        Select Case gszCommand$ '-- what was the last command sent?
            Case "DATA"
                '-- Now we have permission to send the message.
                '   Compose the complete message. Note the date format.
                '   This is very important.
                szFullMsg = "DATE: " & Format$(Now, "dd mmm yy ttttt") & vbCrlf _
                    & "FROM: " & gszFrom & vbCrlf _
                    & "TO: " & gszTo & vbCrlf _
                    & "SUBJECT: " & gszSubject & vbCrlf & vbCrlf _
                    & gszMsg & vbCrlf & "." & vbCrlf

                '-- Don't use SendSMTP command, so the
                '   last command will still be "DATA"
                SendData dsSocket1, szFullMsg


        End Select
```

This is where you tell the user that the message has been sent. It's important that you set the bReceived220 flag back to false here, and do any other reset procedures that your application may need.

Figure 5.10   Sample SMTP message.

DATE: 23 Nov 95 0800

FROM: me@mydomain.com

TO: someone@somedomain.com

SUBJECT: This is a test

Hello. This is the first line of an E-mail message

This is the second line

Above is a blank line. That's perfectly acceptable.

Figure 5.10 *Continued.*

There MUST be a blank line between the SUBJECT
line and the first line of the message.

You can include UUEncoded data (files) anywhere in this
message body.

The message ends with a period on a line by itself.

Sincerely,

Me.

Sending versus Mailing

When you SEND (as opposed to MAIL) a message, the message is delivered directly to the user's terminal if the user indeed *has* a terminal and is logged on. SENDing is really only appropriate for terminal-based Unix shell systems and does not apply throughout the enterprise.

There are four commands for delivering a mail message. MAIL, the standard command for sending mail, sends a message to a user's mailbox. SEND sends the message directly to the user's terminal. SAML (Send And Mail) sends to the user's terminal if available and also MAILs the message to the user's mailbox. Finally, SOML (Send Or Mail) sends directly to the user and only MAILs to the mailbox if there is a problem SENDing.

In today's world, if you are going to write routines to send e-mail, you should stick to the MAIL command.

Replying to Mail

Sending a reply uses the exact same mechanism as sending a standard message. The only difference is really the subject line, which should start with "Re:" (but this is not necessary for delivery), and you may want to quote the original document in the body of the code. In short, sending a reply is sending a message. The content of the subject and body are the only differences, and those differences are optional.

Forwarding Mail

Sometimes when you attempt to send a message, the recipient no longer has an account at the post office you are sending to. The server notifies you after you send the RCPT command if forwarding is necessary. If you receive a 251 reply, then the server will forward the mail for you in which case you don't have to do any special processing. Just tack 251 as a criterion onto the 250 reply handler because 251 is a specific reply that occurs only under this condition. For example:

```
251 User not local; will forward to <Postel@USC-ISIF.ARPA>
```

This can be handled by the same code that handles 250:

```
Case 250, 251
```

However, if the server cannot (or will not) forward the mail, you will receive a 551 reply like so:

```
551 User not local; please try <Mockapetris@USC-ISIF.ARPA>
```

If you receive a 551 you should automatically substitute the new address for the current one, and resend the RCPT command. Figure 5.11 shows how this is handled.

Figure 5.11   Handling e-mail redirection.

```
Select Case nCode

    . . .
    . . .

Case 551
    '-- What was the last command?
    Select Case gszCommand$
        Case "RCPT"
            '-- The specified recipient does not exist here but there is
            '   a forwarding address. Parse it and resend the RCPT command
            gszTo = szParseString(ReceiveData, "<", 2)
            nPos = InStr(gszTo, ">")
            If nPos Then
                gszTo = Left$(gszTo, nPos - 1)
                SendSMTPCommand dsSocket1, "RCPT TO: <" & gszTo & ">"
            End If
    End Select
```

Verifying an SMTP Address

The VRFY command lets you verify that a user does in fact have an account on the post office. The argument is the first part of the user's e-mail address (up to the @ sign), or the first or last name of the user. For example, my e-mail address is carl@franklins.net. If you were to connect to an SMTP gateway and send a VRFY command it would be as follows:

```
SendSMTPCommand dsSocket1, "VRFY carlf"
```

There are four possible responses to a VRFY command. A 250 command returns the full e-mail address of anyone matching the last name specified. For example:

```
250 carlf<carl@franklins.net>
```

If the user does not exist, you will receive a 550 reply like so:

```
550 String does not match anything
```

If the string you specify applies to more than one user you will get a 553 reply like so:

```
553 User ambiguous
```

If the user is not local, the server sends back a 551 reply with the forwarding address:

```
551 User not local; please try <carlf@somewhere.else.com>
```

Figure 5.12 shows how to handle the successful completion of a VRFY command. In this scenario a VRFY command has been sent and a 250 code has been received. If upon receiving a 250 the last command sent was VRFY, a message box simply shows the user the verification message. You might want to use the VRFY command before sending a message to make absolutely sure that mail goes through.

Figure 5.12   Verifying an e-mail address.

```
Case 250, 251     '-- Command OK
    '-- What was the last command?
        Select Case gszCommand$
            Case "MAIL"
                '-- After MAIL, send the RCPT command to
                '   establish the final destination
                SendSMTPCommand dsSocket1, "RCPT TO: <" & gszTo & ">"
            Case "RCPT"
                '-- After RCPT, send the DATA command          Continues
```

Figure 5.12   Verifying an e-mail address. *(Continued)*

```
        '    to request permission to send the mail message.
        '    This should yield a 354 reply.
        SendSMTPCommand dsSocket1, "DATA"
    Case "DATA"
        '-- We have just sent the message successfully.

        '-- Confirmation that the message was delivered.
        MsgBox "Message Delivered", vbInformation, "SMTP Client"

        btnSend.Enabled = True
        btnOK.Enabled = True
        Screen.MousePointer = vbNormal
        bReceived220 = False
    Case "VRFY"
        MsgBox Mid$(ReceiveData, 4), vbInformation, "User Verified"
```

Error Handling

Any code over 400 is considered an error and should at least be reported to the user, if not written to a log.

There may be times when a particular error received after sending a particular command would require some specific action (how's that for mumbo-jumbo?). In this case, you can handle the error the same way positive replies are handled, with a Select Case block.

Post Office Protocol 3 (POP3)

POP3 is the protocol by which e-mail messages are retrieved from an Internet server. Like SMTP, the client sends commands to the server to which the server replies with coded responses. You may think that POP3 has more commands and codes than SMTP but actually this is not the case. POP3 is extremely simple.

POP3 Commands

POP3 uses a series of simple four-character commands such as RETR and LIST that perform the various tasks required to retrieve e-mail messages. These commands are listed in the POP3 Reference Appendix at the back of this book. POP3 Commands are always followed with a CR/LF pair.

Server Responses

After sending a POP3 command, you will receive a reply that begins with either a plus sign (+) to indicate success or a minus sign (–) to indicate failure. These commands begin with either +OK or –ERR. Immediately following either of these responses on the same line is an informative message for the user. Here are a couple of sample replies:

```
+OK message 2 deleted
-ERR message not found
```

Figure 5.13 shows a sample POP3 session modified from RFC 1725. S stands for "server" and C stands for "client," indicating who is doing or sending what. As you can see, it's pretty straightforward. After the client connects, the server sends either a +OK message indicating that the server is available, or a –ERR message if the server is not available. Actually, every command response from the POP3 server either begins with +OK or –ERR.

The client then sends the username and password: First the USER command, then the PASS command. If either the user or password are invalid, the server returns a –ERR message. The server sends a +OK after receiving the USER command, and again after the PASS command.

By the way, an octet is a byte. More specifically, it is eight bits. The word only exists to distinguish eight bits from a byte, which in the world of the Internet can mean a basic data unit containing more than eight bits on some systems.

The STAT command returns the number of messages in the mailbox and the total number of bytes used by the messages. In the preceding example there are two messages that, combined, total 320 bytes, or octets.

Note that the STAT command is being phased out in lieu of the server sending the STAT information in the reply to the PASS command (after the user has successfully logged on). This is really the current state of POP3, but I wanted you to see the example from the RFC untouched.

The LIST command returns the number of bytes for each message. You can optionally specify a message number to get its size. Generally, you won't need this information because you will most likely be receiving data in carriage return/line-feed–delineated lines.

Figure 5.13   Sample POP3 conversation.

S: <wait for connection on TCP port 110>

C: <opens a connection>
S: +OK POP3 server ready <popserver@somewhere.com>

C: USER santaclaus
S: +OK Password required for santaclaus

C: PASS hohoho
S: +OK santaclaus has 2 message(s) (320 octets).

C: TOP 1, 0
S: +OK 120 octets
S: <the POP3 server sends the header for message 1>
S: .

C: RETR 1
S: +OK 120 octets
S: <the POP3 server sends message 1>
S: .

C: DELE 1
S: +OK message 1 deleted

C: TOP 2, 0
S: +OK 200 octets
S: <the POP3 server sends the header for message 1>
S: .

C: RETR 2
S: +OK 200 octets

Figure 5.13 *Continued.*

S: <the POP3 server sends message 2>

S: .

C: DELE 2

S: +OK message 2 deleted

C: QUIT

S: +OK POP3 server signing off (maildrop empty)

S: <closes connection>

S: <wait for next connection>

Another command shown in this example, TOP, returns the header information (From:, Subject:, Date:, etc.) from a specified message. This is used to create a string to present to the user in a list box, say, to identify a message. More on this later.

The RETR command retrieves the text of a specific message. The first line is a +OK response followed by the size of the message. The text of the message is sent with every line ending in a carriage return/linefeed pair. A period on the last line indicates the end of the message.

Finally, the DELE command deletes a message from the server's mailbox, and the QUIT command ends the session by instructing the POP3 server to close the socket connection.

POP3 States

The POP3 client and server enter into three different states during a session. These are as follows:

1. *Authorization*. The client must identify itself to the POP3 server.

2. *Transaction*. The client requests actions on the part of the POP3 server.

3. *Update*. The POP3 server releases any resources acquired during the transaction state and says goodbye.

Authorization State

The authorization state is the first state and exists between the time of initial connection up until the point where the client has successfully logged on. The following commands are legal in the authorization state:

PASS

USER

QUIT

As soon as a connection is established the server sends back a +OK reply indicating that a clean connection has been made. At this point you must send the USER command with your username. The server sends back a +OK reply to the USER command, at which point you must send the PASS command followed by your password.

Once the server validates you then it sends back a +OK reply indicating the number of messages you have like so:

```
+OK <username> has 2 message(s) (320 octets)
```

The number of messages is always preceded by the word HAS and followed by the word MESSAGE. In parentheses at the end of the line is the total number of bytes in your mailbox, or the total size of all your messages added together.

After receiving the previous line, you are now in the transaction state and can exchange transaction commands with the server.

> **TIP** The username and password are the ones you use to log in to your POP3 server. If you only have one username and password for all Internet access, then use this information.

Transaction State

The transaction state begins after the client has logged on and ends when the client sends a QUIT command to end the session. The following commands are legal in the transaction state:

DELE

NOOP

LIST

RETR

RSET

STAT

There are two main ways in which you can go about downloading messages. One way is to first ask for the headers of each message, display the header information on a line in a list box (or equivalent), and then only retrieve the whole message when the user double-clicks on it in the list. The other method is what most implementations do, and that is to download all of the messages and immediately delete them from the post office, keeping them in a local database instead. This way the user has to wait only until all the new mail is downloaded. The other way, the user has to wait every time he or she wants to read a message.

Update State

The update state exists between the time that the server receives the QUIT command and when the client is disconnected. When in the update state, the server removes all messages marked as deleted and removes all locks on the mailbox.

VB Programming Technique

The programming technique I recommend for POP3 access is exactly the same as with SMTP. All logic resides inside the Receive event. Since there are only two types of replies (+OK and –ERR) the first test is for a +OK reply. If you get a positive reply then we look to see what the last command sent was. Action is then taken based on the last command.

Sample Program: POP3.VBP

The POP3 sample application connects you to a POP3 mail server, downloads descriptions of your mail and displays them in a list box, and lets you view any message by double-clicking on a message in the list.

Take a look at Figure 5.14, which shows the Receive event for a simple POP3 mail viewer. Just like the SMTP example, there are two modes for receiving data: Command Mode and Data Mode. The nCommandMode variable is True when receiving commands, its default state. Any time you send a command that returns data, such as TOP or RETR, the flag is switched off so that the program can collect the data in another part of the code.

Figure 5.14   Simple POP3 handler.

```
Private Sub dsSocket1_Receive(ReceiveData As String)

    Static nBeenHere        As Integer
    Static nCurMessage      As Integer
    Static nNumMessages     As Integer
    Static szReceived       As String
    Static szDate           As String
    Static szFrom           As String
    Static szSubject        As String

    Dim nPos                As Integer
    Dim nPos2               As Integer
    Dim szTemp1             As String
    Dim szTemp2             As String
    Dim szTemp3             As String
    '-- nCommandMode is True when we are receiving commands
    If nCommandMode Then
        '-- Is this a positive reply?
        If UCase$(Left$(ReceiveData, 3)) = "+OK" Then
            '-- Yes. Is this the first line we've received?
            If nBeenHere = False Then
                '-- Yes. Send the USER command (user's name)
                SendPOP3Command dsSocket1, "USER " & mszUser
            Else
                '-- Nope, we've been here before.

                '-- What is the last command sent?
                Select Case mszCommand
                    Case "DEL"  '-- DELE
                        MsgBox "Message Deleted", vbInformation

                    Case "LIS"  '-- LIST
                        nCommandMode = False

                    Case "NOO"  '-- NOOP
                        '-- You can set a flag here if you want to
                        '   use the NOOP command.

                    Case "PAS"  '-- PASS
                        '-- Logged in! Get the messages.
                        szTemp1 = UCase$(ReceiveData)
                        szTemp2 = UCase$(mszUser) & " HAS"
                        szTemp3 = "MESSAGE"
```

Figure 5.14 *Continued.*

```
                    nPos = InStr(szTemp1, szTemp2)
               If nPos Then
                    nPos2 = InStr(szTemp1, szTemp3)
                    If nPos2 Then
                         nNumMessages = Val(Mid$(szTemp1, _
                            nPos + Len(szTemp2), nPos2 - _
                            (nPos + Len(szTemp2))))

                         frmMain.Caption = Str$(nNumMessages) & _
                            " New Messages"
                         '-- Once we have the number of messages
                         '    send the TOP command to retrieve the
                         '    header (once for each message).
                         '    nCurMessage keeps track of the message
                         '    we're currently reading the header of.
                         nCurMessage = 1
                         Screen.MousePointer = vbHourglass
                         SendPOP3Command dsSocket1, "TOP 1 0"
                    End If
               End If

          Case "QUI"   '-- QUIT
               '-- Reset the last command
               mszCommand = ""

          Case "RET"   '-- RETR
               '-- Here comes the message
               nCommandMode = False
               Screen.MousePointer = vbHourglass

          Case "RSE"   '-- RSET
               mszCommand = ""

          Case "STA"   '-- STAT

          Case "TOP"   '-- TOP
               '-- Here comes the header data
               nCommandMode = False

          Case "UID"   '-- UIDL

          Case "USE"   '-- USER
               SendPOP3Command dsSocket1, "PASS " & mszPassword
```

Continues

Figure 5.14   Simple POP3 handler. *(Continued)*

```
                    Case ""        '-- First command
                End Select
            End If
        Else
            '-- This is an error reply. Display the error portion
            '   in a message box.
            Screen.MousePointer = vbNormal
            MsgBox SuperTrim$(Mid$(ReceiveData, InStr(ReceiveData, " ") + _
                1)), vbInformation

            '-- Reset the last command sent to nothing.
            mszCommand = ""
        End If
    Else
        '-- Not in command mode. We are instead receiving data. either a list
        '   of messages or a message itself

        '-- Is this the end of the data transmission?
        If ReceiveData = "." & vbCrLf Then
            '-- Yes.

            '-- What was the last command sent?
            Select Case mszCommand
                Case "RET"   '-- RETR (retrieves a message)
                    Screen.MousePointer = vbNormal
                    '-- Display the message
                    frmDisplay.txtText = szReceived
                    frmDisplay.Show vbModal
                    Unload frmDisplay
                    Set frmDisplay = Nothing
                    '-- Go back to Command mode
                    nCommandMode = True
                Case "TOP"
                    '-- Display the header
                    If Len(szFrom) > 19 Then
                        szFrom = Left$(szFrom, 19)
                    End If
                    If Len(szSubject) > 24 Then
                        szSubject = Left$(szSubject, 24)
                    End If
                    lbMessages.AddItem Format$(szFrom, "!" & String$(23, "@")) & _
                        Format$(szSubject, "!" & String$(27, "@")) & _
                        szDate
```

Figure 5.14 *Continued.*

```
                    If nCurMessage < nNumMessages Then
                        nCurMessage = nCurMessage + 1
                        SendPOP3Command dsSocket1, "TOP" & _
                                  Str$(nCurMessage) & ", 0"
                    Else
                        Screen.MousePointer = vbNormal
                        lbMessages.Enabled = True
                    End If
            End Select
            '-- Flush the receive buffer
            szReceived = ""
            '-- Go back to Command mode
            nCommandMode = True
        Else
            '-- No. We are still receiving data.

            '-- What was the last command received?
            Select Case mszCommand
                Case "LIS"  '-- LIST
                    lbMessages.AddItem szTrimCRLF(ReceiveData)
                Case "RET"  '-- RETR (Retrieve a message)
                    szReceived = szReceived & ReceiveData
                Case "TOP"  '-- Retrieves the header
                    szReceived = szReceived & ReceiveData
                    Select Case UCase$(szParseString(ReceiveData, ":", 1))
                        Case "SUBJECT"
                            szSubject = szTrimCRLF(Trim$(Mid$(ReceiveData, 9)))
                        Case "DATE"
                            szDate = szTrimCRLF(Trim$(Mid$(ReceiveData, 6)))
                        Case "FROM"
                            szFrom = szTrimCRLF(Trim$(Mid$(ReceiveData, 6)))
                    End Select
            End Select
        End If
    End If

    '-- Make sure we know we've been here before.
    nBeenHere = True

End Sub
```

Let me first explain the code at the top of the routine, and then I'll get into the signal flow issues. The first thing that happens when a string is received is a test for Command Mode. If indeed we are accepting commands, then we check to see if this reply is positive (+OK) or negative (–ERR).

If the reply is negative, the error message is displayed to the user and the variables are reset. If the reply is positive, then another flag (nBeenHere) is tested. This flag is set at the bottom of the subroutine and merely provides a way to determine if this is the first string being received for a particular session. If it IS the first line received, the code automatically begins the login process by sending the USER command and exiting the routine.

Just like with SMTP, it is absolutely necessary to keep track of the last command issued so that the code can determine how to respond to a given command reply. The SendPOP3Command performs this service. Shown in Figure 5.15, it simply sets the module-level mszCommand variable to the first three letters of the command issued (three characters is enough to identify a POP3 command).

Logging into the Server

To log into a POP3 server you first send a USER command (with your username), wait for a +OK, and then send the PASS command (with your password).

Let's say that the last command we sent was USER. We now know that we've sent the server our username and it replied positively. Now it's waiting for the password. So, send the PASS command.

The next time the Receive event fires, it should fall into the block where PASS is the last command issued. In this block, we determine how many messages the user has based on the reply from the server, and begin to retrieve the headers for these messages. Figure 5.16 shows the code that occurs when a +OK is received after sending the password.

Figure 5.15 Keeping track of the last command sent.

```
Sub SendPOP3Command(DSSock As Control, szCmd As String)

    mszCommand = Left$(szCmd, 3)

    SendData DSSock, szCmd & vbCrLf

End Sub
```

Figure 5.16   After sending the password to log in.

```
Case "PAS"    '-- PASS
    '-- Logged in! Get the messages.
    szTemp1 = UCase$(ReceiveData)
    szTemp2 = UCase$(mszUser) & " HAS"
    szTemp3 = "MESSAGE"

    nPos = InStr(szTemp1, szTemp2)
    If nPos Then
        nPos2 = InStr(szTemp1, szTemp3)
        If nPos2 Then
            nNumMessages = Val(Mid$(szTemp1, nPos + _
              Len(szTemp2), nPos2 - (nPos + Len(szTemp2))))

            frmMain.Caption = Str$(nNumMessages) & " New Messages"
            '-- Once we have the number of messages send the TOP
            '   command to retrieve the header (once for each
            '   message). nCurMessage keeps track of the message
            '   we're currently reading the header of.
            nCurMessage = 1
            Screen.MousePointer = vbHourglass
            SendPOP3Command dsSocket1, "TOP 1 0"
        End If
    End If
```

The server sends back a string like so:

`+OK carlf has 3 message(s).`

To get the number of messages out of this string, the code does a bit of manual string parsing. First the word "HAS" is found in the string (all Instr's are done in uppercase). Then the word "MESSAGE" is located. The number of messages lies between these two words, and is saved into the nNumMessages variable.

Retrieving Message Headers

The next task is to retrieve header information for each of the messages so that they can be displayed in a list box for the user to select. At this point a few things happen. The number of messages is displayed in the caption of the form. The nCurMessage variable, which keeps track of which message's header we are currently retrieving, is initialized to 1. The cursor changes to an hourglass (until the last header has been received), and finally, the TOP command is sent to retrieve the header of the first message. Here is the syntax of the TOP command:

```
TOP 1, 0
```

This tells the server, "give me the header lines for message 1 and zero lines of the message body." The TOP command takes two arguments. First is the message number. Message numbers always start at one and go up from there. You do not have to return a wacky message number for each message. Specifying message number 1 means "for the first message."

After receiving the TOP command, the server returns a +OK reply followed by all the header lines ending with a period on a line by itself. Here is an example header:

```
Received: by upsmot02.msn.com id AA24082; Sat, 25 Nov 95 22:57:32 -0800
Date: Sun, 26 Nov 95 06:49:31 UT
X-UIDL: 817369062.000
From: "Carl Franklin" <CarlFranklin@msn.com>
Message-Id: <UPMAIL02.199511260658180351@msn.com>
To: "'carl@franklins.net'" <carl@franklins.net>
Subject: Hello
Status: RO
```

The header is received one line at a time, telling our code to look for specific header lines like Subject, From, and Date. These header lines are sufficient for creating a string to present to the user to identify a message.

Follow the code down to where we are *not* in command mode, and it is not the end of the data transmission. Figure 5.17 shows that block of code. Once again, knowing the last command issued is critical in determining actions. Look at where the last command is TOP. We know that this is data. We know that this is a header line. All we need to do is look at the first word up to, but not including, the colon. In this manner the subject, from address, and date are all kept in static string variables.

Now jump up to where this *is* the end of data transmission and the last command given was TOP. Figure 5.18 shows this code. If TOP was the last command issued, then we have just received a complete header for one of the messages. The code then concatenates the from address, subject, and date into a complete string and adds it to the list box (lbMessages) on the main screen.

Next, we check to see if the current message is less than the total number of messages. If so, then we have another TOP command to issue (at least one more). The nCurMessage variable is increased, and the TOP command is issued to receive the next header. If this was a TOP command for the last message, the mouse pointer is restored to normal.

Figure 5.17   Parsing a POP3 mail header.

```
'-- No. We are still receiving data.

    '-- What was the last command sent?
    Select Case mszCommand
        Case "LIS"  '-- LIST
            lbMessages.AddItem szTrimCRLF(ReceiveData)
        Case "RET"  '-- RETR (Retrieve a message)
            szReceived = szReceived & ReceiveData
        Case "TOP"  '-- Retrieves the header
            szReceived = szReceived & ReceiveData
            Select Case UCase$(szParseString(ReceiveData, ":", 1))
                Case "SUBJECT"
                    szSubject = szTrimCRLF(Trim$(Mid$(ReceiveData, 9)))
                Case "DATE"
                    szDate = szTrimCRLF(Trim$(Mid$(ReceiveData, 6)))
                Case "FROM"
                    szFrom = szTrimCRLF(Trim$(Mid$(ReceiveData, 6)))
            End Select
    End Select
```

After the successful receiving of a complete block of data (not commands) the szReceived variable is zeroed and Command Mode is set back to True so we can process the next command.

Retrieving Messages

To retrieve a specific message, send the RETR command (with the message number). In our application this is initiated in the list box's double-click event like so:

```
Private Sub lbMessages_DblClick()
    Screen.MousePointer = vbHourglass
    SendPOP3Command dsSocket1, "RETR" & Str$(lbMessages.ListIndex + 1)
End Sub
```

Jumping back now to our Receive code, take a look at the block of code that executes when a positive reply is received after sending the RETR command:

```
Case "RET"  '-- RETR
    '-- Here comes the message
    nCommandMode = False
    Screen.MousePointer = vbHourglass
```

Figure 5.18   Displaying the received POP3 mail header.

```
Case "TOP"
        '-- Display the header
        If Len(szFrom) > 19 Then
            szFrom = Left$(szFrom, 19)
        End If
        If Len(szSubject) > 24 Then
            szSubject = Left$(szSubject, 24)
        End If
        lbMessages.AddItem Format$(szFrom, "!" & String$(23, "@")) & _
            Format$(szSubject, "!" & String$(27, "@")) & _
            szDate

        If nCurMessage < nNumMessages Then
            nCurMessage = nCurMessage + 1
            SendPOP3Command dsSocket1, "TOP" & Str$(nCurMessage) & ", 0"
        Else
            Screen.MousePointer = vbNormal
            lbMessages.Enabled = True
        End If

        '-- Flush the receive buffer
        szReceived = ""
        '-- Go back to Command mode
        nCommandMode = True
```

The only thing we need to do is turn the cursor to an hourglass and flip Command Mode off. The next line to be received is the first line of the message:

```
Case "RET"  '-- RETR (Retrieve a message)
        szReceived = szReceived & ReceiveData
```

All we are doing is adding the new line to szReceived, a static string variable that will contain the whole of the message when it has been completely received.

The server will send a period on a line by itself after completely sending the message. The code snippet in Figure 5.19 shows what happens next. After a message has been received in full, szReceived will contain the entire thing. The sample application simply throws it in a read-only text box and displays it. As always, the code then goes back to Command Mode.

Figure 5.19   Displaying an e-mail message.

```
'-- What was the last command sent?
        Select Case mszCommand
            Case "RET"   '-- RETR (retrieves a message)
                Screen.MousePointer = vbNormal
                '-- Display the message (with a definite lack of imaginative UI)
                frmDisplay.txtText = szReceived
                frmDisplay.Show vbModal
                Unload frmDisplay
                Set frmDisplay = Nothing
                '-- Go back to Command mode
                nCommandMode = True
```

Sending and Receiving Binary Files

Before a binary file can be sent via e-mail, it must be encoded such that all the characters that represent the file's data are printable and viewable with any ASCII editor. A process called UU encoding converts binary data into printable ASCII. The reciprocal process is called UU decoding. There are many simple utilities available for free on the Internet that encode and decode files; however, I could not find any BASIC or Visual Basic source code to do the deed.

After acquiring the C source for UU encoding and decoding from my friend Tory Toupin (ttoupin@du.edu) and figuring out how it would work in VB, I wrote some routines with a little help from Steve Cramp of Dolphin Systems (stephenc@dolphinsys.com) to make it easy to encode and decode on the fly in your Visual Basic apps. The routines are included in UUCode.bas on the CD-ROM, and we will discuss them here.

How UU Encoding Works

The basic idea behind UU encoding is that for every three characters or bytes of data, you must convert into four 6-byte characters that are offset by the space character, or 32. In other words, three 8-bit characters is 24 bits. Four 6-bit characters is also 24 bits. A value of 32 is added to each 6-bit character, to insure that the character is printable, or greater than a space character. Here is another way to visualize the two ways to interpret 24 bits of data:

```
1 2 3 4 5 6 7 8 1 2 3 4 5 6 7 8 1 2 3 4 5 6 7 8

1 2 3 4 5 6 1 2 3 4 5 6 1 2 3 4 5 6 1 2 3 4 5 6
```

You may already be thinking there is no easy way to access 6-bit characters in Visual Basic, and you are right. There is not. The process requires the use of the bitwise AND operator, and division to coerce the right values out of the 8-bit characters we use exclusively in Visual Basic.

Let me show you how it works. Let's say we have a file in which the first three bytes are GSU. The UU encoding process works on three ASCII characters at a time, converting them into four printable ASCII characters. Here is the Visual Basic code to retrieve a UU-encoded character from the first of three bytes:

```
szA_1 = "G"
szUU_1 = Chr$(((Asc(szA_1) And 252) \ 4) + 32)
```

Here is the same logic using binary arithmetic:

```
71              =       1000111    (ASCII 71 = "G")
252             =      11111100
4               =           100

71 AND 252      =       1000100    =       68
\ 4             =         10001    =       17
+ 32            =        110001    =       49


UU encoded Character 1 = Chr$(49) = "1"
```

Notice how in order to get 6 bits, you have to AND the 8-bit value with a binary number where all the desired bits are true. Then, dividing by 4 shifts the bits to the right by two places, resulting in a 6-bit value. Adding 32 to this value gives us a UU-encoded character.

There are four characters, however, to every three bytes. So the two unused bits on the right side of the first ASCII character make up the first two bits of the second UU character. The first four bits of the second ASCII character make up the rightmost four bits of the second UU character. Got it? This is the kind of stuff that turns a mild-mannered VB programmer into "Code-zilla."

To accomplish this in VB, you must multiply the remaining bits from the first ASCII character by 16 to shift them left four bit positions, and then add this value to the first four bits of the second ASCII character, which have been shifted to the right four places using the same method as the first character. The only difference is, you AND the second ASCII character by 240 and divide by 16 instead of ANDing with 252 and dividing by 4. Add 32 to the result to get the UU-encoded value. Here is the VB Code to get the remainder from the first character and create the second UU-encoded character:

```
szA_2 = "S"

nRemainder = (Asc(szA_1) And 3) * 16
szUU_2 = Chr$(nRemainder + ((Asc(szA_2) And 240) \ 16) + 32)
```

Figure 5.20 shows how the binary arithmetic works. Retrieving the third UU-encoded character from the three 8-bit characters uses the same logic. The last four bits of the second ASCII character make up the first four bits of the third UU character. The first two bits of the third ASCII character are the last two bits of the third UU character.

The first four bits must be shifted left two places, which is done by ANDing the ASCII character with 15 and multiplying by 4. The next two bits, which come from the third ASCII character, must be shifted right by six positions. This is done by ANDing the character with 192 and then dividing by 64. As before, adding 32 to

---

Figure 5.20   Encoding the first of three characters.

```
Acquiring the Remainder:
========================

71              =       1000111     (ASCII 71 = "G")
3               =            11
16              =         10000

71 AND 3        =            11     =       3
* 16            =        110000     =       48



Acquiring the rightmost four bits:
==================================

83              =       1010011     (ASCII 83= "S")
240             =      11110000
32              =        100000
16              =         10000
83 AND 240      =       1010000     =       80
\ 16            =           101     =       5
+ 32            =        100101     =       37
+ 48 (rem)      =       1111010     =       122

UU encoded Character 2 = Chr$(122) = "z"
```

---

the result renders the UU-encoded character value. Here is the VB code to retrieve the third character:

```
szA_3 = "U"

nRemainder = (Asc(szA_2)) And 15) * 4
szUU_3 = Chr$(nRemainder + ((Asc(szA_3) And 192) \ 64) + 32)
```

Figure 5.21 shows the binary arithmetic, which illustrates the method clearly.

Finally, the last UU character is equal to the remaining six bits of the third ASCII character. To get the UU-encoded value, AND it with 63 and add 32. Here is the VB code:

```
szUU_4 = Chr$((Asc(szA_3)) And 63) + 32)
```

Figure 5.21   Encoding the second of three characters.

```
Acquiring the Remainder:
=======================

83                  =       1010011     (ASCII 83= "S")
15                  =          1111
4                   =           100

83 AND 15           =            11      =      3
* 4                 =          1100      =     12



Acquiring the rightmost two bits:
================================

85                  =       1010101     (ASCII 85 "U")
192                 =      11111100
64                  =       1000000

85 AND 192          =       1000000      =     64
\ 64                =             1      =      1
+ 32                =        100001      =     33
+ 12 (rem)          =        101101      =     45

UU encoded Character 3 = Chr$(45) = "-"
```

Figure 5.22   Encoding the third of three characters.

```
85              =           1010101    (ASCII 85 "U")
63              =            111111

85 AND 63       =             10101 =      21
+ 32            =            110101 =      53

UU encoded Character 4 = Chr$(53) = "5"
```

Figure 5.22 shows the binary arithmetic. Therefore, the ASCII values GSU become UU encoded into 1z-5.

UUCODE.BAS Encoding and Decoding Routines

The UUCODE.BAS file contains two routines, UUEncode and UUDecode, which accept a source file and a destination file, and produce an encoded ASCII file and a decoded binary, respectively.

UUEncode

Here is the prototype for UUEncode:

```
Function UUEncode(szFileIn As String, szFileOut As String, _
   nAppend As Integer) As Integer
```

It accepts an input file and an output file and a flag that tells UUEncode to append the new data to the output file. The input file is the fully qualified path and name of any binary file, and the output file is the encoded ASCII file to be created. You can specify a full path for the output file as well, so that you can save your encoded file anywhere. If nAppend is False, the output file is overwritten, otherwise it is appended.

UUEncode returns zero if no error occurs, or the error number if an error occurs while encoding. The error number represents a standard Visual Basic error. If an error occurs you can retrieve a descriptive error message by using the Error$ function. Here is an example of how you would call UUEncode:

```
Dim nErrCode    As Integer
nErrCode = UUEncode("C:\MYFILE.EXE", "C:\MYFILE.UUE", False)
If nErrCode Then
    MsgBox Error$(nErrCode), vbInformation
End If
```

UUDecode

Here is the prototype for UUDecode:

```
Function UUDecode(szFileIn As String, szFileOut As String) As Integer
```

Just as with UUEncode, UUDecode accepts two filenames, one for input and one for output. The input file is the full path- and filename of an encoded ASCII file, and the output file is the name of the binary file which will be created. You can specify a full path for the output file as well, so that you can save your decoded file anywhere.

UUDecode returns zero if no error occurs, or the error number if an error occurs while decoding. The error number represents a standard Visual Basic error. If an error occurs you can retrieve a descriptive error message by using the Error$ function. Here is an example of how you would call UUDecode:

```
Dim nErrCode    As Integer

nErrCode = UUDecode("C:\MYFILE.UUE", "C:\MYFILE.EXE")

If nErrCode Then
    MsgBox Error$(nErrCode), vbInformation
End If
```

Sending an Encoded File with SMTP

To embed an encoded file into an e-mail message, simply tack on the encoded data to the end of your e-mail message. To do this, you should first create the complete message including all encoded files (you can send more than one) using the nAppend flag of UUEncode, and then send the file as your message. Now, I know that probably involves some code, but you're going to have to write it yourself. Ha! Just kidding. I already wrote it for you.

nSendFileAsMsg

Shown in Figure 5.23, this is a function in SMTP.BAS that sends a file via e-mail. The file can contain one or more encoded files and text. Here is a list of the parameters.

szFileName. The full path and filename of your encoded file (e.g., c:\myfile.txt).

dsSocket. The sockets control being used.

lBlockSize. The maximum size of each chunk of data sent.

szFrom. The sender's e-mail address.

szTo. The recipient's e-mail address.

szSubject. The subject of the message.

szText. The textual portion of the message (if not already contained in the file).

nSendFileAsMsg. Returns an error code if an error occurs, otherwise it returns zero.

Figure 5.23   The nSendFileAsMsg function sends a file via SMTP. The file can contain one or more encoded files.

```
Function nSendFileAsMsg(szFileName As String, dsSocket As Control, _
    lBlockSize As Long, szFrom As String, szTo As String, _
    szSubject As String, szText As String)

'**********************************************************
'   nSendFileAsMsg (by Carl Franklin)
'
'   This function sends a file via email.
'   If you want to send binary files you must
'   first UUEncode them. Use the function
'   nMakeMsgWithFiles (in UUCODE.BAS) to create
'   a file that has a text message and one or
'   more binary files embedded in it.
'
'   Parameters: szFileName  Full path and filename
'               dsSocket    Sockets control
'               lBlockSize  The maximum size of each block
'                              (default is 8192)
'               szFrom      Sender's email address
'               szTo        Recipient's email address
'               szSubject   Subject of the message
'               szText      Any text you want to tag on
'                              to the top of the message.
'**********************************************************

    Dim nMsgFile    As Integer
    Dim szLine      As String
    Dim szBuffer    As String
```

Continues

Figure 5.23   The nSendFileAsMsg function sends a file via SMTP. The file can contain one or more encoded files. *(Continued)*

```
On Error GoTo nSendFileAsMsg_Error
'-- Default block size = 8K
If lBlockSize = 0 Then
    lBlockSize = 8192
End If

'-- Open the message file
nMsgFile = FreeFile
Open szFileName For Binary As nMsgFile

'-- szBuffer holds up to <blocksize> number of bytes
'    and is sent when it becomes full.

'-- Send the header first
szBuffer = "DATE: " & Format$(Now, "dd mmm yy ttttt") & vbCRLF _
    & "FROM: " & szFrom & vbCRLF _
    & "TO: " & szTo & vbCRLF _
    & "SUBJECT: " & szSubject & vbCRLF & vbCRLF _
    & szText & vbCRLF
SendData dsSocket, szBuffer

'-- Send the file in chunks
Do Until EOF(nMsgFile)
    szBuffer = Space$(lBlockSize)
    Get #nMsgFile, , szBuffer
    SendData dsSocket, szBuffer
Loop

Close nMsgFile

'-- Send the final period.
SendData dsSocket, vbCRLF & "." & vbCRLF

Exit Function
nSendFileAsMsg_Error:

    nSendFileAsMsg = Err
    On Error Resume Next
    Close nMsgFile
    Exit Function

End Function
```

Using the cfSMTP and cfPOP3 Objects

Now that you know how SMTP and POP3 work you can use the cfSMTP and cfPOP3 objects in your own projects without having to cut and paste my sample code into your project. Chapter 9 shows you how to drop these objects into your own projects with just a few lines of code.

Epilogue

E-mail is a powerful medium for moving data from one person to another anywhere in the world. By now you know my mantra: Apply this technology to your own real-world problems and opportunities. You can use SMTP and POP3 to integrate nicely into any enterprise. Do you need the results of some computer-based research? E-mail them. Do you need to supply up-to-date product information to your customers? E-mail them.

How about this? You have a team of beta testers hammering on your program. They are all connected to the Internet. Install an error handler in your application. Anytime someone has an error, e-mail yourself important information about the state of your program and the machine. You'll have a report in your hands before the tester has time to pick up the phone and call you (well, maybe not that fast). The point is that e-mail is a medium. How you use it is completely up to you.

FILE TRANSFER PROTOCOL

Introduction

U p until 1994, when the World Wide Web took over the Internet, File Transfer Protocol (FTP) was the most widely used Internet client application besides e-mail. It is used as a remote shell for file access on an Internet host. Using an FTP application, you can connect to an FTP server, navigate through the available directories, and transfer files.

An FTP site can be public, private, or both. With a private account, you can be given access to the entire network's directory structure, or just specific areas. For the longest time I used a private FTP account to manage the files on Carl & Gary's Visual Basic Home Page (www.cgvb.com).

The Internet is also home to thousands of public access FTP servers that allow anyone to connect and transfer files to and from specific directories regardless of whether they have an account on the host. This is called *anonymous FTP.* When you connect to an anonymous FTP site, you usually specify "anonymous" as your user name and "guest" or your e-mail address as your password. Anonymous FTP sites are used, for example, to publish a large listing of public domain and/or shareware files. One of the most famous public FTP sites for shareware is ftp.cica.indiana.edu, which has mirror sites all over the world for its famous CICA shareware library.

FTP was designed mainly for use by programs, but the FTP application itself has turned out to be a critical part of any TCP/IP implementation. FTP.EXE is also an application that is installed when you use Microsoft TCP/IP drivers in Windows for Workgroups 3.11, Windows95 or Windows NT.

In fact, FTP is built into Netscape and other World Wide Web browsers so you can browse FTP servers with the same program that you use to browse the web.

As stated in RFC 959, there were four objectives in the design of the FTP protocol:

1. To promote sharing of files (computer programs and/or data).
2. To encourage indirect or implicit (via programs) use of remote computers.
3. To shield a user from variations in file storage systems among hosts.
4. To transfer data reliably and efficiently.

When Should You Use FTP?

If you are writing an application that does a fair amount of file transfer and are considering using FTP as your primary means of transferring files, you should know a few things. First of all, FTP is a client/server protocol. Using FTP to transfer files from one application to another on the same machine is not practical. You should consider FTP only if you have to transfer files with a known FTP server, or if you are writing a general-use FTP client program.

Sometimes it's a good idea to use an FTP server as a repository for files shared by all the users of your application. It completely depends on what your project goals are. If you want to give your users access to a bunch of shared files, FTP is a good tool for the job.

FTP does not have file control commands such as VB's Open, Input #, and Print # commands. If your project requires that you open a file remotely and have file-level access to it then FTP will not work. FTP is used primarily for getting directory listings and transferring files.

This chapter includes code that lets you connect to, navigate, and transfer files to and from any FTP server. I will show you how to use these routines in your VB applications, as well as how they work.

The FTP Program

FTP refers to both the FTP protocol and an FTP application. The FTP protocol defines a series of commands that the client sends the server, and how the client and server transfer data. An FTP application is usually a character-based terminal-type application in which you connect to an FTP server. The purpose for the FTP application is to provide English-like commands and help/error messages, as well as higher-level functionality than just a terminal could provide.

If you are using Microsoft's built-in TCP/IP drivers then you should have a file in your Windows directory called FTP.EXE. This is an FTP client application. I have noticed that many Windows users are not hip to FTP at all. I feel that knowing how to use FTP ranks right up there with knowing how to use the Windows File Manager or Explorer. Given that, I feel I should educate you on how to use it.

Figure 6.1 shows the FTP window. You may notice that it looks like a DOS window. It is a character-based terminal program. You can view it either in a window or full screen, just like any DOS text-mode application. If you are using Windows NT you can enjoy some nicer features such as scrolling back through your commands with the uparrow.

Connecting and Logging In

When you first run FTP you are presented with the following prompt:

```
ftp> _
```

You can connect to any FTP site with the OPEN command. Type OPEN followed by the name of the FTP server. For example, to connect to Microsoft's public FTP site type the following:

```
ftp> open ftp.microsoft.com <enter>
```

Figure 6.1   FTP window. FTP.EXE is a simple FTP client that comes with Windows 95/98/NT, and MS TCP/IP drivers for WFW 3.11.

At this time the program attempts to connect to the server on port 21. Once connected, you will receive a 220 reply followed by a welcome message. Here's the welcome message at ftp.microsoft.com:

```
Connected to ftp.microsoft.com.
220 ftp Microsoft FTP Service (Version 1.0).
```

Next, you get a prompt to enter your username. If you have an account on the server you can enter your username, but for public access (anonymous FTP) just type anonymous:

```
User (ftp.microsoft.com:(none)): anonymous
331 Anonymous access allowed, send identity (e-mail name) as password.
```

Next you are asked for a password. Again, if you have an account you can enter your password here, but if you are connecting for public access, just enter your e-mail address. Note that your password is not echoed to the screen.

```
Password:
```

The server then grants you access with another welcome message, and you finally get the FTP prompt again. Think of this like a DOS prompt. There are a fixed set of commands that you can use to navigate through the directories on the server and download files.

```
230-This is ftp.microsoft.com.  See the index.txt file
  in the root directory for more information
230 Anonymous user logged in as anonymous.
```

Listing Directories

One of the commands you can use to navigate through directories is DIR. In reality there is no DIR command in the FTP protocol spec. However, the standard user interface for accessing FTP servers has brought this command forward from the operating system because it's more user friendly (as if typing a bunch of commands into a terminal is at all user friendly).

Figure 6.2 shows what you get when you type DIR at an FTP prompt. Note that there's a lot more information here than you were probably expecting. In the rightmost column is the file or directory name. To the right of that is the file date and size. All the way to the left is a field of 10 bits. These are attributes. In DOS there are a limited number of attributes for files and directories such as Hidden, Read-Only, and Archive. However, Unix has a much more extensible set of attributes. You can create masks that give access to certain groups of users or prevent other users from gaining access. You can tell which is a file and which is a directory by the "d" attribute, which is displayed in the far-left attribute field. If there is a "d" then it's a directory.

Changing Directories

You can change directories with the CD command. CD works exactly like it does in DOS but using forward slashes instead of backslashes. Here is the command to change to the /developr/vb directory:

```
ftp> cd developr/vb
250 CWD command successful.
```

Once again, typing DIR gives you a list of files and directories. Figure 6.3 shows the result of typing DIR in the /developr/vb directory on ftp.microsoft.com.

Figure 6.2   The DIR command displays a directory listing.

```
ftp>dir
200 PORT command successful.
150 Opening ASCII mode data connection for /bin/ls.
d-----    1 owner    group          0  Jul  3 13:52  bussys
d-----    1 owner    group          0  Aug  9  3:00  deskapps
d-----    1 owner    group          0  Oct 27  7:35  developr
-----     1 owner    group       7905  Oct  5  8:53  dirmap.htm
-----     1 owner    group       4510  Oct  5  8:52  dirmap.txt
-----     1 owner    group        712  Aug 25  1994  disclaimer.txt
-----     1 owner    group        860  Oct  5  1994  index.txt
d-----    1 owner    group          0  Aug 31 12:17  KBHelp
-----     1 owner    group    7393252  Nov 28  4:04  ls-lR.txt
-----     1 owner    group     914179  Nov 28  4:05  ls-lR.Z
-----     1 owner    group     766409  Nov 28  4:04  LS-LR.ZIP
d-----    1 owner    group          0  Oct 20  9:27  MSCorp
-----     1 owner    group      28160  Nov 28  1994  MSNBRO.DOC
-----     1 owner    group      22641  Feb  8  1994  MSNBRO.TXT
d-----    1 owner    group          0  Oct 11  3:00  peropsys
d-----    1 owner    group          0  Aug 23 21:55  Products
d-----    1 owner    group          0  Oct  5  8:46  Services
d-----    1 owner    group          0  Nov 22 14:38  Softlib
-----     1 owner    group       5095  Oct 20  1993  support-phones.txt
-----     1 owner    group        802  Aug 25  1994  WhatHappened.txt
226 Transfer complete.
1407 bytes received in 0.99 seconds (1.42 Kbytes/sec)
```

Figure 6.3   Listing of the /developr/vb directory of Microsoft.

```
ftp> dir
200 PORT command successful.
150 Opening ASCII mode data connection for /bin/ls.
d-----   1 owner     group                 0 Oct 25  6:39 kb
d-----   1 owner     group                 0 Feb 24 11:35 public
-----    1 owner     group              1571 Aug 24  1994 README.TXT
d-----   1 owner     group                 0 Aug 24  1994 unsup-ed
226 Transfer complete.
270 bytes received in 0.22 seconds (1.23 Kbytes/sec)
```

Downloading

Downloading a file is simple and straightforward. Before you download, however, you must make sure you are in *binary* mode. There are two modes, ASCII and binary. To change to binary mode just type BIN:

```
ftp> bin
200 Type set to I.
```

To change back to ASCII mode type ASC. You do not have to change back and forth. In fact, I usually leave FTP in binary mode all the time so I don't forget and download a file in ASCII mode. (Don't run that .EXE! I used ASCII mode! Yikes!)

The GET command is used to retrieve a file. If you want to download with its original filename in the default directory, just type GET <filename> <enter>. Figure 6.4 shows this interaction.

You can also just type GET, after which you are prompted for the file you want to download, and then again for the name of the file (and path) on your system. This makes it easier to move files from a Unix or Win32 system (where filenames are long) to a Windows for Workgroups machine, or just to download to a directory other than where your FTP.EXE application is.

Figure 6.4   The Get command retrieves a file from the server.

```
ftp> get readme.txt
200 PORT command successful.
150 Opening BINARY mode data connection for readme.txt(1571 bytes).
226 Transfer complete.
1571 bytes received in 3.46 seconds (0.45 Kbytes/sec)
```

Figure 6.5   The SEND command sends a file to the server.

```
ftp> send
(local-file) myfile.zip
(remote-file) myfile.zip
200 PORT command successful.
150 Opening BINARY mode data connection for myfile.zip.
226 Transfer complete.
3018 bytes sent in 0.06 seconds (50.30 Kbytes/sec)
```

Uploading

You can upload a file in much the same way with the SEND command. You must be in a public area that allows uploads, of course. Figure 6.5 shows an example of uploading a file to Carl & Gary's VB file upload area (ftp.cgvb.com/uploads).

Supported Commands

If you want to view a list of supported commands, just type HELP. Figure 6.6 shows what you get on ftp.microsoft.com when you type HELP.

Ending the Session

You can end your FTP session at any time by typing BYE at any FTP prompt.

```
ftp> bye
<the server disconnects the client>
```

Figure 6.6   The Help command returns a list of supported commands.

```
ftp>help
Commands may be abbreviated.   Commands are:

!            delete        literal      prompt       send
?            debug         ls           put          status
append       dir           mdelete      pwd          trace
ascii        disconnect    mdir         quit         type
bell         get           mget         quote        user
binary       glob          mkdir        recv         verbose
bye          hash          mls          remotehelp
cd           help          mput         rename
close        lcd           open         rmdir
ftp>
```

Using a Web Browser to Download Files

There is a much easier way to download files from an anonymous FTP site. Use a web browser—you can download any file by either making a link to it in an HTML document and clicking the link, or simply entering an FTP URL in the location edit window (which most web browsers display at the top of the window directly under the menu section). Using a web browser for FTP access is good and fast, but it is limited in what you can access. For example, you cannot send files (at least, there is no standard way). But for downloading files from public sites, you can't beat it.

Here is an example URL that downloads a Winsock API Trace utility from Carl & Gary's VB Home Page FTP server:

```
ftp://ftp.cgvb.com/pub/misc/tpwins32.zip
```

If you enter the URL directly from the browser make sure you turn on the "save to disk" option. If you create an HTML file with a link, the file should look like this:

```
<a href="ftp://ftp.cgvb.com/pub/misc/tpwins32.zip">tpwins32.zip</a>
```

Using your web browser you can click on the link while holding down the Shift key to save to disk.

The FTP Protocol

The commands you give to an FTP application are a bit different from the commands that an FTP application gives to an FTP server. For example, to get a directory listing with an FTP application you would use the DIR command. However, the FTP application uses the LIST command. When I refer to FTP from now on, I am referring to the protocol, unless otherwise noted.

If there is any one big difference between FTP and the protocols that we've covered up to this point, it is that FTP uses more than one port. Port 21, the control connection, is used for transferring commands, and another port, the data connection, is used for transferring data. The default port for the data connection is 20, but any other port can be used also. This makes FTP a wee bit more difficult to code than, say, SMTP or POP3.

FTP Errata

Yes, there is plenty of weirdness concerning FTP, and why not? FTP has long been the staple file transfer mechanism of the Internet community. Because it is so popular, everyone has a way to improve on it. Therefore, there is tons and tons of addenda, comments, and additions to the FTP protocol. This has yielded some inconsistencies in FTP commands between servers. For that reason you must exercise a bit of caution when extending the power of FTP to your users.

For example, if your client only connects to your server and you have tested the connection then you needn't worry. On the other hand, if you incorporate FTP as a means to grab any file from any FTP server, and extend that functionality to the user, you may be in for a headache. Most third-party FTP tools maintain a list of server types and the different commands that the server may or may not understand. Using the FTP protocol, if you send the SYST command, the FTP server will send you back the FTP server name and version. It is beyond the scope of this book to list all of the different inconsistencies among FTP servers.

I am not trying to make it sound like FTP is not a standard. For the most part, FTP server implementations stick to the standard commands. The commands in this chapter were taken from RFC 959, which is the standard FTP protocol definition. Any deviation from this standard is a risk, and software shops should know this.

Connections

The FTP server accepts initial connections on port 21. Unlike HTTP, which reconnects on every command, FTP keeps the connection open. This connection is for the processing of FTP commands only. A separate connection is used for data transfer. These two connections are called the control connection and the data connection, respectively.

For example, when retrieving a file the client usually sends the PORT command, accepts a connection on port 20 and then tells the server to send the file using the RETR command. The server then sends the data, and closes the connection. The reason this method is used and not the familiar *send data ending with a period on a line by itself* method, is because FTP sends binary data. There is no practical way to interpret an end-of-line character when every possible character could be interpreted as data.

Another option is for the client to tell the server to listen to a particular port with the PASV command (indicating passive mode), and then connect to that port for the data connection. I like to use passive mode because you don't have to accept a connection, which isn't always possible.

If you are going to use the PORT method, it is best to open either port 20 or the next available port over 1024 and then send a PORT command to the server. That way, if the user is already transferring a file with a standalone FTP application, there is no chance of interfering with it. (I say to use ports over 1024 because ports 1–1024 are reserved for TCP/IP and standard protocols.)

FTP Commands

FTP uses a series of simple commands such as LIST and RETR that perform the various tasks of navigating directories and transferring files with an FTP server. These commands are listed in the FTP Reference in Appendix D at the back of this book. FTP commands are always followed with a CR/LF pair.

Server Responses

After sending an FTP command, you will receive a reply that consists of a three-digit number followed by a space and a text message. Figure 6.7 shows a list of reply codes in numeric order. The full descriptions of these codes can be found in RFC 959.

Figure 6.7   Reply codes.

110 Restart marker reply.

   In this case, the text is exact and not left to the particular implementation; it must read:

   MARK yyyy = mmmm

   where yyyy is User-process data stream marker, and mmmm is server's equivalent marker (note the spaces between markers and "=").

120 Service ready in nnn minutes.

125 Data connection already open; transfer starting.

150 File status okay; about to open data connection.

200 Command okay.

202 Command not implemented, superfluous at this site.

211 System status, or system help reply.

212 Directory status.

213 File status.

214 Help message.

   On how to use the server or the meaning of a particular nonstandard command. This reply is useful only to the human user.

215 NAME system type.

   NAME is an official system name from the list in the Assigned Numbers document.

Figure 6.7   *Continued.*

220 Service ready for new user.

221 Service closing control connection.

    Logged out if appropriate.

225 Data connection open; no transfer in progress.

226 Closing data connection.

    Requested file action successful (for example, file transfer or file abort).

227 Entering Passive Mode (h1,h2,h3,h4,p1,p2).

230 User logged in, proceed.

250 Requested file action okay, completed.

257 "PATHNAME" created.

331 User name okay, need password.

332 Need account for login.

350 Requested file action pending further information.

421 Service not available, closing control connection.

    This may be a reply to any command if the service knows it must shut down.

425 Can't open data connection.

426 Connection closed; transfer aborted.

450 Requested file action not taken.

    File unavailable (e.g., file busy).

451 Requested action aborted: local error in processing.

452 Requested action not taken.

Insufficient storage space in system.

500 Syntax error, command unrecognized.

    This may include errors such as command line too long.

501 Syntax error in parameters or arguments.

502 Command not implemented.

503 Bad sequence of commands.

504 Command not implemented for that parameter.

530 Not logged in.

532 Need account for storing files.   *Continues*

Figure 6.7   Reply codes. *(Continued)*

550 Requested action not taken.

   File unavailable (e.g., file not found, no access).

551 Requested action aborted: page type unknown.

552 Requested file action aborted.

   Exceeded storage allocation (for current directory or dataset).

553 Requested action not taken.

Filename not allowed.

Reply Code Categories

Each digit of the reply code has a specific meaning. There are five values for the first digit of the reply code: 1 indicates a positive preliminary reply (the command was accepted, and this is the first of more than one positive reply from the server); 2 indicates a permanent positive reply; 3 indicates a positive intermediate reply, in which case the server is waiting for more information; 4 indicates that the command was not accepted and the requested action did not occur, yet the condition may be temporary; 5 indicates absolute failure.

The second digit indicates the category of the reply: 0 indicates a syntax error; 1 indicates informational content; 2 indicates a message concerning the transmission channel; 3 refers to authentication or accounting messages; 4 is not used; and 5 indicates a message regarding the file system status. The third digit merely specifies the level of granularity of messages in a particular category.

Figure 6.8 shows a quick summary of how to interpret FTP reply codes. You should consult RFC 959 for a complete discussion.

Visual Basic Code

The project FTPDEMO.VBP is an FTP client application. With it, you can connect to any FTP server, navigate and list directories, and send and receive files. Figure 6.9 shows the FTPDemo program. FTPDemo does not have a command parser, such as does the FTP.EXE application. Instead, it has a series of command buttons for FTP actions.

Figure 6.8   Interpreting FTP reply codes.

1xx   Positive Preliminary Reply

2xx   Positive Reply

3xx   Positive Intermediate Reply

4xx   Transient Negative Completion Reply

5xx   Permanent Negative Completion Reply

x0x   Syntax error

x1x   Information

x2x   Connections

x3x   Authentication and accounting

x4x   Unspecified as yet

x5x   File system

Figure 6.9   FTPDemo program.

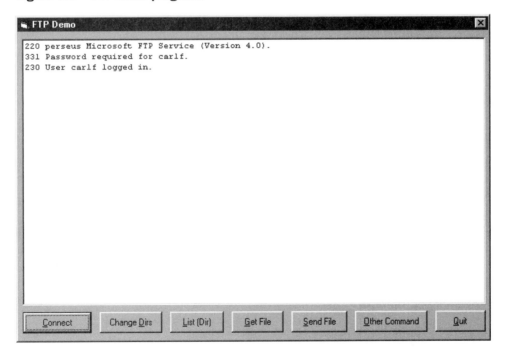

Though this code is a terrific teaching tool, you should use the cfFTP object outlined in Chapter 9 if you want to use FTP code in your own VB applications. Since cfFTP is an object, it can be accessed easily from any VB application.

The form, frmFTP, has three DSSock controls on it; one for the control connection (dsSocket1), one to accept a data connection, and the third for the data connection itself. The module FTP.BAS then has FTP routines such as FTPLogon that log you into the FTP server. FTP.BAS requires FTP.FRM and vice versa. First, I'll show you how to use the FTP routines, and then we'll get into how they work.

Using a Display Terminal

The FTP code has a provision for using a list box or a text box to display messages and directory listings from the FTP server. If you want to use this feature, you need to modify one line of code in FTP.BAS. Specifically, the DisplayMessage routine has a line that sets a local object called Display to a list box or a text box. Simply change this line to point to your list box or text box on any form:

```
'-- Set your control name here (Text Box or List Box)
Set Display = frmMain.List1
```

You can, of course, modify this routine to display text in any type of display control. The Demo project (FTPDemo) uses a list box as a display window.

FTPLogon

The first thing you need to do is connect to an FTP server. Use the FTPLogon function for this. Here is the syntax:

```
Success% = FTPLogon (ServerName$, UserName$, Password$, Timeout%)
```

The return value is True if successfully connected and authorized, and False if there was any problem either connecting or logging in. ServerName$, UserName$, and Password$ are self-explanatory. Timeout% is the number of seconds to wait for a successful connection.

Here is an example of calling FTPLogon that connects to Carl & Gary's Visual Basic Home Page FTP Server anonymously as santaclaus@northpole.com, and waits up to 30 seconds for a connection:

```
If FTPLogon ("ftp.cgvb.com", "anonymous", "guest", 30) Then
    MsgBox "Connected!"
Else
    MsgBox "There was a problem connecting or logging in"
End If
```

SendFTPCommand

SendFTPCommand has provisions for any command that requires a data connection, such as RETR and STOR. If a data connection is required, it first sends the command to set up the data connection, and then it sends the command. Here is the syntax:

```
SendFTPCommand FTPCommand$, BinaryMode%, FileName$
```

FTPCommand$ is any valid FTP command.

FileName$ is an optional argument that specifies a FileName when sending a file with STOR or STOU, or retrieving a file with RETR.

When retrieving a file using the RETR command, FileName$ is the local name that the file will be saved to. When sending a file using STOR or STOU, FileName$ specifies the name of file on the server that will be created.

BinaryMode indicates whether or not the output from the server is sent in binary mode or ASCII mode. Setting BinaryMode to True indicates binary mode. In general you should send and receive all files using BinaryMode True. When retrieving directory listings with LIST, you should specify BinaryMode False.

Here is an example in which MYFILE.ZIP is downloaded:

```
SendFTPCommand "RETR", True, "MYFILE.ZIP"
```

Retrieving a Directory Listing

To retrieve a directory listing of the current directory on the FTP server, use the RETR command with the following syntax:

```
SendFTPCommand "LIST", False
```

Note that you do not have to specify a filename if it is not required. SendFTPCommand uses the Visual Basic 4.0 Optional keyword for the FileName argument, so it is not required.

You can also return a listing of files that match a particular spec. For example, the following command returns all files with an extension .zip:

```
SendFTPCommand "LIST *.zip", False
```

If you are using a display terminal then the directory listing will be displayed. If not, then you will have to intercept the data in the frmFTP.dsSocket2_Receive event, which is where all data received via the data connection enters your application.

Changing Directories

To change to a new directory, send the CWD (Change Working Directory) command specifying the directory name. For example, to change to /uploads:

```
SendFTPCommand "CWD /uploads", False
```

Downloading a File

To download a file, send the RETR command with the name of the file. The FileName$ argument is the name to which the downloaded file will be saved. When sending RETR, make sure you specify nBinaryMode as True. Here is an example that downloads a file in the current FTP server directory called MYFILE.ZIP and saves it locally to C:\FILES\MYFILE.ZIP:

```
SendFTPCommand "RETR MYFILE.ZIP", True, "C:\FILES\MYFILE.ZIP"
```

GetFileFromURL

You can also use the GetFileFromURL to connect to an anonymous FTP server, download a file, and disconnect all in one shot. This is similar to using a web browser to download a file from an anonymous FTP site. Here is the syntax:

```
Success% = GetFileFromURL%(URL$, DestPath$, Email$, Timeout%)
```

The return value is True if the file was downloaded and False if there was a problem with either connecting or downloading. URL$ is a URL pointing to an anonymous FTP file. It can either start with file:// or ftp://. DestPath$ is a local directory name where the file will be saved. Email$ is your e-mail address (used to connect anonymously). If you leave this blank, then "guest" is used as an e-mail address (some sites don't allow this). Timeout% is the number of seconds to wait for a connection before the function returns False.

Here is an example that downloads the file sleigh.zip from ftp.northpole.com in the directory /pub/games and saves it to the local C:\ directory. The user's e-mail address is specified as me@here.com, and the routine will wait up to 30 seconds for a connection.

```
If GetFileFromURL("file://ftp.northpole.com/pub/games/sleigh.zip", _
 "c:\", "me@here.com", 30) Then
    MsgBox "Success!"
Else
    MsgBox "Failure"
End If
```

The GetFileFromURL function does not return to your code until it has either successfully downloaded the file or determined that there was an error.

Uploading a File

To send a file to an FTP Server you can either use SendFTPCommand or the SendFile routine. SendFile is a wrapper for SendFTPCommand, and adds the benefit of automatically setting the transfer mode to binary, and waiting until your file is sent before it returns. Here is the syntax for SendFile:

```
ErrCode% = SendFile%(SourceFileName$, DestFileName$, ErrorMessage$)
```

SendFile% returns zero if all goes well; otherwise it returns the FTP reply that represents an error that occurred. To use SendFile you must already be connected to the FTP server (see FTPLogon).

SourceFileName$ is the name of a local file to be sent. DestFileName$ is the path and filename of the file that will be written on the server. The path uses forward slashes (/) not backslashes (\) and must not contain wildcard characters. ErrorMessage$ returns with an error message if an error occurs.

Here is an example that sends the file c:\myfile.zip to /pub/uploads on the server:

```
Dim szErrMsg As String

If SendFile("c:\myfile.zip", "/pub/uploads/myfile.zip", szErrMsg) Then
    MsgBox szErrMsg, vbInformation
End If
```

Debugging

My FTP code (in fact, all the code) comes with an excellent debugging tool for those times when you just want to know what's going on in the code. Stepping through the code is impossible during an FTP session, so the only way to see the flow of data is to write a log file.

The WriteLogFile function is a routine that writes a string to a file in the current directory called ERRORLOG.TXT. It writes the date and time, and the string to the file. If the file is not open it is opened. The string is automatically appended to the file. WriteLogFile writes to the log file only if you use /D on the command line of your application.

Even if you are not having trouble with the code, chances are that sooner or later someone is going to have trouble. You can tell them to start your application with /D and then send you the LOG file. That way you can trace what happens; the last line written to the log indicates the last successful action that the program took before the error occurred.

Figure 6.10 WriteLogFile writes error message to a file.

```
Sub WriteLogFile(szData As String)

    '-- File handle for the log file (if used)
    Dim nLogFileNum As Integer

    On Error Resume Next

    If InStr(UCase$(Command$), "/D") Then
        '-- Open The File
        nLogFileNum = FreeFile
        Open App.Path & "\" & szLogFileName For Append As nLogFileNum

        '-- Write the string
        Write #nLogFileNum, Str$(Now) & Chr$(9) & szData

        '-- Close the file
        Close nLogFileNum
    End If

End Sub
```

Figure 6.10 shows the WriteLogFile routine, contained in DSSOCK.BAS. The code checks the command line for /D. The string is written to the file only if it has been specified. Notice that the date and time is also written to the log file.

You can use WriteLogFile in any of the applications (or any of your own for that matter). I find it an invaluable little debugging tool for real-time communications.

WriteLogFile is called at every critical point in the FTP code, as listed here.

Routine	Description
SendData	Sending data to a server (writes the data).
dsSocket1_Close	When the control connection is closed by the server.
dsSocket1_Connect	When the control connection is made between you and the server.
dsSocket1_Exception	When a WinSock error occurs in the control connection (writes the error).
dsSocket1_Receive	When data is received on the control connection (writes the data).

dsSocket1_SendReady	When the control connection becomes ready to send data.
dsSocket2_Accept	When a data connection has been established with the server by means of the server connecting to you (PORT).
dsSocket2_Close	When the data connection is closed by the server.
dsSocket2_Connect	When a data connection has been established with the server by means of you connecting to the server (PASV).
dsSocket2_Exception	When a WinSock error occurs in the data connection (writes the error).
dsSocket2_Receive	When data is received on the data connection (writes the data).
dsSocket2_SendReady	When the data connection becomes ready to send data.
CloseDataConnection	When the code closes the data connection (even if it's not open).

As you can see, using /D will create quite a nice little error log for you to study. I used it several times in debugging the FTP code.

Inside the FTP Code

The FTP Code is a bit complex because of the flags and globals that help bridge the gap between the routines and the FTP form, where all the data transfer occurs. Instead of going over the code line by line, I will instead walk through the data flow using the typical example uses of FTP, connecting to a server, getting a directory, and transferring files. If you are the curious type, you can read the well-commented code.

Take a look at the FTP Form. There are two dsSocket controls: the first (dsSocket1) is used for the control connection and the second (dsSocket2) is used for the data connection. Because there can be more than one data connection, this control is an array, having an index of zero.

Connecting to the Server

This is done with FTPLogon. FTPLogon does more than just connect you to the server, it logs you into the server and waits for the server to say you are logged in. Figure 6.11 shows the FTPLogin function.

The first thing this routine does is make sure that dsSocket1 (the control connection) is in Line mode (not binary) and that the end-of-line character is a linefeed.

Figure 6.11   The FTPLogon routine connects and logs into an FTP server.

```
Function FTPLogon(szHostAddress As String, szUserName As String, _
    szPassword As String, nTimeout As Integer)

    Dim EndTime

    Screen.MousePointer = vbHourglass

    '-- Set Line Mode and EolChar (Linefeed)
    frmFTP.dsSocket1.LineMode = True
    frmFTP.dsSocket1.EOLChar = 10

    '-- Set the username and password
    gszUserName = szUserName
    gszPassword = szPassword
    gnFTPReady = False

    '-- Connect (with a timer)
    If SocketConnect(frmFTP.dsSocket1, 21, szHostAddress, nTimeout) = 0 Then
        '-- Use the same timer value to wait for gnFTPReady
        '    which is set in dsSocket1_Receive

        EndTime = DateAdd("s", nTimeout, Now)
        Do
            DoEvents
                If Now >= EndTime Then
                    Exit Do
                End If
        Loop Until gnFTPReady

        '-- Success?
        If gnFTPReady Then
            '-- Yes! We be connected
            FTPLogon = True
        Else
            '-- Error. disconnect
            SocketDisconnect frmFTP.dsSocket1
        End If
    End If

    Screen.MousePointer = vbNormal

End Function
```

Next it sets two globals (gszUserName and gszPassword) to the username and password passed to FTPLogin. These will be used in the dsSocket1_Receive event to answer the server's request for the username and password.

Also, the flag gnFTPReady is initialized to False. This is set to True when we have received login confirmation from the server.

Next, SocketConnect is called to connect to the FTP server. If you remember back in Chapter 2 on Winsock programming, SocketConnect is the generic connect routine for any type of Internet host.

Check out the next block of code:

```
EndTime = DateAdd("s", nTimeout, Now)
Do
    DoEvents
        If Now >= EndTime Then
            Exit Do
        End If
Loop Until gnFTPReady = True
```

This code waits for gnFTPReady to be set to True, indicating a successful FTP login, but exits after nTimeout number of seconds has expired.

The timing code uses the Now function, which returns a date/time value of the exact moment when it is called. The DateAdd function adds nTimeout number of seconds to Now, and returns a value that represents nTimeout number of seconds in the future. Inside the loop, Now is tested against EndTime and exits if the number of seconds has elapsed.

If indeed the loop exits because of a timeout then gnFTPReady will be false. If this is so, then we did not connect; otherwise FTPLogin returns True to indicate success.

Let's look at the data flow that actually happens when you connect. Immediately after connection, the FTP Server sends a 220 reply with a welcome string. For example:

```
220 ftp.cgvb.com FTP server (Version wu-2.4.2-academ[BETA-16](1) Sun Apr 26 07:0
9:33 EDT 1998) ready.
```

In the dsSocket1_Receive event, a Select Case statement is set up on the value of the reply code (the value of the leftmost three digits of ReceiveData). If the code is 220, then we have just logged into the server and should send the USER command with the user name. Here is the code to handle this precise moment:

```
Case 220    '-- Service ready for new user.

    SendData dsSocket1, "USER " & gszUserName & vbCrLF
```

Now the USER command (specifying the username) has been sent and we should get back a 331 reply indicating that the username requires a password. Here is the code to handle this (also in dsSocket1_Receive):

```
Case 331    '-- User name okay, need password.

    SendData dsSocket1, "PASS " & gszPassword & vbCrLf
```

Now, if the password is accepted, then we will get back a 230 command. If this occurs, then gnFTPReady is set to True in the following clause:

```
Case 230    '-- User logged in, proceed.

    '-- This flag tells FTPLogin that we're actually logged in.
    gnFTPReady = True
```

Once the gnFTPReady flag is set to True, then the loop in FTPLogin exits, FTPLogin is set to True, and we're in!

Reality Break

About this time is where most people want to put the book down and use a custom control to do all this. Believe me, it's not as complex as you think, and you should avoid using controls whenever possible. Remember, I am showing you the innards of the code that you can access at a high level. The dirty work is done. You have the added benefit of being able to tinker with the code, which you don't get with an FTP control. However, I must stress that if you want to use this code in your own applications you should probably use the cfFTP class outlined in Chapter 9.

So take a few deep breaths, count to 11,239, pour a cup of coffee, put on your fuzzy slippers, and forge ahead. Just think of all the boneheads you'll impress with just the buzzwords alone, let alone the fact that you'll be able to communicate with FTP servers in Visual Basic, something that my cats can't even do (and they're not stupid!).

Inside SendFTPCommand

Figure 6.12 shows the SendFTPCommand routine. I want to bring to your attention right off the bat the block of code that begins with:

```
If gszLastCmdSent <> "TYPE" Then
```

This code determines if the user has specified a change of transfer mode (binary to ASCII or vice versa). If so, the command string passed in to SendFTPCommand is saved in the global gszDataCommand variable, the TYPE command is sent to change the mode, and the routine is exited. When the OK reply (200) is received after sending the TYPE command, the original command (gszDataCommand) is then issued.

Figure 6.12   SendFTPCommand command lets you send any FTP command to the server.

```
Sub SendFTPCommand(szCommand As String, szFileName As String, _
   nBinaryMode As Integer)

'-- This function sends any command that requires a data connection.
'    These commands are "RETR", "APPE", "LIST", "NLST", "STOR", and "STOU".
'    Add more as they become necessary.

    Dim nPos1       As Integer
    Dim nPos2       As Integer
    Dim nPos3       As Integer
    Dim nSpace      As Integer

    Dim szAddr      As String
    Dim szPort      As String

    '-- Set up an error handler
    On Error GoTo ERR_SendDataCommand

    WriteLogFile "SendFTPCommand: " & szCommand & ", " _
        & szFileName & "," & Str$(nBinaryMode)

    '-- Save the command internally
    gszLastCmdSent = UCase$(Left$(szCommand, 4))
    gnFileOK = False

    If gszLastCmdSent <> "TYPE" Then
        '-- Handle the data mode (binary or ASCII)
        If gnLastMode <> nBinaryMode Then
            gnLastMode = nBinaryMode
            gszDataCommand = szCommand
            gszLastCmdSent = "TYPE"
            gszFileName = szFileName
            If nBinaryMode Then
                SendData frmFTP.dsSocket1, "TYPE I" & gszCRLF
            Else
```

Continues

```
            SendData frmFTP.dsSocket1, "TYPE A" & gszCRLF
        End If
        Exit Sub
    End If
End If

gszFileName = szFileName

Select Case gszLastCmdSent

    Case "RETR", "APPE", "LIST", "NLST", "STOR", "STOU"
        '-- These commands require setting up a data connection.
        gnBinaryMode = nBinaryMode

        '-- Make sure the data connections are closed
        CloseDataConnection

        '-- Close the data file if open.
        If gnFileNum Then
            Close gnFileNum
        End If
        gnFileNum = 0

        '-- Save this command
        gszDataCommand = szCommand
        '-- If gnPassiveMode is True, then we connect to the
        '   FTP server, otherwise it connects to us (for a
        '   data connection).

        If gnPassiveMode Then
            gszLastCmdSent = "PASV"

            '-- Send the PASV command
            SendData frmFTP.dsSocket1, "PASV" & gszCRLF

        Else
            On Error Resume Next
            frmFTP.dsSocket2(0).Action = SOCK_ACTION_CLOSE
            On Error GoTo ERR_SendDataCommand

            '-- Tell the data connection socket to listen to
            '   the next available port.
            frmFTP.dsSocket2(0).LocalPort = 0
```

Figure 6.12 *Continued.*

```
                   frmFTP.dsSocket2(0).LocalDotAddr = ""
                   frmFTP.dsSocket2(0).ServiceName = ""
                   frmFTP.dsSocket2(0).Action = SOCK_ACTION_LISTEN

                   '-- Devise a PORT command to tell the FTP server where
                   '   to connect.
                   szAddr = frmFTP.dsSocket2(0).LocalDotAddr
                   nPos1 = InStr(szAddr, ".")
                   nPos2 = InStr(nPos1 + 1, szAddr, ".")
                   nPos3 = InStr(nPos2 + 1, szAddr, ".")

                   szPort = "PORT " & Left(szAddr, nPos1 - 1) & ","
                 szPort = szPort & Mid(szAddr, nPos1 + 1, nPos2 - nPos1 - 1) & ","
                  szPort = szPort & Mid(szAddr, nPos2 + 1, nPos3 - nPos2 - 1) & ","
                  szPort = szPort & Mid(szAddr, nPos3 + 1, _
                       Len(szAddr) - nPos3) & ","

                   szPort = szPort & frmFTP.dsSocket2(0).LocalPort \ 256 & ","
                   szPort = szPort & frmFTP.dsSocket2(0).LocalPort Mod 256

                   gszLastCmdSent = "PORT"

                   '-- Send the port command
                   SendData frmFTP.dsSocket1, szPort & gszCRLF

              End If

         Case Else
              '-- Send the specified command
              SendData frmFTP.dsSocket1, szCommand & gszCRLF

      End Select


      Exit Sub

ERR_SendDataCommand:

      Debug.Print "Error" & Str$(Err) & ": " & Error
      On Error Resume Next
      Exit Sub

End Sub
```

This intermediate step takes the burden off you as the programmer of constantly sending a TYPE command before every single command.

At the top of the routine the leftmost four characters of the command are saved as the global gszLastCmdSent. This variable always contains the last command sent via SendFTPCommand, and is necessary for determining action to be taken based on the codes received.

Changing Directories

The CWD command is extremely simple. Use the following example as a model for syntax:

```
SendFTPCommand "CWD /pub/cdrom/win95", False
```

When you send this command, the server will change directories and send back a 250 reply to notify success. There is no special handling for the CWD command in the code, but you can add it by simply looking at gszLastCmdSend. If it's CWD, then you have yourself a handler.

Creating a Data Connection

The next thing the code does is determine if the command requires a data connection. There are two basic types of FTP commands: those that require a data connection and those that don't. For example, the CWD command does not require a data connection. The commands RETR, APPE, LIST, NLST, STOR, and STOU all require a data connection.

```
Select Case gszLastCmdSent

   Case "RETR", "APPE", "LIST", "NLST", "STOR", "STOU"
```

A data connection can be created one of two ways. You can either connect to the FTP server on a port that the server gives you, or you can tell the server to connect to you on a port you give it. The PORT command tells the server to connect to you, and the PASV (passive) command asks the server for a port to connect to for the data connection.

Usually the PORT command is used, but there are situations when you want to connect to the server for a data connection, such as when you are behind a firewall that does not allow incoming connections. It is for this reason that I use PASV in the demo code as the default method of creating a data connection.

The gnPassiveMode variable determines who connects to whom for the data connection. Set gnPassiveMode to False if you want to accept the data connection, otherwise leave it set to True (the default).

If gnPassiveMode is True, then the PASV command is sent; otherwise a connection is created with dsSocket2(1). In the case that gnPassiveMode is False, the code that begins with the following comment devises a string to be sent to the server that defines the IP address and port that dsSocket2(0) is listening on:

```
'-- Devise a PORT command to tell the FTP server where
'   to connect.
```

Once the new control is listening, the PORT command is sent with the aforementioned string that defines the IP address and port for the data connection, and the routine exits.

At this point we've sent the PORT command and are waiting for a reply. When dsSocket2(0) answers the connection, it passes the socket to dsSocket2(1) and the data connection is established, and the FTP server sends an OK reply (200). If, when this is received, the last command sent was PORT, then the original command (gszDataCommand) is sent. Figure 6.13 shows the code in dsSocket1_Receive that handles this precise moment.

Figure 6.13   After receiving a PORT command, the server sends a 200 reply, at which point you send the original commands such as RETR or STOR.

```
Case 200    '-- Command okay.

    '-- What was the last command sent?
    Select Case gszLastCmdSent
        Case "TYPE" '-- Type toggles between Binary and Ascii
                    '    modes too.
            '-- Set the binary mode flag accordingly
            If InStr(UCase$(ReceiveData), "SET TO A") > 0 Then
                gnBinaryMode = False
            ElseIf InStr(UCase$(ReceiveData), "SET TO I") > 0 Then
                gnBinaryMode = True
            End If
            gnLastMode = gnBinaryMode
            If Len(gszDataCommand) Then
                SendFTPCommand gszDataCommand, gszFileName, gnBinaryMode
            End If

        Case "PORT"
            '-- Send the actual command that the PORT command
            '    was sent to prepare for.
            DisplayMessage "Sending command: " & gszDataCommand
            SendData dsSocket1, gszDataCommand & gszCRLF
    End Select
```

If the last command was PORT, that means that the data connection is made (or is in the process of being made) and the server is ready to accept the original command that required a data connection. At this time, the original command is sent, and the results are returned via the data connection. When the sending side of the connection has finished sending, it closes the connection.

Retrieving a Directory Listing

A directory listing involves the use of a display terminal (see Using a Display Terminal). All you need to do to get a directory is send the LIST command.

LIST takes a filespec parameter just like DOS's DIR command. Here is an example that asks for a directory listing of all the ZIP files in /pub/files/new:

```
SendFTPCommand "LIST /pub/files/new/*.zip", False
```

Unix Wildcards

FTP uses Unix wildcards in filespecs. Here are a few of the most commonly used Unix wildcards:

?   matches a single character. Unlike DOS, "hell?" will match "hell" but not "hello".

*   matches any sequence (including a period).

[xxx]   where xxx is a collection of letters or a range of letters (like A–Z). "hello.[A-Za-z]" matches "hello.z" but not "hello.9".

The LIST command requires the use of the data connection. The data connection must be created on the fly before sending the actual LIST command or any other command that requires it (see Creating a Data Connection).

When you call SendFTPCommand with LIST as the command, first a data connection is made using either PORT or PASV, depending on gnPassiveMode. Once the data connection is made, then the LIST command gets sent. The server immediately sends the directory information and the dsSocket2_Receive event fires upon receiving the data. Figure 6.14 shows the code in this event.

Look at the statement "Case LIST." This is where the code arrives after sending the LIST command. By default the code simply calls DisplayMessage, which displays the text in either a list box or a text box, depending on which you want to use. The demo program uses a list box.

Figure 6.14 Receiving data via the data connection.

```
Sub dsSocket2_Receive(Index As Integer, ReceiveData As String)

    WriteLogFile "RD: " & Str$(Len(ReceiveData)) _
        & " bytes. First 10 = " & Left$(ReceiveData, 10)

    '-- What was the last command sent?
    Select Case UCase$(Left$(gszDataCommand, 4))
        Case "RETR" '-- The retrieve command is the same as a
                    '    Download command, the purpose is to
                    '    retrieve a file. If we are here then
                    '    we are receiving file data.
            '-- Is the file not open?
            If gnFileNum = 0 Then
                '-- Was a file specified?
                If Len(gszFileName) Then
                    '-- Yes. Open the file in binary mode (always)
                    gnFileNum = FreeFile
                    Open gszFileName For Binary As gnFileNum
                End If
            End If

            '-- If the file is open, write the data.
            If gnFileNum Then
                Put gnFileNum, , ReceiveData
            End If

        Case "LIST"

            '-- This is a line of a directory listing. If you wish to parse
            '    it to determine the properties of the files, you should do
            '    so here, but be warned... The format of this listing may
            '    change from server to server.

            DisplayMessage ReceiveData


        Case Else
            '-- We are not retrieving a file, so display the
            '    received data. Of course, you can modify this
            '    logic to also display retrieved file data (if
            '    in text mode, or something like that) or to save
            '    all received data to a file.                    Continues
```

Figure 6.14   Receiving data via the data connection. *(Continued)*

```
            DisplayMessage ReceiveData
    End Select

    '-- Update the number of bytes received.
    glBytesReceived = glBytesReceived + Len(ReceiveData)

End Sub
```

Uploading a File

When you call the SendFile Routine (shown in Figure 6.15) the first thing that happens is the STOR command is sent with SendFTPCommand. The data connection is
created using either the PASV command or the PORT command, and the STOR (or
STOU) command string is temporarily stored in the gszDataCommand variable.
Now, the server sends either a 125 or a 150 code indicating that the transfer is starting. Figure 6.16 shows the code in the dsSocket1_Receive event that handles this precise moment.

Figure 6.15   The SendFile routine sends a file to the server.

```
Function SendFile(szSourceFile As String, szDestFile As String, _
  szErrorMessage As String) As Integer

    Dim nRetVal As Integer

    SendFTPCommand "STOR " & szDestFile, szSourceFile, True
    nRetVal = WaitForFileResponse()
    If nRetVal = 226 Then
        nRetVal = False
    Else
        szErrorMessage = gszErrMsg
    End If
    SendFile = nRetVal

End Function
```

Figure 6.16   The dsSocket2_Close event occurs when the server closes the data connection.

```
Sub dsSocket2_Close(Index As Integer, ErrorCode As Integer, ErrorDesc As String)

    WriteLogFile "dsSocket2(" & Trim$(Str$(Index)) & ")_Close"

    DisplayMessage "Connection Closed. Total bytes received = " _
        & glBytesReceived & gszCRLF

    '-- Close the file if its open
    If gnFileNum Then
        Close gnFileNum
        gnFileNum = 0
    End If

    '-- You cannot unload dsSocket2(0)
    If Index = 1 Then
        Unload dsSocket2(Index)
    End If

    gszDataCommand = ""
    glBytesReceived = -1

End Sub
```

Simply put, the file is opened in Binary mode and sent in chunks. The chunk size is set with the variable gnSendBlockSize, which you can set in the Form_Load event of frmFTP. The default is 16000. The basic rule is that there is more overhead in sending two blocks of *n* bytes than sending one block of 2*n* bytes. In other words, the bigger the buffer, the better. So, try to avoid bagging bugs by barking with big buffers. Once the file has been sent, the data connection is closed.

SendFile makes use of another handy routine, called WaitForFileResponse. This routine waits in a loop for the gnFileOK global integer variable to be set, and returns the value of gnFileOK. gnFileOK is set to any 200 completion code or error code. It is not set by interim codes such as 200, but is set only after a command has been completely carried out. Using WaitForFileResponse is an easy way to return control to your program after a command has been carried out. I use it in the FTPdemo project to disable the form temporarily until a command is complete.

This prevents the user from stacking up commands on top of each other, which could yield unpredictable results.

Downloading a File

The RETR (Retrieve) command downloads (receives) a file from the FTP server. The file can be anywhere on the server (that's available to you, of course) and you can specify a full server-side path with the filename.

Here is the syntax to download a file:

```
SendFTPCommand "RETR MYFILE.ZIP", True, "C:\FILES\MYFILE.ZIP"
```

When you send this command, just like with LIST, SendFTPCommand saves the RETR command to gszDataCommand and sends the PORT command (or the PASV command) to initiate a data connection. Once the data connection is made, the original command (RETR) is sent. The server responds positively with a 150 reply to indicate that it's OK to start the transfer, or a 125 if the data connection is already open.

At this time you are ready to start receiving the file. Look at Figure 6.14 again, which shows the dsSocket2_Receive event. If the last command sent was RETR then you are receiving binary file data. The code opens the file if it is not open and writes the received data to the file.

When the server has finished sending the data, it closes the data connection. Figure 6.17 shows the dsSocket2_Close event that occurs when the server closes the data connection. gnFileNum, the VB file handle of the received file, is closed when the data connection is closed. Also, the data connection control dsSocket2(Index) is unloaded from memory. To clean up, gszDataCommand is zeroed and the number of bytes received is set to −1 to indicate an end of file to the code in dsSocket1_Receive.

Figure 6.17   The dsSocket2_Close event.

```
Sub dsSocket2_Close(Index As Integer, ErrorCode As Integer, ErrorDesc As String)

    WriteLogFile "dsSocket2(" & Trim$(Str$(Index)) & ")_Close"

    DisplayMessage "Connection Closed. Total bytes received = " & glBytesReceived &
vbCrLf

    '-- Close the file if its open
    If gnFileNum Then
```

Figure 6.17 *Continued.*

```
      Close gnFileNum
      gnFileNum = 0
   End If

   gszDataCommand = ""
   glBytesReceived = -1

End Sub
```

Using the cfFTP Object

Now that you know how FTP works you can use the cfFTP object in your own projects without having to cut and paste my sample code into your project. Chapter 9 shows you how to drop this object into your own projects with just a few lines of code.

Epilogue

The FTP protocol isn't difficult on paper, but it requires a sort of state-machine mentality to write in Visual Basic, hence all the gszLastCommand variables and what-not. In all honesty, because of this, the FTP code took me the longest to write. Fortunately for you, you can just drop this code in your project and be sending and receiving files in no time. Please be sure and stop by the Visual Basic 6.0 Internet Programming site (http://carl.franklins.net/vbip) for code updates and utilities.

ACCESSING THE WORLD WIDE WEB

The World Wide Web

Just since early 1994, the World Wide Web has brought the elusive world of the Internet into homes all over America. Once the sole realm of universities and research firms, the Internet is now a household word. This is all due to the growing popularity of the World Wide Web.

The World Wide Web is the Internet. It is a term for the huge collection of web servers out there on the Internet. The reason it is called a "web" is because of how it is accessed. With the click of a mouse, you can connect to any web server anywhere in the world. Once you've connected, you can view documents that have hypertext jumps, or *links*, to other web servers anywhere else in the world. The act of jumping around from server to server is called *surfing the net*.

I know you've either read the preceding paragraph somewhere before, or maybe you heard it on the radio or saw that episode of *Beyond 2000*. It seems like everyone is talking about the World Wide Web, and why shouldn't they? This is the future. That's why you are reading this book, because you want to know how to be a part of the future in a big way.

Let's forget about the hype for a minute and take a look at what's really going on under the hood of the web, so to speak. First, a couple of definitions.

HTTP—Hypertext Transfer Protocol

HTTP is the protocol by which web clients, such as Netscape and MS Internet Explorer, communicate with web servers, such as WebSite or MS Internet Information Server. In this chapter I make references to HTTP servers and web servers. The two are the same. HTTP is the protocol of the World Wide Web.

Like all protocols, there is a set of rules. I am not going to go into the innermost workings of HTTP, but you will undoubtedly pick up on some of them as you read this chapter and implement the code.

HTML—Hypertext Markup Language

HTML is in the same category as RTF (Rich Text Format). HTML is the source code of the World Wide Web. Using any good web browser, you can connect to any site and view the HTML source for the page you are looking at.

In a nutshell, HTML is an enhanced text format. Certain commands, or *tags* as they are called, are embedded in the text, and tell the HTML display program what to display. To display a GIF file, you use the <IMG> tag like so:

```
<IMG SRC=PICTURE.GIF>
```

To display text in bold, you would do this:

```
<B>This is some bold text</B>
```

and so on. There are tags for creating lists, displaying text input fields, buttons, horizontal ruler lines, and many other things.

Do not confuse HTML with HTTP. The latter is the protocol, or the set of rules by which HTML and other data is transmitted between web clients and web servers. HTML is a markup language, the specific purpose of which is the display of text, graphics, and hypertext jumps.

If you want to know more about HTML and writing it, there are lots of places on the web that have tutorial and reference documents. The best source of these documents can be found at the Yahoo! database (Stamford University). Here is the link for that list:

```
http://www.yahoo.com/Computers_and_Internet/Information_and_Documentation/Data_Formats
/HTML/
```

I also recommend the *HTML Sourcebook* by Ian S. Graham (John Wiley & Sons, 1995).

Understanding the World Wide Web

Basically, an HTTP server is a Winsock application that listens to port 80. When a blind connection is made, it sends the default document (i.e., INDEX.HTML) from its default document directory to the client using the HTTP protocol and immediately closes the connection. The client is now viewing the index page complete with text and graphics. On that page, there are links to other pages, which may be anywhere in the world. In HTML, a link is defined as follows:

```
<A HREF="http://some.server.somewhere.com/">This is the link text</A>
```

The A stands for *anchor*. An anchor is a reference to another HTML page (or program) running on an HTTP server somewhere in the world. When the user clicks on that anchor, the client makes a new connection to the HTTP server defined in the anchor. In this case, the server name is some.server.somewhere.com. Since the port is already defined as 80, there is no need to specify the port.

An anchor can also contain the name of a specific file, for example:

```
<A HREF="http://carl.franklins.net/default.asp">Carl's Page</A>
```

This anchor points to my personal page on my private network, Franklin's Net. The name of the file is /default.asp. The root directory is defined by the HTTP server.

You may have been wondering why files and directories are defined with forward slashes as opposed to backslashes. The reason is Unix. Since the web started with Unix machines, it naturally follows that HTTP and HTML separate files and directories the same way Unix does, with forward slashes. It does not matter what platform you run your HTTP server on—HTML and HTTP will always use forward slashes, even when the operating system does not, as is the case with Windows NT.

It is easy to see why the problem of *dead links* exists on the web. There is no referential integrity. Any web site has the right to change its paths and HTML filenames if it wants to. When this happens, any existing outside references to the page are considered dead. It is for that reason that most people leave a page that proclaims "This site has moved to the following address" at the old site.

This chapter shows you how to use the Hypertext Transfer Protocol, or HTTP, the protocol of the World Wide Web. The primary focus is on how to connect to and manipulate web pages programmatically, and interpret the data that comes back from the web site. There is nothing in this chapter about writing back-end server CGI applications. That topic is covered in Chapters 10 and 11. In this chapter we write several interesting programs. One program retrieves a text file from Carl & Gary's Visual Basic Home Page, and another downloads ad hoc street-level maps of anywhere in the United States.

I must preface this chapter with a hideous invention of the legal profession called a disclaimer. It is sometimes unlawful to extract and present data that exists on web pages for your own purposes. Before setting out to write any kind of application that uses data gleaned from somebody's web page, or any existing Internet host for that matter, make sure you have permission. John Wiley and Sons, Inc. and myself (Carl Franklin) will in no way be held responsible by your actions. There, that wasn't so bad was it?

I learned about this legal issue the old fashioned way. I wrote a VB program that connects daily to a stock quote server, retrieves several quotes, and logs them to an Access database. I was debugging the application when all of a sudden it stopped working. The message that was coming back from the web page was that I had asked for more than 100 quotes in one day, which was not allowed. In the same message, they explained that it was unlawful to run automated scripts against their server, and they would prosecute those who did. Whoops!

Another point I'd like to make is that the sites listed in this chapter, as elsewhere in this book, existed at the time I wrote the book. Since the Internet has a tendency to change, I cannot guarantee that they are still in existence. You should use the code set forth as a guide for creating your own little demons of death and destruction. Heck, for all I know by the time you read this, Microsoft may have bought the rights to the Internet and this book may be banned!

How to Read a URL

URL stands for Universal Resource Locator. A URL identifies an object (HTML page, document, or a file) that exists on any web site anywhere in the world. Using Netscape or some other web browser, you can enter a URL at the top of the screen in the location field, and you will soon be downloading (and with a little luck, viewing) the object defined by the URL. Everything you need to know to retrieve a document or file on the web is contained in the URL. Consider this URL for WorldTRAIN: http://www.worldtrain.com:80/about.asp.

Figure 7.1 shows the different portions of a URL. The first portion (http://) identifies the protocol used to retrieve the resource. The second part is the machine name or IP address (www.worldtrain.com). The third part of the URL identifies the port of the web site (:80). This is usually not used unless the port is other than 80. Port 80 is the default port for all HTTP servers. Next comes the full path and filename of the resource (/about.asp).

If you simply specify a directory name with no filename, then the default file will be sent. Usually this is called index.html or default.asp, but webmasters can set the default file to any file.

The best way to learn how HTTP works is to look at the data that flows between client and server during a session. You can do this with a program like the Listen

Figure 7.1 Portions of a URL.

```
Portion Examples
-------------------------

Protocol http://

Machine Name     www.worldtrain.com
        199.105.125.50

Port Number      :80
        <none>

Full Path Of File        /about.asp
        /about.asp
        <none> (implies default file)
```

utility written by Ian S. Graham, author of the *HTML Sourcebook* (John Wiley & Sons, 1995), an excellent book on HTML with quite a bit of information on HTTP. The Listen utility that comes with Graham's book displays all data that is sent from the web client to the server. Getting the server's response data is a bit trickier. You have to use the Terminal program (see Chapter 2) to connect to the web server on port 80 and manually type in or paste in the exact data that the client sends the server. The server will send you the data exactly as your web client receives it.

Let's take a look at what really happens when you click on a URL in Netscape or any other web client. This is exactly what gets sent to Carl & Gary's VB Home Page when you enter the URL to read the Suggestion Box Page, from Internet Explorer 4.01:

```
GET /suggest.boa HTTP/1.1
Accept: application/msword, application/vnd.ms-powerpoint, application/vnd.ms-excel,
image/gif, image/x-xbitmap, image/jpeg, image/pjpeg, */*
Accept-Language: en-us
Accept-Encoding: gzip, deflate
User-Agent: Mozilla/4.0 (compatible; MSIE 4.01; Windows NT)
Host: www.cgvb.com:80
Connection: Keep-Alive
<CRLF>
```

All HTTP messages end with a carriage return/linefeed on a line by itself. That is how the receiver identifies the end of the message.

HTTP Message Headers

All HTTP messages contain a header that serves several purposes. First and fore-most, the header is for identification. The message sent to the server is called a *request message*, and consists entirely of an HTTP *request header*. The request header has several fields, a field being a line ending with a carriage return/linefeed. The first field is called the *method field*, which is followed by several *request fields*. The method field has the following format:

```
<HTTP method> <identifier> <HTTP version>
```

In this case, the HTTP method is GET, which retrieves a document from the server. There are several other methods defined by HTTP, which are shown in Figure 7.2. The request fields provide additional information about the client (or server). For example, several Accept: fields are sent to tell the server which types of data the client can view. If your web client can decode inline GIF images, it will send the following request field:

```
Accept: image/gif
```

Otherwise, it won't. The client identifies itself to the server with the User-Agent request header:

```
User-Agent: Mozilla/2.0 (compatible; MSIE 3.02; Update a; Windows NT)
```

This could be useful, for example, if a client-of-tomorrow connects to a server-of-tomorrow, which supports neural communication via ESP. The server could detect that the client is "one of its kind" and send it special commands. This type

---

Figure 7.2   Methods of accessing a web page.

Method	Description
GET	Retrieves the indicated URL (document or otherwise).
HEAD	Retrieves the HTTP Header information for the indicated URL.
TEXTSEARCH	Sends a query to the URL using a GET method against a URL that contains query data.
LINK	Links one object (file or executable) to another.
UNLINK	Removes the link between two objects.
POST	Sends data to a URL. The URL must already exist.
PUT	Replaces data sent by a POST method to a URL. The URL must already exist.

---

of built-in intelligence is part of the reason why web browsers work so well on many different platforms.

The request fields are optional. If you know what you are getting back from the server, there is no need to go crazy with the request fields. This method field itself is usually enough to return a text or HTML file from any server.

Interpreting the Server's Response

When the server receives the request message it performs the requested method on the object specified and returns a result message back to the client. Figure 7.3 shows the server's response to the earlier request message from the client.

Figure 7.3   Sample response from Carl & Gary's Visual Basic Home Page.

```
HTTP/1.1 200 OK
Date: Fri, 23 Oct 1998 13:44:45 GMT
Server: Apache/1.3.0 (Unix)
Last-Modified: Thu, 25 Jun 1998 11:03:20 GMT
Keep-Alive: timeout=15, max=100
Connection: Keep-Alive
Transfer-Encoding: chunked
Content-Type: text/html


b61
<html>
<head>
<title>VB Home Page Suggestion Box</title>
</head>
<body text="#000000" bgcolor="#FFFFFF" face="verdana,arial">
<font face="verdana,helvetica,arial" size="-1"><table cellpadding=10>
<tr><td valign="middle"><center><a href="/"><img src="/img/smalmast.gif" border=0
height=92 width=211></a><br><small><a href="/links/maint">Add Your Own
Link</a></small></center></td>
<td><h2><font color="#CC0000" face="verdana,arial,helvetica">
VB Home Page Suggestion Box</font></h2></td></tr></table>
<blockquote>
<font size=2 face="verdana,arial,helvetica">
<p>
<p>
<i><Font color="#FF0000" face="verdana,arial,helvetica">Note: This page is not for VB
questions</font></i><p>
Tell us what you think.  Praise, suggestions, flames, or funny stories
if you have any. We're committed to providing a great page, and any ideas you have
```

Continues

---

could easily show up sometime soon. Just fill in your suggestion or comment below and click Send or Cancel. If you have any problems submitting suggestions using this interface, you can send mail directly to
<a href="mailto:vb-admin@cgvb.com">vb-admin@cgvb.com</a> as well.
Please provide an e-mail address if we need to get back to you.
You don't need to include one if you don't want any replies from us.

```
<p>
<hr size=7>
<p>
<FORM METHOD="POST" ACTION="suggest-reply.boa">
<p>
E-mail address (please include):<br>
<input name="email" size=50>
<p>
Topic: <select name="topic">
<option>General Comment
<option>Broken Link
<option>Suggestion for Improvement
<option>Complaint
<option>Technical Problem with Site
<option>Other
</select>
<p>
Enter your comment below.  If you are telling us about a broken
link, or problem with a particular page or file, please include
as much information as you can to assist us.<br>
<textarea name="comments" rows=15 cols=60></textarea>
<p>
<input type="submit" value="Send"> <input type="reset" value="Clear Form">
</form>

<p>
<hr size=7>
</font>
</blockquote>
<center>
<p>
<font size=2 face="verdana,arial,helvetica">
<map name="navmap">
<area coords="1,1,59,59" href="/">
<area coords="60,1,125,59" href="/lsearch.boa">
<area coords="425,1,482,59" href="/suggest.boa">
```

Figure 7.3 *Continued.*

```
<area coords="127,1,182,59" href="/whatsnew.boa">
<area coords="184,1,230,59" href="/gcgi/news_form">
<area coords="231,2,302,59" href="/links">
<area coords="304,2,377,59" href="/links/lpage.boa/TOOLVENDOR">
<area coords="378,2,424,59" href="/links/lpage.boa/FILE">
</map>
<center>
<a href="/img/toolbar.map"><img ismap usemap="#navmap" src="/img/tbnew.gif" border=0
width=483 height=60 ALT="Navigation Toolbar"></a>
<p>
<a href="/"><img src="/img/cgvbhome.gif" height=34 width=119 border=0></a>
<br><font size="-2" face="verdana,arial,helvetica"><i>Copyright (c) Carl Franklin and
Gary Wisniewski,
1994-1998.  All rights reserved.</i>
<br>Design and production courtesy
<a href="http://www.spidereye.com.au/">Spider Eye Studios</a></font>
</center>
</font></body>
</html>
```

The first line of the header, like the request header, is a status line that usually follows this format:

```
<HTTP Version> <Status Code> <Explanation>
```

The status code is a three-digit number that tells the client exactly what the response is. As defined in the HTTP 1.0 draft document, Figure 7.4 shows the possible status codes that the server sends the client.

Figure 7.4   Status codes returned by the HTTP server.

```
"200"   ; OK
"201"   ; Created
"202"   ; Accepted
"204"   ; No Content
"301"   ; Moved Permanently
"302"   ; Moved Temporarily
"304"   ; Not Modified
"400"   ; Bad Request
"401"   ; Unauthorized
"403"   ; Forbidden
"404"   ; Not Found
```

Continues

Figure 7.4 Status codes returned by the HTTP server. *(Continued)*

```
"500"   ; Internal Server Error
"501"   ; Not Implemented
"502"   ; Bad Gateway
"503"   ; Service Unavailable
```

In this case, the status is 200, or OK. As a general rule, codes between 200 and 299 indicate success. Codes 300 to 399 indicate a redirection to another object (more on this later). Codes from 400 to 599 indicate error messages.

The explanation is a short description of the status code. Unlike status codes, however, the explanation can vary from server to server. The main benefit of the explanation is for the human user.

Every line below the status line is some sort of response header information field. The *Date* field sends the date and time of the transmission in Greenwich Mean Time (GMT). The *Server* field identifies the name and version of the HTTP server software, with the name and version separated by a forward slash. The *Content*-type field tells the client the MIME data-type of the object. Sometimes you will also receive a MIME-version field, which identifies the version of the MIME protocol. Finally, the *Last-modified* field gives the date and time of the last modification to the object being sent, and the Content-length field gives the object's size in bytes. HTTP headers always end with a carriage return/linefeed on a line by itself (an empty line).

Accessing HTTP Servers in Visual Basic

The WebDemo sample project shown in Figure 7.5 and listed in Figure 7.6 shows how to connect to Carl & Gary's VB Home Page and retrieve a text file. You can change the name of the document in the GET command to any publicly accessible file that exists on the server.

Take a look at the code in Figure 7.6. In the Form_Load event, the program connects to www.cgvb.com on port 80, after which the command GET /greeting.txt HTTP 1.0 is sent followed by two carriage return/linefeed pairs. As the text file is received from the server, it is appended to the text in the txtText text box (whew!, that's a mouthful!). It's really a very simple program.

Comment out the line in btnGo_Click that retrieves welcome.txt and uncomment the line that retrieves index.html and run the program again. Looks a bit different, doesn't it? You are looking at the source code of the *what's new* page. The function of a web client program like MS Internet Explorer or Netscape is to take this raw HTML text and make it look like a web page.

Figure 7.5   The WebDemo program retrieves a text file from a web site.

Figure 7.6   The HHTP command GET tells a web server to send you the contents of a file. In this case it is a personal greeting from the author.

```
DSSOCK.BAS (included in project)


Option Explicit

Dim szReceived As String
Private Sub Form_Load()
    '-- Use Line Mode
    dsSocket1.LineMode = True
    dsSocket1.EOLChar = 10

    '-- Temporarily disable the form and set the hourglass cursor
    Enabled = False
    Screen.MousePointer = vbHourglass

    '-- Show the form
```

Continues

```
Show

If SocketConnect(dsSocket1, 80, "www.cgvb.com", 20) Then
    '-- There was an error. Re-enable the form
    '   and reset the mouse pointer
    Screen.MousePointer = vbDefault
    Enabled = True

    '-- Display the error
    MsgBox "Error connecting: " & Error
    Exit Sub
Else
    '-- Send the command to get a file from the server
    SendData dsSocket1, "GET /greeting.txt" & vbCrLf & vbCrLf
End If

End Sub

Private Sub dsSocket1_Close(ErrorCode As Integer, ErrorDesc As String)

    '-- Before you add a received line to a text box, you must make
    '   sure it ends with a CRLF and not just a LF
    szReceived = szStripHTML(szLFToCRLF(szReceived))

    '-- Append the line to the Text Box
    Me.txtText.SelStart = Len(Me.txtText) + 1
    Me.txtText.SelText = szReceived

    szReceived = False

    '-- Re-enable the form and reset the mouse
    '   pointer
    Screen.MousePointer = vbDefault
    Enabled = True
    gnConnected = False

End Sub

Private Sub dsSocket1_Connect()

    '-- Set this flag indicating we've connected
```

Figure 7.6 *Continued.*

```
    gnConnected = True

End Sub

Private Sub dsSocket1_Receive(ReceiveData As String)

    '-- Append the received data to szReceived
    szReceived = szReceived & ReceiveData

End Sub

Private Sub dsSocket1_SendReady()

    gnSendReady = True

End Sub
```

Now go to the Receive event and uncomment the line that calls szStripHTML. This function removes the HTML codes from the text, making it a bit more readable. Figure 7.7 shows the szStripHTML routine.

Figure 7.7   szStripHTML removes HTML codes from a string and does some simple reformatting with CRLFs and horizontal rulers. It is not intended to be a complete HTML parser.

```
Function szStripHTML(szString As String) As String
'-- szStripHTML by Carl Franklin
'    This function strips HTML codes from a string
'    and attempts to reformat with CRLFs.


    Dim szTemp As String
    Dim szResult As String
    Dim nPos As Integer
    Dim nMarker As Integer

    '-- Copy the argument into a local                    Continues
```

Figure 7.7   szStripHTML removes HTML codes from a string and does some simple reformatting with CRLFs and horizontal rulers. It is not intended to be a complete HTML parser. (Continued)

```
'   string so the original does not
'   get whacked.
szTemp = szString

'-- Remove HTML codes
Do
    nPos = InStr(szTemp, "<")
    If nPos = False Then
        Exit Do
    Else
        '-- szResult contains the final
        '    product of this routine.
        szResult = szResult & _
            Left$(szTemp, nPos - 1)
        '-- szTemp is the working string,
        '    which is continuously
        '    shortened as new codes
        '    are found
        szTemp = Mid$(szTemp, nPos + 1)
        nPos = InStr(szTemp, ">")
        If nPos = False Then
            '-- No complimentary arrow
            '    was found.
            Exit Do
        Else
            '-- What was the code?
            Select Case szParseString(UCase$(Left$(szTemp, nPos - 1)), " ", 1)
                Case "P", "/H1", "/H2", "/H3", "/H4", "/H5", "DL"
                    szResult = szResult & vbCrLf & vbCrLf
                Case "BR"
                    szResult = szResult & vbCrLf
                Case "HR"
                    szResult = szResult & vbCrLf & String$(50, "-") & vbCrLf
            End Select


            '-- Shorten the working
            '    string
            szTemp = Mid$(szTemp, _
                nPos + 1)
```

Figure 7.7 *Continued.*

```
        End If
    End If
Loop


'-- Find a marker byte by looking for
'    a char that does not already exist
'    in the string.
For nMarker = 255 To 1 Step -1
    If InStr(szResult, Chr$(nMarker)) = 0 Then
        Exit For
    End If
Next

'-- Remove carriage returns
Do
    nPos = InStr(szResult, vbCr)
    If nPos Then
        szResult = Left$(szResult, _
            nPos - 1) & Mid$(szResult, _
            nPos + 1)
    Else
        Exit Do
    End If
Loop

'-- Replace linefeeds with Marker bytes
Do
    nPos = InStr(szResult, vbLf)
    If nPos Then
        szResult = Left$(szResult, _
            nPos - 1) & Chr$(nMarker) _
            & Mid$(szResult, nPos + 1)
    Else
        Exit Do
    End If
Loop

'-- Replace marker bytes with CR/LF pairs
Do
    nPos = InStr(szResult, Chr$(nMarker))
    If nPos Then
        szResult = Left$(szResult, _
```

Continues

```
                nPos - 1) & vbCrLf _
                & Trim$(Mid$(szResult, nPos + 1))
        Else
            Exit Do
        End If
    Loop

    '-- Thats all for this routine!
    szStripHTML = szResult

End Function
```

You can use this technique to write applications that retrieve news or other timely documents from any web page and use it in your personal applications. Someday, I'd like to write myself an application that goes and gets news from a variety of sources (web sites, Usenet groups, etc.), picks out stories of interest, and creates one big document that I can then view in the morning when I get up.

Accessing Forms

The coolest part of accessing the World Wide Web has to be manipulating forms. With some simple code and HTTP savvy you can connect to a form page, enter values into the text boxes or select options, and press buttons. This is all done programmatically, of course. There are no "virtual buttons" you have to press. Your code bypasses the user interface, talking directly to the web site in HTTP.

There are two ways in which you can send data to a web site: the POST method and the PUT method. POST is the most common command used to send data to a web site. You have probably come across many web forms in your time. A form is a page that has input fields that you fill in and a button that lets you send the data.

A Brief Overview of the Common Gateway Interface (CGI)

A form assigns names to each of the input fields. When you fill out these fields and press a Submit button on the form, the client sends a POST method message to the server along with all the values for each of the field names.

The server then runs a program (called a *gateway* program) at the web site and passes it the data that you have entered into the form. The interface between the HTTP server and the gateway program is called the Common Gateway Interface, or CGI.

The gateway program does its thing (whatever it does) and returns HTML text to the HTTP server, which passes it through to the client.

In Chapter 10, I show you how to create your own gateway programs in Visual Basic using Windows CGI, a special version of CGI made specifically for Visual Basic programmers. In Chapter 11, I show you how to use ActiveX objects written in Visual Basic as CGI programs with Microsoft's Internet Information Server.

As I said before, every input field on a form has a name. Take a look at the form section of Carl & Gary's Suggestion Box HTML page in Figure 7.8. All form definitions start with the <FORM> tag and end with the </FORM> tag. Every form has a method associated with it. The method is sent when the Submit button is pressed.

Figure 7.8   An HTML snippet from Carl & Gary's Visual Basic Home Page Suggestion Box.

```
<FORM METHOD="POST" ACTION="suggest-reply.boa">
<p>
E-mail address (please include):<br>
<input name="email" size=50>
<p>
Topic: <select name="topic">
<option>General Comment
<option>Broken Link
<option>Suggestion for Improvement
<option>Complaint
<option>Technical Problem with Site
<option>Other
</select>
<p>
Enter your comment below.  If you are telling us about a broken
link, or problem with a particular page or file, please include
as much information as you can to assist us.<br>
<textarea name="comments" rows=15 cols=60></textarea>
<p>
<input type="submit" value="Send"> <input type="reset" value="Clear Form">
</form>
```

A Submit button is a button whose job it is to execute the form's method. In the case of our suggestion box, the form uses the POST method to send the data in the fields to the server application, which is defined in the ACTION portion of the FORM tag as vb-bin/post-sug.pl. This is a Unix script written in the Perl scripting language.

Yes, I know, Carl & Gary's runs on a Unix machine! How are we supposed to promote Microsoft with an attitude like that? Well, the fact is that when we started all the really good web software (and most Internet software in general) ran on Unix, but that is changing. Windows NT is the future of operating systems. NT does take up much more memory than SunOS or any other Unix flavor, but it does so many great things. (Well, that's another book, isn't it?) Anyway, Carl & Gary's uses MS Internet Information Server for some of the pages, which, of course, run on an NT box.

The input fields are defined with the INPUT and TEXTAREA tags. You can create a Submit button by setting VALUE=SUBMIT. The VALUE parameter identifies the text on the button.

Let's say for the sake of argument that you connect to this suggestion box page with your web browser and enter your e-mail address as reader@myhouse.com, and enter a suggestion that reads, "Carl & Gary are the coolest VB programmers I know!" When the Submit button is pressed, the data in Figure 7.9 is sent to the server.

Figure 7.9   A sample of data sent to a server when a Submit button is pressed.

```
POST vb-bin/post-sug.pl HTTP/1.0
Accept: application/msword, application/vnd.ms-powerpoint, application/vnd.ms-excel,
image/gif, image/x-xbitmap, image/jpeg, image/pjpeg, */*

Accept-Language: en-us

Accept-Encoding: gzip, deflate

UA-pixels: 800x600
UA-color: color24
UA-OS: Windows NT
UA-CPU: x86
User-Agent: Mozilla/4.0 (compatible; MSIE 4.01; Windows NT)

Host: www.cgvb.com:80

Connection: Keep-Alive

Content-type: application/x-www-form-urlencoded
Content-length: 90
&email=reader@library.com&comments=Carl+%26+Gary+are+the+coolest+VB+programmers+I+know%21
<CRLF>
```

There are two sections to the POST command, a header section and a data section. The header section contains the Content-type and other HTTP headers. Like the GET request message, the header section begins with a status line. The command is POST, the identifier is the CGI script post-sug.pl located in the vb-bin directory on the server, and the protocol is HTTP version 1.0.

Notice the Content-type field. When sending data to an HTTP 1.0 server, there is only one content type and that is application/x-www-form-urlencoded. There is no other option. Also, the Content-length field is used in the request method because data is being sent in the message body. The content length is the length of this data.

By the way, that's not a typo. Urlencoded is the word, not uuencoded. URL = Universal Resource Locator, hence urlencoded.

The data section is composed of a string of "variable=data" pairs like so:

```
&variable1=data1&variable2=data2
```

These variables are defined by the server in the HTML that defines the form.

You might have noticed that spaces are replaced with the plus character (+). As well, there are some strange numbers in the place of the ampersand and the exclamation point. Those numbers are the hexadecimal values of the characters. As a general rule, if a character in your data is being used by the protocol and has special meaning, encode it as a percent sign followed by its hex value (26 is the hex value of the ampersand, and 21 is the hex value of the exclamation point).

You can encode any character using Visual Basic with the following code:

```
Encoded$ = "%" & Hex$(Asc(Character$))
```

Mapping with the TIGER Map Service

While writing this book, I stumbled on a most interesting web site, the TIGER Map Service (TMS). This site is operated by the U.S. Bureau of the Census. The goal of the service is to provide a public resource for generating high-quality, low-detail maps of anywhere in the United States using public geographic data. In short, you can send a query to this page specifying an exact location in the United States using longitude and latitude values, and the picture size, and it returns to you a GIF file of a map. The URL of the TIGER Mapping Service (shown in Figure 7.10) is http://tiger.census.gov/.

Figure 7.10   TIGER Mapping Service.

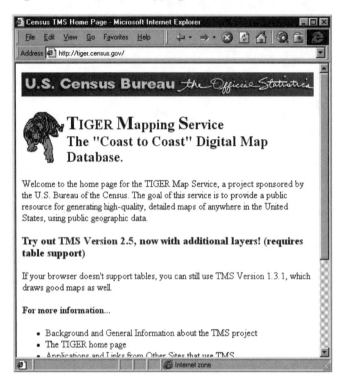

There is an interactive page, where you can generate maps and look at them, and then there is a page that tells you how to send queries.

Basically, you connect on port 80 to tiger.census.gov and send a POST command with the coordinate data tagged on at the end. Here is a list of some of the variables you can specify.

lon=number. The longitude, in decimal degrees, of the center of the map. Remember that longitudes for the Western Hemisphere are negative numbers. Longitudes for the contiguous United States range between about –67 and –125 degrees.

lat=number. The latitude, in decimal degrees, of the center of the map. Latitudes for the contiguous United States range between about 24 and 49 degrees.

wid=number. The desired width, in decimal degrees of longitude, of the coverage of the map. The actual coverage of the map may vary slightly from this number, due to fitting the requested coverage to the shape of the image.

ht=number. The desired height, in decimal degrees of latitude, of the coverage of the map. It may turn out slightly different, for the reason given earlier.

iwd=number. The image width, in pixels. If none is specified, the default is 512.

iht=number. The image height, in pixels. If none is specified, the default is 256.

legend=on. If included, the legend graphic is returned rather than the map.

To get an idea of what these maps look like, check out Figure 7.11. This is a map of Washington, D.C. Since you can specify the image's pixel width and height, you can render a graphic suitable for printing. Not bad!

The page has some sample URLs that generate maps. One example is a shot of Manhattan. Here is the URL:

```
http://bluefs.census.gov/cgi-bin/mapper/map.gif?lat=40.739&lon=-73.99&
wid=0.06&ht=0.08&iht=500&iwd=240
```

Figure 7.11   Washington, D.C.

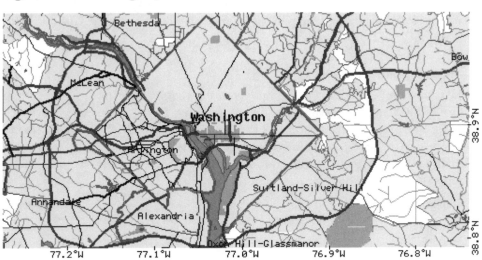

```
POST /cgi-bin/mapper/map.gif HTTP/1.0
Accept: image/gif
Content-type: application/x-www-form-urlencoded
Content-length: 57
 <CRLF>
?lat=38.89&lon=-77.028&wid=.06&ht=.01&iht=300&iwd=400&mark=-77.03
64,38.8973,redpin,White+House;-77.01,38.8895,blueball,Capitol
<CRLF>
```

From this we can extrapolate that this is a POST command with the following variables:

lat = 40.739

lon = 73.99

wid = 0.06

ht = 0.08

iht = 500

iwd = 240

Figure 7.12 shows the data you should send once you've connected to tiger.census.gov on port 80. Now, wouldn't it be cool if you had a program that let you enter coordinates and displayed a map in a Visual Basic picture or image control? Well, bust my buttons! I wrote one for you.

Sample Application—MAP

MAP (shown in Figure 7.13) is a sample program that lets the user retrieve a map from TIGER Map Service from specified coordinates. Figure 7.14 shows the source code for this project. When you press the Generate button, MAP first connects to the server with the SocketConnect routine, and then calls the GetMap routine with all the user-defined data and options. GetMap is the heart of the program. It accepts the following data for parameters:

longitude

latitude

width

Figure 7.13   TIGER retrieval program.

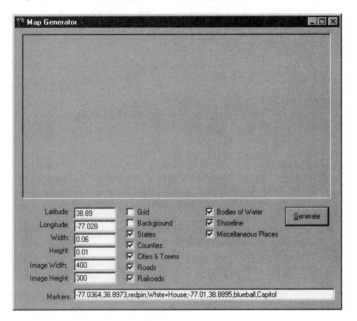

height

image width (in pixels)

image height (in pixels)

marker string

grid

background

states

counties

places (cities and towns)

roads

railroads

water (bodies of water)

shoreline

miscellaneous places (like parks and schools)

Figure 7.14   The GetMap routine, which uses the specified coordinates and options and sends a query to the TIGER Map Service, which then sends back the map as a GIF file and closes the connection.

```
Sub GetMap(szLat As String, szLon As String, szWid As String, _
    szHgt As String, sziWid As String, sziHgt As String, _
    szMark As String, nGrid As Integer, nBack As Integer, _
    nStates As Integer, nCounties As Integer, nPlaces As Integer, _
    nRoads As Integer, nRailroads As Integer, nWater As Integer, _
    nShoreline As Integer, nMisc As Integer)

    Dim szSendMe    As String
    Dim szData      As String
    Dim szOn        As String
    Dim szOff       As String

    If nGrid Then
        szOn = szOn & "GRID,"
    Else
        szOff = szOff & "GRID,"
    End If

    If nBack Then
        szOn = szOn & "BACK,"
    Else
        szOff = szOff & "BACK,"
    End If

    If nRoads Then
        szOn = szOn & "roads,majroads,"
    Else
        szOff = szOff & "roads,majroads,"
    End If

    If nStates Then
        szOn = szOn & "states,"
    Else
        szOff = szOff & "states,"
    End If

    If nCounties Then
        szOn = szOn & "counties,"
    Else
        szOff = szOff & "counties,"
    End If
```

Figure 7.14 *Continued.*

```
If nPlaces Then
    szOn = szOn & "places,CITIES,"
Else
    szOff = szOff & "places,CITIES,"
End If

If nRailroads Then
    szOn = szOn & "railroads,"
Else
    szOff = szOff & "railroads,"
End If

If nWater Then
    szOn = szOn & "water,"
Else
    szOff = szOff & "water,"
End If

If nShoreline Then
    szOn = szOn & "shorelin,"
Else
    szOff = szOff & "shorelin,"
End If

If nMisc Then
    szOn = szOn & "miscell"
Else
    szOff = szOff & "miscell"
End If

szData = "lat=" & szLat & "&lon=" & szLon _
  & "&wid=" & szWid & "&ht=" & szHgt _
  & "&iht=" & sziHgt & "&iwd=" & sziWid _
  & "&mark=" & szMark _
  & "&on=" & szOn _
  & "&off=" & szOff

szSendMe = "POST /cgi-bin/mapper/map.gif HTTP/1.0" & vbCrLf
szSendMe = szSendMe & "Accept: text/plain" & vbCrLf
szSendMe = szSendMe & "Content-type: application/x-www-form-urlencoded" & vbCrLf
szSendMe = szSendMe & "Content-length:" & Str$(Len(szData)) & vbCrLf
szSendMe = szSendMe & vbCrLf
szSendMe = szSendMe & szData & vbCrLf & vbCrlf
SendData dsSocket1, szSendMe

End Sub
```

Complete documentation of the accepted parameters for the TIGER Map Service are listed at the following URL: http://tiger.census.gov/instruct.html.

Once the POST command is sent, the map service whips up a GIF file and starts sending it. The code in dsSocket1_Receive writes the data to a local file named MAP.GIF. When the file has been completely sent, the server closes the connection, and the dsSocket1_Close event fires. Here the file is displayed in the picture control.

Figure 7.15 shows a detail map of my hometown, Mystic, CT. If you ever saw the movie *Mystic Pizza*, this is where I spent the first 20 years of my life. To answer your question, yes there really is a Mystic Pizza. I used to go there every summer on the last day of school when I was a kid.

NetPaper

NetPaper is a program that I wrote to download weather maps or other timely GIF and BMP files from both Web and Gopher sites, and displays them on the desktop as wallpaper. For images on web sites, it simply uses the GET command just as WebDemo does. The files are downloaded on a timer, and you can tell NetPaper to download a different image from the list each time, one after another. While I'm not going to dissect NetPaper in this book, this is a good program for you to look at and try to understand. It uses the same programming technique used in MAP.VBP.

Tips for HTTP Programming

If you see a page that you like and want to write a program to access it, look at the source. Most web browsers allow you to look at the HTML source for any page. Using the source you can determine the names of the input fields and construct the string of data to send it using the earlier HTTP messages as a model.

Think before you distribute an application that accesses someone else's page. That is an easy way to make enemies on the net, and no programmer wants that. (See the ugly disclaimer at the top of this chapter.)

Further Reading

This chapter is by no means meant to be a complete discussion of HTTP. For a more complete description of HTTP and HTML, pick up a copy of Ian S. Graham's *HTML Sourcebook*, published by John Wiley & Sons, 1995. I highly recommend it. Also, read the HTTP 1.0 Draft for a detailed technical description of HTTP.

Figure 7.15   Map of Mystic, CT.

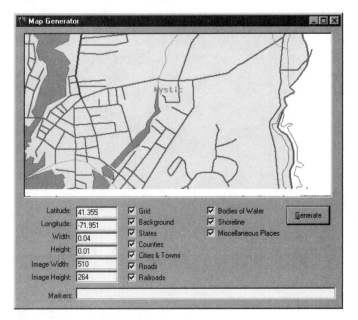

Epilogue

The possibilities for programs that use the resources available on the World Wide Web go way beyond what I can possibly cover in this chapter. Hopefully, these sample applications have sparked your curiosity and have given your imagination a jump start. I'd like to hear about any really cool ways in which you've used these techniques yourself. Please send any comments to me at carl@franklins.net.

AN INTRODUCTION TO OBJECTS IN VISUAL BASIC

Introduction

The first time I looked into using objects I remember being very confused. Not only was there a new vocabulary that I had to learn, but I never had to think at such a high level. So, I guess what I'm trying to say it is "I feel your pain." Hopefully, this will be a good introduction to the concept of programming objects in Visual Basic (VB).

Objects are to Visual Basic code what ActiveX controls are to the Windows API. Just think about what an ActiveX control is for a moment. A control is a way to encapsulate completely the function of a particular program element in some sort of self-contained thingy. Before the advent of controls, Windows programmers had to do things with top-down programming. For example, to create a scrollbar on a window, a Windows programmer had to call the Windows API. The code that had anything at all to do with the scrollbar was scattered throughout the application, making the code very difficult to maintain.

Let's talk some more about scrollbars. A scrollbar is an object. You put a scrollbar object on the form, and you can program it by setting properties, calling its methods, and responding to its events. Everything in your application that has to do with the scrollbar is inside the scrollbar control. Now, of course, the code that you write to program the scrollbar and respond to its events is within your application. However, the code just to perform the scrollbar functions is all contained within the scrollbar object.

Remember Type Variables?

What exactly is an object in terms that a Visual Basic programmer can understand? Did you ever use a Type declaration in Visual Basic? A Type declaration defines a custom variable type. It defines how the memory of that variable is divided up. Take a look at the Type declaration in Figure 8.1. The top line is the name of the variable type, and the next several lines define elements within that type. Now, since we know that an integer takes two bytes, and a long integer takes four bytes, we can determine that the size of this new Type variable is eight bytes .

If you're wondering what Type variables have to do with objects, it's very simple. Objects are a lot like an extended Type variable. So, understanding user-defined data types is a good prerequisite to understanding objects.

I also like the analogy of the cookie cutter, because it truly does characterize the nature of the Type declaration. A Type declaration is a cookie cutter. It defines a variable type just as you would say an Integer is two bytes of memory that is accessed as a number; so the Type variable declaration says that the TIMESTAMP variable type is eight bytes long, and here is a list of all of its elements.

The Type declaration is the cookie cutter and a variable of that type is the cookie. The cookie cutter determines the shape of the cookie. It is a tool. There is only one cookie cutter, but there can be many cookies made from the same cookie cutter. The code in Figure 8.2 creates a variable (a cookie) from the Type definition shown in Figure 8.1 (the cookie cutter) and accesses the elements of that variable.

And so it is with objects. An object definition is called a *class*. A class is a cookie cutter for an object cookie. The major difference between that Type declaration and a class is that classes can define code as well as data elements.

An object is nothing more than a custom control, except that although an object can have user-interface elements, it does not have to. For example, Microsoft Word is made up of many different objects: objects that handle file operations, objects that handle the display, objects that import data from other documents, etc. There is an

---

Figure 8.1   TIMESTAMP data type definition.

```
Type TIMESTAMP
      Hours As Integer
      Minutes As Integer
      Seconds As Long
End Type
```

Figure 8.2   Creating a TIMESTAMP variable.

```
Private Sub Form_Load()
    Dim Stamp As TIMESTAMP
    Stamp.Hours = 3
    Stamp.Minutes = 180
    Stamp.Seconds = 10800

End Sub
```

application object, which has information about the application itself, Microsoft Word. And, there is a document object, which is the top-level object of the document you are editing or creating. Inside that document object are paragraph objects, and the paragraph object has information about the paragraph, its formatting, etc. And so, if you think of an object like an invisible ActiveX control, you'd be doing pretty well for the time being.

Anyone who has Microsoft Word and Visual Basic can open a Word document with VB simply by accessing the objects that already exist within Microsoft Word. In fact, all of Microsoft Office is built on objects. You can access these objects from VB since they are registered with the system.

A big consideration for using objects is maintainability. It is easy to understand programs that are written with objects because we humans understand what those objects represent in the real world. If you wrote a program, for example, that accesses a book, you might have a book object and a page object, a paragraph object and a sentence object, and a word object and a letter object. I know that's going little overboard, but you get the point.

To open a book, you would call the book object's open method, and inside the book would be a collection of page objects, just like an array. The collection is a special type of object that is used to hold an array of other objects. It includes code to manage those objects. For example, have you ever created an array and wanted to delete an element from the middle of the array? How do you do it? Well, you have to delete the item that you want to delete and then copy every single other item that follows down to its previous position. Well, the collection object in Visual Basic allows you to manage those lists by doing all of their work for you. You can add, delete, access, and retrieve the total number of items in the collection.

Another big advantage of using objects is granularity. You know how systems work in the real world. Often times, a computer program is a simulation of something that is done in the real world. Maybe it could be done on paper, as in balancing a check-book. Maybe it could be done with a file cabinet full of papers, as in a database application. Whatever the task, there is generally a real world equivalent of that task.

More Analogies

Writing objects lets you make a model of each of the specific elements that play a role in the completion of that task. And each element is responsible only for what it does. You can think of it as building a tool chest. You have a bunch of tools that do specific things. When you put those tools together you make an organ, or something that works as a unit. If you have a pencil and a piece of paper for example, the pencil does one thing. It draws on the paper. The pencil doesn't know anything about the paper and paper doesn't know anything about the pencil. But, when you put them together, you can make pictures.

If I were to model the process of drawing, I would start with a paper object and a pencil object. The pencil object has properties. What would they be? Maybe there is a sharpness property that indicates how sharp the pencil's point is. Maybe this is a number from 0 to 10, with 0 being broken and unusable and 10 being extremely sharp. Maybe there is a size property that returns the length of pencil in inches or whatever scale you want. Maybe there is a color property that allows you to change the color of the pencil.

And what about the paper object? The paper object would have some obvious properties such as color, size, and shape. The pencil object might have a message called draw where you give the coordinates of the page and you tell it to draw. Maybe the paper object has a property that points to a pencil object, so that you can associate a particular pencil with a piece of paper. That way, when you tell the pencil to draw, it knows what to draw on.

These are all considerations that a programmer must take into account when developing an object-based application. The first thing that you do is to define the objects. What will they represent? What will the properties and methods be? Will they have events? I have clearly illustrated what an object is and why it is important. You may not think that using objects is important, but just wait until you get two years into developing a Visual Basic application. Simple maintenance turns into a nightmare, because the code is so interdependent. With objects, you create black boxes that do exactly as they are told. The traditional method allows a programmer to create dependencies. For example, when you write code into an event of a textbox, for the sake of argument, you all are making that code dependent on that textbox. If the textbox object should change for any reason, that code will have to be rewritten. When developing a system with objects, however, you need to rewrite only the code that behaves incorrectly for the object that it is modeling in the real world. It makes for much simpler program maintenance, and scales very well.

Now, consider the automobile. The car is like an application. A car is made up of lots and lots of different systems, all based on objects. The clutch is an object, the brake pedal is an object. Each of these objects has its own unique task, its own job or function to perform. That's the beauty of object-based programming. You can set up the objects to respond with a particular behavior, or perform specific calculations, or whatever. The application, then, simply ties all of the objects together to form a cohesive unit.

How Do We "Make" an Object?

So, how do you create objects in Visual Basic? An object is defined with a class module. A class module is just like a standard code module in every way, except that it represents a single class. A class is a cookie cutter, and an object is the cookie that the cookie cutter makes. The class module is the cookie cutter for an object. An object is a variable type just like an Integer or String. The specific elements of the object are defined in the class module. Think of a class module as a giant Type declaration, in which you can not only have data elements, but code elements as well.

Objects can have properties, methods, and events just like custom controls. An object can also have simple public members, which do not have the same level of support as properties do. Take a look at Figure 8.3. This is a simple class called Card that defines a playing card. There are two public String members. The Suit member sets and returns the suit as Hearts, Diamonds, Spades, or Clubs. The Value represents the card and can be A, 2, 3, 4, 5, 6, 7, 8, 9, 10, J, Q, or K.

If you are actually creating this class in VB, you would first create a new Standard EXE project, add a class module, name it Card, save it as Card.Cls, and enter the code from Figure 8.3 in the class module.

Figure 8.3   Card.Cls simple object class.

```
Option Explicit

Public Suit As String
Public Value As String
```

Note the word Public; this means that the variable is accessible from outside the class. You may be wondering what the difference is between Public and Global. Global variables are accessible anywhere in the project, but a Public member of a class is accessible only by way of the object. Figure 8.4 creates a card object from this class and sets the value of the card by accessing these public members.

Note the use of the New keyword. Objects have an extra step that needs to occur in order for them to be brought to life. They must be initialized. The statement

```
Dim ThisCard As Card
```

does not initialize the object. It merely states that ThisCard is of the data type Card. When you use the New keyword, the object is initialized. Consider initialization to be like when you load a form and the Form_Load event runs. Only with a class, this routine is called Class_Initialize. This gives you a chance to set default values for public members and properties, load data, or do any other initialization necessary.

Properties

Properties are different from publicly declared members, such as in our Card class. By changing these members to properties, the class will get control whenever the property is read or set. Replace the code in the Card class with the code in Figure 8.5.

Now when the calling code sets the ThisCard.Suit property, the Let Suit property procedure runs, and your code sets the value of a private member, m_Suit, which holds the actual contents of the property.

Figure 8.4   Creating a card object.

```
Option Explicit

Dim ThisCard As Card

Private Sub Form_Load ()

    Set ThisCard = New Card
    ThisCard.Suit = "Hearts"
    ThisCard.Value = "J"

End Sub
```

Figure 8.5 Adding properties.

```
Option Explicit

Private m_Suit As String
Private m_Value As String

Public Property Get Suit() As String
    Suit = m_Suit
End Property

Public Property Let Suit(NewValue As String)
    m_Suit = NewValue
End Property

Public Property Get Value() As String
    Value = m_Value
End Property

Public Property Let Value(NewValue As String)
    m_Value = NewValue
End Property
```

If all this stuff seems very daunting and overwhelming, good! I thought I smelled smoke! Now might be a good time to put the book down, get some cheese sandwiches, and watch a Lost In Space marathon. However, if you trust me to lead you in the right direction, and you have faith in yourself that you will understand this, then read on!

Collections

And now comes the monkey wrench! Just kidding. Enter the collection. A collection is like an array object with built-in array management functions. In Visual Basic if you wanted to add a string to an array, you have to allocate space for that string, and then set the value of the new array element. With a collection, you use the Add method, passing the object that you want to add to the collection. To remove an item from an array, you must first delete the item, and then move all of the consecutive array elements down.

Why use a collection: Although it may not be clear right now, there will be situations where having a collection of objects with array-kind of accessibility is necessary, and using collections is much easier and more powerful than using an array of objects.

If you have done any work with DAO, RDO, or ADO (all database engines), you have probably used a collection. A Recordset is essentially a collection object that contains returned data from a query. It has custom methods like MoveFirst and MoveNext that help navigate through the data. Although it is more complex than a simple collection, a Recordset is a collection nonetheless.

The code in Figure 8.6 returns a collection that contains 52 Card objects, and initializes the card values.

Figure 8.6   Accessing a collection in VB.

```
Private Function NewDeck() As Collection

    Dim SuitNum As Integer
    Dim CardNum As Integer
    Dim ThisCard As Card
    Dim ThisDeck As New Collection

    For SuitNum = 1 To 4
        For CardNum = 1 To 13
            Set ThisCard = New Card
            Select Case SuitNum
                Case 1
                    ThisCard.Suit = "Hearts"
                Case 2
                    ThisCard.Suit = "Diamonds"
                Case 3
                    ThisCard.Suit = "Clubs"
                Case 4
                    ThisCard.Suit = "Spades"
            End Select
            Select Case CardNum
                Case 1
                    ThisCard.Value = "A"
                Case 2 To 10
                    ThisCard.Value = Trim$(Str$(CardNum))
                Case 11
                    ThisCard.Value = "J"
                Case 12
                    ThisCard.Value = "Q"
                Case 13
                    ThisCard.Value = "K"
            End Select
            ThisDeck.Add ThisCard
```

Figure 8.6 *Continued.*

```
        Next
    Next

    Set NewDeck = ThisDeck

End Function
```

Figure 8.7   Change Form_Load to initialize a new deck.

```
Private Sub Form_Load()

    Dim Deck As Collection

    Set Deck = NewDeck

    Debug.Print Deck.Item(24).Value & " of " & Deck.Item(24).Suit
    Debug.Print Deck.Item(31).Value & " of " & Deck.Item(31).Suit

End Sub
```

Finally, the Form_Load event of our test form has been changed to initialize a deck of cards and print out a couple of them in the debug window, just for the purposes of demonstration. Figure 8.7 shows this code.

If you really want to continue with this project, write a routine to shuffle the deck!

Epilogue

Let's review.

1. Objects are important because they model the real world. When you use objects, a little bit of forethought and planning can save you countless hours of aggravation down the road.

2. Object programming is to traditional Visual Basic programming what customs controls are to the Windows API.

3. An object is a cookie. A class module is a cookie cutter.

4. A class module is like a user-defined variable type that includes code elements as well as data elements.

5. Object is a data type in Visual Basic, just like String or Integer.

6. An object can contain another object as one of its members.

7. A collection is an object that contains a manageable collection of other objects.

8. Nothing goes better with Lost In Space than cheese sandwiches.

Although this chapter is not meant to be a complete primer to objects in Visual Basic, it should give the intermediate VB programmer a context in which to understand the next few chapters, which deal with objects. For further reading on VB Objects, I suggest *Doing Objects in Microsoft Visual Basic* by Deborah Kurata as an excellent one-stop source for VB Object design and development issues.

And now, fair knave, turn the page and let's talk objects!

USING THE CFINTERNET OBJECTS

9

In this chapter, I'll introduce the cfInternet objects, and show you how to use them. Very simply, cfInternet is a DLL that contains all of the code from Chapters 4, 5, 6, and 7, all written as separate classes. In short, cfInternet is the easiest way for you to access the Internet in your Visual Basic applications, and it comes free with this book. And you thought you were just buying another book. Surprise!

Because it is an ActiveX DLL, you can add it to your VB project by selecting References from the Project menu, and then selecting *Carl Franklin's Internet Objects* in the list of references.

Figure 9.1 shows the different objects in the cfInternet project. All of these objects are part of the cfInternet project, and can all be accessed with a single reference.

First Things First—cfWinsock

Before we go head over teakettle into using these objects, I'd like to explain how they were developed. I wanted to make it easy to use either the dsSocket control or the Microsoft Winsock control, depending on the user preference. So, I created two objects—cfWinsockDS and cfWinsockMS—that encapsulate the dsSocket control and the Microsoft Winsock control, respectively.

Both versions of cfWinsock include all the support routines from DSSOCK.BAS, such as IsDotAddress and SendData. The only difference is that one uses dsSocket and the other uses the Microsoft control. This idea is extended to cfInternet, which comes in two versions—cfInternetDS and cfInternetMS.

Figure 9.1   cfInternet object classes.

cfFTP	File Transfer Protocol class
cfNNTP	Usenet News class
cfPOP3	E-mail retrieval class
cfSMTP	E-mail sending class
cfMsg	E-mail and Usenet message class
cfUUCode	UU encoding and decoding class

cfWinsockDS uses the dsSocket type library instead of the control. If you remember from Chapter 8, you can use the WithEvents keyword to create an object that has events, and respond to those events just as if it were a control.

Before you can use the dsSocket object, you must go to the References windows (select References from VB's Project menu), click the Browse button, and select DSSOCK32.TLB from your System directory. This will add a reference to the dsSocket Type Library.

Figure 9.2 shows the minimal VB code for creating the dsSocket object. Note that you must use the word WithEvents when creating a reference to dsSocket. Also, you cannot say:

```
Private WithEvents Socket As New dsSocket
```

When you use WithEvents, you cannot use the New keyword. So, you have to instantiate the dsSocket object in the Form_Load event, or Class_Initiailize if you are accessing it from another object.

The Socket_Connect event is not required, but I'm showing it to you so you can get used to the idea of using objects that have events. This is the same as the Connect event of the dsSocket custom control, except that you don't need a form, or even a control to use it.

Go ahead and load the cfWinsockDS project. You'll find it in \Winsock\ClientDS. This is an ActiveX DLL that encapsulates the dsSocket con-

Figure 9.2 Creating an object with events.

```
Option Explicit

Private WithEvents Socket As dsSocket

Private Sub Form_Load ()

    Set Socket = New dsSocket

End Sub

Private Sub Socket_Connect ()

    MsgBox "Connected!"

End Sub
```

trol, and adds some handy routines as well. Figure 9.3 shows the declaration section of the cfWinsockDS class. Note the events.

The events (wsAccept through wtSendReady) are simply encapsulations, or wrapper routines, for the dsSocket events. Figure 9.4 shows the Control_Receive event, in which cfWinsockDS simply raises his own wsReceive event, passing the ReceiveData string as a parameter.

Figure 9.3 cfWinsockDS declaration section.

```
Option Explicit
'-------------------------------------------------
'Copyright 1998 by Carl Franklin
'Unauthorized reproduction in any medium of this
'source code is strictly prohibited without written
'permission from the author and John Wiley & Sons.
'-------------------------------------------------

Public WithEvents Control    As dsSocket

Private m_DebugMode          As Boolean
Private m_Connected          As Boolean
Private m_SendReady          As Boolean

Event wsAccept(SocketID As Integer)
```

Continues

Figure 9.3   cfWinsockDS declaration section. *(Continued)*

```
Event wsConnect()
Event wsClose(ErrorCode As Integer, ErrorDesc As String)
Event wsAsyncComplete(AsyncType As Integer, ErrorCode As Integer, ErrorDesc As
String)
Event wsException(ErrorCode As Integer, ErrorDesc As String)
Event wsListen()
Event wsReceive(ReceiveData As String)
Event wsSendReady()

Const SOCK_ERR_OPERATIONWOULDBLOCK = 21035
Const ERR_TIMEOUT_CONNECTING = 2
Const ERR_TIMEOUT_DISCONNECTING = 3
Const ERR_CONNECT = 4

'local variable(s) to hold property value(s)
Private mvarLogFileName As String 'local copy
```

So, when the dsSocket object in cfWinsockDS receives data, it fires its Receive event, and then cfWinsockDS fires its wsReceive event, passing the received data through. This behavior is the same for all of the events. This is probably a critical piece of new information for you. If you are not yet comfortable with the idea that you can use and create objects that have events, then put the book down, go play Forsaken or Quake for an hour or so, grab a soda, put your feet up on your desk, and think about it.

Before we move on, I'll pause to let you put on a clean shirt. Now, not only are cfWinsockDS and cfWinsockMS objects that have events, but so are all the objects in cfInternet. They all use the cfWinsock object with events, and they all have events that you can use in your own project. And while we have our neck stuck out, let's just review a bit.

1. There are two cfWinsock objects—cfWinsockDS and cfWinsockMS.

Figure 9.4   Receive event.

```
Private Sub Control_Receive(ReceiveData As String)

    RaiseEvent wsReceive(ReceiveData)

End Sub
```

2. Both are exactly the same, except that one uses dsSocket and one uses the MS Winsock control.

3. There are two cfInternet objects—cfInternetDS and cfInternetMS.

4. Both are exactly the same, except that one uses cfWinsockDS and one uses cfWinsockMS.

Using the cfWinsock Object

Using cfWinsock is easy. Just add a reference to it in the References window of Visual Basic (Select References from the Project menu). Select either cfWinsockDS or cfWinsockMS and press OK. Then, add the code in Figure 9.5 to your form, module, or class module.

If you are accessing this object from a class module instead of a form, then just instantiate the object in the Class_Initialize event, rather than the Form_Load event. This approach works for both cfWinsockDS and cfWinsockMS.

You can connect to a server like so:

```
Socket.SocketConnect 80, "www.someplace.com", 30
```

This example connects to www.someplace.com on port 80, and waits 30 seconds before timing out. When it connects, the wsConnect event will fire. All of the events of cfWinsockDS and cfWinsockMS start with *ws*. The events correlate exactly to the events of the dsSocket control, except that they begin with *ws*.

The Control Property

cfWinsock has a Control property that is a reference to the actual Winsock control. In the case of cfWinsockDS, this is a dsSocket control. With cfWinsockMS it points to the Microsoft Winsock control. You can use this in situations where you need to access the control directly. Here is an example of accessing the DataSize property of the dsSocket control inside cfWinsockDS:

```
Socket.Control.DataSize = 5000
```

Figure 9.5 Using cfWinsock.

```
Option Explicit

Private WithEvents Socket As cfWinsockDS

Sub Form_Load ()
    Set Socket = New cfWinsockDS
End Sub
```

The rest of the object is fairly straightforward. You get all of the routines from DSSOCK.BAS in this object, such as IsDotAddress and ParseString. In addition, some HTML helper routines such as StripHTML are also included. StripHTML removes all HTML codes from text, and substitutes CRLF characters for <P> codes, etc.

Inside cfInternet

cfInternet is simply the result of my moving all the code from previous chapters into public class modules and converting them to use cfWinsock instead of dsSocket. I made a few enhancements here and there to take advantage of the class model, such as adding events, but for the most part the code is exactly the same. Only now, you can drop it into your projects much more easily than you could before.

In addition to adding events, I created a new class, cfMsg, which represents a message. This could be either a Usenet article or an e-mail message. I made it so that it would support both. Of course, these class modules are created for the purpose of teaching how to program for the Internet, and are not intended to be a complete product. In fact, I would encourage you to make modifications yourself, and share them with the rest of the world by sending them to me by e-mail, so I can post them on my book web site: carl.franklins.net/vbtip.

There are two sample group projects in the \cfInternet directory, TestDS.grp and TestMS.grp that demonstrate how to use all of the objects in cfInternet. In most cases, I just took the forms from the original sample code and modified them to use the new object. Feel free to load one of these projects now and follow along as you read the rest of this chapter.

These projects are groups. A group is a collection of one or more projects that all run together. In this case, the cfInternet code runs in the VB environment, so you can watch the code as it works its magic.

cfNNTP

The cfNNTP object, like all the other objects, is much more useable than its sample code counterpart from the previous chapters. It is completely event driven. As such, there are several events that you can use to complete the tasks of reading and posting messages.

Take a look at Figure 9.6. It shows the test form with some buttons on it. Simply, each button loads the test form for the protocol displayed on the button. Press the NNTP button to display the NNTP test form (shown in Figure 9.7).

Figure 9.6   cfInternet Test project.

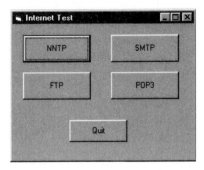

Check out the Declarations section of frmNNTP. The only line besides Option Explicit is this:

```
Private WithEvents News As cfNNTP
```

Here again we come back to the WithEvents keyword. I keep mentioning it because I have noticed that not many VB programmers have a keen grasp of objects in Visual Basic. If you feel you need a refresher, please go back and read Chapter 8 before continuing.

Figure 9.7   Test form.

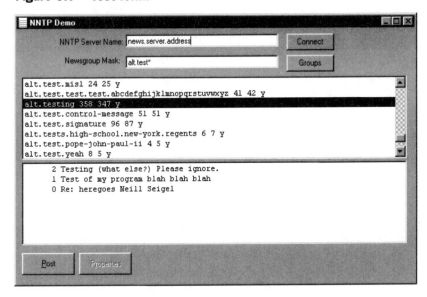

The WithEvents keyword is necessary in order to access an object's event procedures. Also, this statement does not create the object. It merely creates an object variable. To create the object, you must use the New keyword. This is done in the Form_Load event as follows:

```
Set News = New cfNNTP
```

OK. Now that we have a cfNNTP object called News, we can use it to access a Usenet server. In design mode, double-click on the Connect button. There are several lines of setup code that clear the list boxes and disable buttons while the code is connecting, and then one line of code that actually does the work:

```
News.Connect txtHost
```

txtHost is the name of the text box control on the form where you specify the address of the news server. The port is hard-coded to 119, as most NNTP servers use this port. But, if you want to get your hands dirty, you can alter the cfNNTP object to include a Port property.

The result of calling the Connect method will yield a Connect event. The Connect event fires and passes a Boolean value called Connected. If a connection is made successfully, then Connected is True; otherwise, it is False.

Retrieving Articles

Normally before you can retrieve articles you might select a newsgroup. This can be a long process. However, you can specify a mask with this object, and cfNNTP will return only the newsgroups that fit the mask. Use the asterisk character on either side of a word to create a simple mask. Here are a few examples:

alt.fan.*	Selects all newsgroups that begin with alt.fan
*.television	Selects all the groups that end with the word television
music	Selects all the groups that contain the word music

Double-click the Groups button. You will notice one line of code that accesses the News object:

```
News.GetGroups txtMask
```

The GetGroups method selects a list of groups based on a specified mask string. When each group is received, cfNNTP fires the GroupList event, passing the group name as a string.

Take a look at the News_GroupList event procedure. Note that there is only one line of code here, too. This code adds the group name to the list box lbGroups:

```
lbGroups.AddItem Group
```

When all the groups have been returned, the GroupListReceived event fires. That is how you know you have received the entire list of groups. In the case of our demo, I am just enabling the list boxes so you can use them.

The next thing you might do is to select a particular group and retrieve all the articles in that group. This is done with the SelectGroup method. Take a look at the code that does this by double-clicking the top list box (lbGroups). Figure 9.8 shows the code.

The only thing I'm doing here that might seem strange to you is parsing the newsgroup name from the selected text in the list box. The newsgroup name is the leftmost characters up to, but not including, the first space. The ParseString function of the cfWinsock object returns a portion of a string within another string given a delimiter. In this case, we are asking for the first segment using a space as a delimiter. Once I have the group name, I select it with the SelectGroup method.

When you select a group, cfNNTP starts sending article headers, firing the ArticleList event and passing an article in the form of a cfMsg object. Take a look at the News_ArticleList Event, as shown in Figure 9.9. This is a good time to discuss the cfMsg object a bit.

The cfMsg object is simply a data object. It holds data about a message. The message can be a Usenet article, or it could be an e-mail message. In this case, it's

---

Figure 9.8   Selecting a newsgroup.

```
Private Sub lbGroups_DblClick()

    Dim GroupName As String

    Screen.MousePointer = vbHourglass

    lbArticles.Clear
    lbArticles.Enabled = False
    btnProperties.Enabled = False
    btnPost.Enabled = False

    GroupName = News.Socket.ParseString(lbGroups.List(lbGroups.ListIndex), " ", 1)
    News.SelectGroup GroupName

End Sub
```

Figure 9.9   ArticleList event.

```
Private Sub News_ArticleList(Article As cfMsg)

    Dim Msg     As String

    Msg = Format$(Trim$(Str$(Article.Lines)), "@@@@@@@") & " " &
News.Socket.SuperTrim(Article.Subject)

    '-- Display the item
    lbArticles.AddItem Msg
    lbArticles.ItemData(lbArticles.ListCount - 1) = Article.MsgNumber
    lbArticles.TopIndex = lbArticles.ListCount - 1

End Sub
```

a Usenet article. It has properties like Subject, FromName, and MsgText. You
don't need to know every property, but you should know that a cfMsg object represents a Usenet article or an e-mail message.

Back to Figure 9.9. This code displays the article subject and the number of
lines. It also places the message number in the ItemData property of the lbArticles
list box. The Format function creates a string with a fixed number of spaces. I'm
using it here to display the number of lines so that they line up with each other.

When you double-click on an article in the lbArticles list box, the article is
retrieved via the GetArticle method. Figure 9.10 shows this code.

Figure 9.10   Retrieving an article with the GetArticle method.

```
Sub lbArticles_DblClick()

    Dim ID  As Long

    ID = lbArticles.ItemData(lbArticles.ListIndex)
    If ID Then
        Screen.MousePointer = vbHourglass
        lbArticles.Enabled = False
        News.GetArticle ID
    End If

End Sub
```

This code simply gets the Message ID from the list box and calls the GetArticle method, passing the ID. If you remember from Chapter 4, the Message ID is simply a number that identifies the article to the NNTP server.

After the article is received, cfNNTP fires the Article event and passes the entire article as a cfMsg object. Look at the News_Article event procedure. You'll see that I'm just displaying the MsgText property of the cfMsg object, which holds the entire article, headers and all.

Posting an Article

To post an article, you first call the NewMessage method, then set the properties of the built-in Message object, and then call the Post method. Double-click on the Post button in design mode. Figure 9.11 shows this code.

This code first shows the frmPost form, which is shown in Figure 9.12. This form is just for data entry. I show it modally, and then use the data from the text fields to post the article.

Note that the News object has a Message object. This is a cfMsg object that you use to post a message. Simply fill in the properties shown in Figure 9.11 and then call the Post method of cfNNTP to post a message. Upon posting the message, the Post event will fire.

Figure 9.11   Posting an article.

```
Sub btnPost_Click()

    frmPost.txtNewsgoup = News.Socket.ParseString(lbGroups.List(lbGroups.ListIndex),
" ", 1)
    frmPost.Show 1
    If Len(frmPost.Tag) = 0 Then
        News.NewMessage
        News.Message.FromAddr = frmPost.txtEmail
        News.Message.Newsgroup = frmPost.txtNewsgoup
        News.Message.Subject = frmPost.txtSubject
        News.Message.MsgText = frmPost.txtArticle
        News.Post
    End If
    Unload frmPost
    Set frmPost = Nothing

End Sub
```

Figure 9.12   Post form.

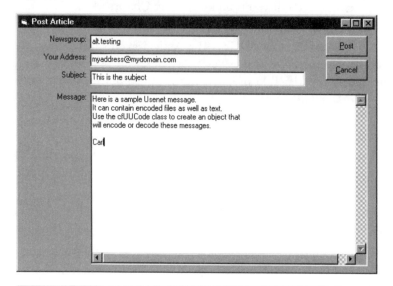

The only tricky thing here is the Newsgroup field. This can be more than one newsgroup. Just list each group separated by commas, and your message will be posted to all groups in the list.

Now, that seems pretty darned easy doesn't it? I thought so. Like I said, how-ever, cfInternet is not meant to be a complete product. It is not perfect. It is meant to be used as a teaching tool. Maybe you could think of some ways in which it could be enhanced. Write your ideas on the back of a $50 bill and send it to me in a case of Scotch, and I'll send you back a well-deserved thank you card! *Kids, please don't drink and drive. You might spill some, and then your folks will really be mad.*

cfSMTP—Simple Mail Transport Protocol

One thing is for sure about the cfSMTP test form. It's much better than the sam-ple code form. This is mostly because I have added a Recipients collection, which lets you send a message to multiple recipients. Take a look at frmSMTP, shown in Figure 9.13. Let's go right to what's behind the Send button here. Figure 9.14 shows this code.

Before sending a message, you have to call the NewMessage method to clear all the internal variables. Then, set the Mailhost property to the address of the SMTP server. Set the FromName and FromAddr properties to your full name and

Figure 9.13   SMTP form for sending e-mail.

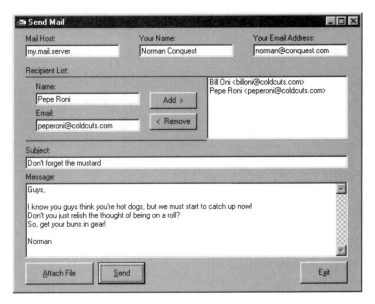

Figure 9.14   Sending e-mail.

```
Private Sub btnSend_Click()

    Dim i As Long
    Dim ThisName      As String
    Dim ThisAddr      As String
    Dim Data          As String

    Smtp.NewMessage

    Smtp.MailHost = txtMailHost
    Smtp.Message.FromName = txtMyName
    Smtp.Message.FromAddr = txtMyAddress
    Smtp.Message.Subject = txtSubject
    Smtp.Message.MsgText = txtMessage

    For i = 0 To lbRecipients.ListCount - 1
        Data = lbRecipients.List(i)
        ThisName = Smtp.Socket.ParseString(Data, " <", 1)
```

Continues

Figure 9.14   Sending e-mail. (Continued)

```
        ThisAddr = Smtp.Socket.ParseString(Data, "<", 2)
        ThisAddr = Left$(ThisAddr, Len(ThisAddr) - 1)
        Smtp.Recipients.Add ThisName, ThisAddr
    Next

    Smtp.Send

End Sub
```

e-mail address. Set the Subject property to the subject of the message, and set the MsgText property to the text of the message itself.

Now it gets tricky. The Recipients collection is a collection of cfRecipient objects, which simply hold a name and e-mail address. This is a custom collection. The Add method accepts a name and address. Use the Add method for each address you wish to send the message to.

Then, call the Send method. If you specify a Timeout number of seconds, then the Send method will not return until either the message has been sent, or the time has expired. If you don't specify a number of seconds, Send will return immediately, and you can use the MessageSent and NNTPError events to determine when and if the message is sent.

cfPOP3—Post Office Protocol 3

Just to recap: cfSMTP is for sending e-mail, and cfPOP3 is for retrieving it. Figure 9.15 shows the frmPOP3 form. Enter the mail server name, and your account name and password, and press the Connect button. All of your headers will be downloaded, and the header information will display in the lbHeaders list box.

 This program does not auto-download the messages, just the headers. That gives you a bit more flexibility in situations where there are big messages in your mailbox that you don't want to read. You can download a message individually by double-clicking on it in the list.

In the list you'll see the size of the message in bytes, followed by the sender's name and address, and finally the subject (if it all fits on one line). Remember that

Figure 9.15   POP3 form.

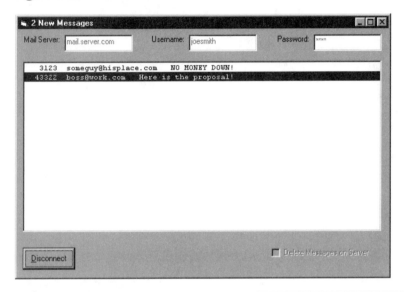

this is for demonstration purposes only. If I wanted to make this a real e-mail application, I would not use a list box to display all this information.

To download a message, double-click on it. After downloading, the message will pop up in a display window.

So, how does this work? Well, it's all pretty straightforward, with one exception, which I'll show you in a minute or two. First of all, when you press the Connect button, I set the MailServer property, the UserName property, and the Password property to the values on the form. Then I call the Connect method.

Upon connection, the Connect event fires, and it passes a Boolean value representing whether or not you've connected. Look at the Connect event now, in Figure 9.16.

Figure 9.16   cfPOP3 Connect event.

```
Private Sub Pop3_Connect(Connected As Boolean)

    '-- Connect or disconnect. This event
    '   gives you a chance to enable and disable
```

Continues

Figure 9.16   cfPOP3 Connect event. *(Continued)* °

```
'   UI elements.

If Connected Then
    Caption = "Connected"
    btnConnect.Caption = "&Disconnect"
    chkDelete.Enabled = False
    txtMailServer.Enabled = False
    txtUsername.Enabled = False
    txtPassword.Enabled = False
    Timer1.Enabled = True
Else
    Caption = "Not Connected"
    btnConnect.Caption = "&Connect"
    lbHeaders.Clear
    chkDelete.Enabled = True
    txtMailServer.Enabled = True
    txtUsername.Enabled = True
    txtPassword.Enabled = True
End If

End Sub
```

Note the bold line, Timer1.Enabled = True. I am turning on a Timer control here. When the Timer control is enabled, the Timer1_Timer event fires after one second. The Timer1_Timer event has only two lines of code, and they are as follows:

```
Private Sub Timer1_Timer()

    Timer1.Enabled = False
    POP3.GetHeaders

End Sub
```

When the Timer event fires, I turn off the timer and call the GetHeaders method to retrieve the e-mail headers. This may seem like a strange way to do this, but let me explain.

If you recall, POP3 has two states, or modes: Command and Transaction. You can only retrieve the headers in the Transaction state. When connecting, however, the code is in the Command state. If you were to try and call POP3.GetHeaders in the Connect event, you'd get an error " -ERR that command is valid only in the

Figure 9.17 cfPOP3 HeaderList event.

```
Private Sub pop3_HeaderList(Header As cfMsg)

    '-- Message header received
    lbHeaders.AddItem Format$(Trim$(Str$(Header.Bytes)), "@@@@@@@") & "  " &
Header.FromAddr & "  " & Header.Subject
    lbHeaders.ItemData(lbHeaders.ListCount - 1) = Header.MsgNumber

End Sub
```

TRANSACTION state!" So, the Connect event has to complete, and then you can call GetHeaders. The easiest way around this is to use a timer.

When you call the GetHeaders routine, the mail server sends back the headers. For each header received, cfPOP3 fires the HeaderList event, passing a cfMsg object with only the header filled in. In the HeaderList event, I display the header information in the list box. Figure 9.17 shows the HeaderList event.

Once all the headers have been received, the HeaderListReceived event fires, and I re-enable the list box (I disable it prior to downloading so that the user could try and retrieve a message while the headers are downloading). Again, not a very elegant solution, but these are good things to think about.

When the user double-clicks on a message, I call the POP3.GetMessage method. You can see this if you double-click on the list box. There is only one line of code:

```
POP3.GetMessage lbHeaders.ItemData(lbHeaders.ListIndex)
```

When a message is received, the Message event fires, passing the complete message as a cfMSG object. I simply display it using the frmDisplay form. Figure 9.18 shows the code that displays the message.

All I'm doing here is placing the message text (Msg.MsgText) into a multiline text box on a form and showing it.

There are two hidden features with cfPOP3. First, if you set the AutoDelete property to True, then messages are deleted from the server after they are completely retrieved. This is how most e-mail programs work. In this sample program, there is a check box that says "Delete Messages on Server" that sets this property.

Second, all the messages that are retrieved are accessible via the Messages property, a collection of cfMsg objects that represents all of the downloaded messages. When you first download the headers, they are available via the Messages property, but only the headers are filled in. After you retrieve a message, its MsgText property will be filled in.

Figure 9.18   cfPOP3 Message event.

```
Private Sub pop3_Message(Msg As cfMsg)

    '-- Message downloaded

    frmDisplay.txtArticle = Msg.MsgText
    frmDisplay.Show 1
    Unload frmDisplay
    Set frmDisplay = Nothing

End Sub
```

cfFTP—File Transfer Protocol

As evidenced in Chapter 6, FTP is perhaps the most complicated Internet protocol to program. However, using cfFTP is not complicated. There are some differences between the sample code and cfFTP; namely, cfFTP is more event-driven. Instead of waiting in a loop for an action to finish, cfFTP code fires events while actions (such as retrieving a file or a directory listing) are being processed, and after they have been completed.

You should already know how to use FTP. If not, go back and read Chapter 6. Let's just walk through the process of connecting, changing directories, retrieving a directory listing, sending (uploading) a file, and retrieving (downloading) a file.

Figure 9.19 shows the FTP window. Press the Connect button, and you will be prompted to enter an FTP host name, your username, and your password on the system. If you want to connect to a public FTP site, enter "anonymous" for the username, and your e-mail address for the password.

To connect, call the FTPLogon method, passing the host name, username, and password. Then, if everything worked, the Logon event fires. If a connection could not be made, the Connect event will fire, passing a Connected value of False. The Connect event fires when a Winsock connection is made (or not made). The Logon event is fired after Connect, and when the server has validated you. Slight difference.

Once you're logged in, press the "List (Dir)" button to get a directory listing of the root directory. When you press this button, you are prompted for a filespec. By pressing Enter and accepting the default, you are telling the FTP server to list all the files (*.*).

Figure 9.19   FTP window.

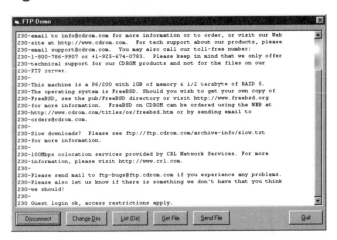

The code then calls the GetDirectoryListing method of the cfFTP object. This establishes a data connection and, just like in the sample code from Chapter 6, the server sends the directory listing. Now, cfFTP handles this data a couple different ways.

First, for every line in the directory listing, it fires the DirectoryLine event, passing the line of text. Also, cfFTP fires the DirectoryInfo event for each line, passing the details of the file (Name, Size, and Date). This was no small feat to pull off since there are variations in how all the various FTP servers display file information. However, my brother, Jay Franklin (jay.franklins.net) was able to come up with some string parsing code that works with many of the major FTP servers. Hats off to Jay for implementing this feature.

In addition to that, the entire directory listing is passed as a string through the Directory event when the listing is complete. That should be enough data for you to get the information you need in your application from a directory listing.

You can change the working directory using the ChangeDirectory method. This is the same as sending a CWD command. In fact, cfFTP does exactly that.

You can retrieve a file using the GetFile method, passing the source filename and the destination filename. The source filename must be relative to the server. If the README.TXT file on the server is in the /Pub/Misc directory, you could say:

```
FTP.GetFile "/Pub/Misc/README.TXT", DestFileName
```

The destination filename must be relative to your machine. If you want to save the README.TXT file to the C:\ drive, it would look like this:

```
FTP.GetFile "/Pub/Misc/README.TXT", "C:\README.TXT"
```

When retrieving a file, there are two events that fire. The FileData event fires when a new file buffer has been received. FileData passes the FileName (server relative) and a string buffer containing a chunk of file data. The second event is FileReceived, which fires after the file has been completely retrieved.

You can use the FileData event along with the Size information from the DirectoryInfo event to create a progress meter as the file is being downloaded (*Hey, I can't do EVERYTHING for you!*). The total size of the file is given, and the size of each block is given. With that information, you can determine the percentage of completion every time the FileData event fires.

Sending a file is just as easy. Use the SendFile method, passing a source filename (relative to your machine) and a destination filename (relative to the server). There are no extended methods for the SendFile method, except the generic CommandOK event, which fires after successful completion of any command.

The only other thing to talk about here is the FTPError event, which fires when an error occurs. Basically, it passes the error message. If you need to, you can look at the first three characters of the error message to determine the specific error that occurred.

cfFTP also has a Receive event, which fires every time a line of text is received from the server on the control connection. This provides a handy way to display all the received text in a list box, such as my demo does.

Epilogue

If you want to learn the innermost workings of SMTP, POP3, NNTP, and FTP, I suggest you read Chapters 4, 5, and 6. If you want to get up and running quickly with these protocols and look into the guts of it at a later time, the cfInternet objects provide that flexibility.

Visual Basic 5.0 and 6.0 have powerful object-oriented features that let everyday shmucks like you and me do some incredibly powerful things. The combination of VB objects and Internet programming make for some really useful tools for doing any kind of Network application. I hope you find cfInternet as useful as I do.

CGI4VB: SERVER-SIDE PROGRAMMING

10

The Common Gateway Interface (CGI)

The CGI is an interface between an HTTP server and an application. CGI is what allows users of the World Wide Web to access data and processes that do not specifically exist within the realm of the HTTP server and HTML documents. Have you ever connected to a web-searching page, such as WebCrawler (webcrawler.com/) or Altavista (altavista.digital.com) that finds web pages from keywords that you specify? Where does the information come from? The answer is a database. Since today's sophisticated databases cannot be accessed directly by the HTTP protocol, some other application must be accessing the database. The tasks, then, are (1) to give the application that accesses the database the user's input data (the search terms), and (2) to return the output of the application to the HTTP server, which in turn presents it to the user.

CGI is implemented differently on different platforms. A CGI application, or one that interacts with an HTTP server, is sometimes called a *script* because it is written in a scripting language, or what us DOS people call batch language. Under the Unix platform CGI scripts are typically written in either the Perl, TCI, or Unix shell, all of which are Unix-based scripting languages. Perl is the language of choice for Unix because of its high-level control and low-level speed.

CGI4VB

When writing this chapter I wanted to find a CGI solution for VB that did not require an additional purchase. When I wrote the VB4 version of this book, I chose Windows CGI (or WinCGI), because it could be used with a shareware web server that I also included with the book. When updating the book, I wanted to find something else that could be used easily with Internet Information Server. Enter CGI4VB.

CGI4VB is a freeware implementation of CGI for VB programmers developed by Kevin O'Brien (obrienk@ix.netcom.com). The heart of CGI4VB is a VB module (.bas file) that you can include in a VB program to create a CGI application. When you compile, you have a standard CGI application that uses the standard in and out (STDIN and STDOUT) devices to communicate. If you don't know what that means then you must have a life. STDIN and STDOUT are the equivalent of command line input and the text output of a character-based program, such as an MS-DOS or Unix program in character mode.

There are currently several Windows NT-based HTTP servers available. They range from free to up to thousands of dollars. I can assure you that paying a lot of money for a web server is a thing of the past since the market is booming. Anyway, here are five inexpensive HTTP servers that exist at the time of this writing:

- *Microsoft Internet Information Server (MIIS)*. Microsoft's Web and FTP Server application for Windows NT. It is included with Windows NT 4.0 Server.

- *The European Microsoft Windows NT Academic Center (EMWAC) in the Czech Republic*. Distributes a freeware Windows NT-based HTTP server. It also supports CGI.

- *WebSite*. A very nice commercial Windows NT HTTP server. At the time of this writing, WebSite 2.3 was going for $799. Its creator also defined Windows CGI, the first CGI platform for VB. So, you can bet this server will always be state of the art. I have used WebSite, and I can offer you my honest opinion. I think it's very slick. The user interface is simple enough for anyone to use, and the security is entirely adequate. You can get the latest information on WebSite at website.ora.com.

- *Netscape offers a couple of excellent servers starting at around $295*. You can check them out at home.netscape.com/comprod/server_central/index.html. Their introductory web server, FastTrack, supports CGI.

CGI Speed Issues

When writing CGI applications, speed is critical. Each time the application is invoked a new instance gets loaded on the server. The speed at which a VB application loads can be slow, depending on the server configuration and the size of the application. It is for this reason that you must keep custom controls and excessive code in your CGI applications to a minimum. For best results, use a single module.

The more forms and controls you have in your project, the slower it will load. If your site starts getting hundreds of requests per minute, your system could really slow down.

Carl & Gary's Visual Basic Home Page (www.cgvb.com) runs partially on a Sun Sparc 2 Unix workstation. We use Perl to write our Unix CGI scripts. In this configuration, about 35–50 Perl scripts can run per second. That's pretty fast, but that kind of performance is required for high-traffic sites like ours. If we were to use CGI on an equivalent NT server, it might take two or more seconds to load and run a simple Visual Basic 5.0 application that opens a database and writes data. Assuming that the VB application was stripped down to one or two modules, this kind of performance is adequate for a small- to medium-traffic web site, but could be slow when traffic gets high.

Figure 10.1   Acme production information. A sample HTML form.

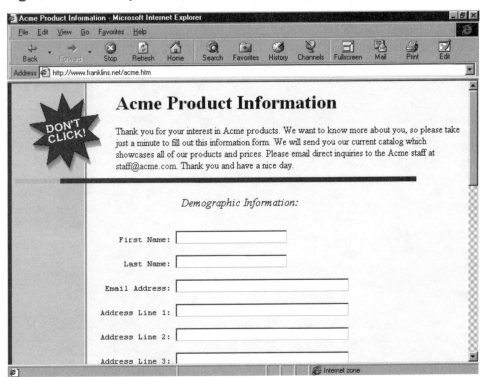

HTML Forms and the ACME.HTM Sample Form

An HTML form is a special type of web page that has input fields to let the user enter data. Usually, forms have a Submit button that tells the HTTP server to run a CGI application and pass the data that the user entered to it. The form user interface is all defined with HTML.

There are some excellent books on the subject of writing HTML forms, so I won't go into a lot of detail on the subject. Instead, I will discuss some of the features of our sample form, a request form for Product Information sponsored by the Acme company (and my mother used to tell me that watching the Road Runner was a waste of time!). Figure 10.1 shows the form as it looks in Netscape Navigator, and Figure 10.2 shows the HTML source.

Figure 10.2   The Acme form's HTML source.

```
<HTML>
<HEAD>
<TITLE>Acme Product Information</TITLE>
<BODY BACKGROUND=ACMEBACK.GIF>
<A HREF="SLMONK.WAV"><IMG SRC=DONT.GIF BORDER=0 ALIGN=LEFT HSPACE=20></A>

<H1>Acme Product Information</H1>

Thank you for your interest in Acme products. We want to know more about you, so
please take just a minute to fill out this information form. We will send you our
current catalog which showcases all of our products and prices. Please email
direct inquiries to the Acme staff at <A HREF="MAILTO:staff@acme.com">staff@acme.com</A>.
Thank you and have a nice day.

<BR CLEAR=LEFT>
</HEAD>
</CENTER>
<FORM ACTION="/cgi-bin/acme.exe" METHOD="POST">
<IMG SRC=BACK2.GIF>
<P>

<CENTER><FONT SIZE=4><I>Demographic Information:</FONT SIZE=4></I></CENTER>
<PRE>
                First Name:          <INPUT SIZE=25 NAME="FirstName">
                Last Name:           <INPUT SIZE=25 NAME="LastName">
                Email Address:       <INPUT SIZE=40 NAME="Email">
                Address Line 1:      <INPUT SIZE=40 NAME="Address1">
                Address Line 2:      <INPUT SIZE=40 NAME="Address2">
```

Figure 10.2 *Continued.*

```
                 Address Line 3:     <INPUT SIZE=40 NAME="Address3">
                 City, State & Zip:  <INPUT SIZE=20 NAME="City">, <INPUT SIZE=2
NAME="State">  <INPUT SIZE=12 NAME="Zip">
                         Home Phone: <INPUT SIZE=12 NAME="HomePhone">
                         Work Phone: <INPUT SIZE=12 NAME="WorkPhone">

</PRE>

<IMG SRC=BACK2.GIF>
<P>

<CENTER><FONT SIZE=4><I>Professional Information:</FONT SIZE=4></I></CENTER>
<PRE>
                    Operating System: <SELECT NAME="OperatingSystem">
     <OPTION>Windows NT
     <OPTION>Windows 95
     <OPTION>OS/2 Warp
     <OPTION SELECTED>Windows 16-Bit
     <OPTION>UNIX
     <OPTION>Mac
     <OPTION>DOS
     <OPTION>Other
     </SELECT>

                    Primary Language: <SELECT NAME="PrimaryLanguage">
     <OPTION SELECTED>Visual Basic
     <OPTION>Visual C++
     <OPTION>C
     <OPTION>Delphi
     <OPTION>Other Pascal
     <OPTION>Smalltalk
     <OPTION>Other
     </SELECT>
           Years in Development: <SELECT NAME="Years">
     <OPTION SELECTED>This is my first year
     <OPTION>2
     <OPTION>3
     <OPTION>4
     <OPTION>5
     <OPTION>6-9
     <OPTION>10+
     </SELECT>

<IMG SRC=BACK2.GIF>
```

Continues

Figure 10.2   The Acme form's HTML source. (Continued)

```
                          Clicking this button will transfer your
                          information to our database, and you will
                          be sent a catalog as soon as possible.

                          <INPUT TYPE="submit" VALUE="Register">

</PRE>

<P>

<IMG SRC=BACK2.GIF>

<FONT SIZE=1>
<BR>
<I>
<BLOCKQUOTE>
<BLOCKQUOTE>
<BLOCKQUOTE>
<BLOCKQUOTE>
Copyright 1995, 1996 Acme Software Inc<BR>
All rights reserved<BR>
</BLOCKQUOTE>
</BLOCKQUOTE>
</BLOCKQUOTE>
</BLOCKQUOTE>
</I>
</FONT SIZE=1>
<P>
</FORM>
</BODY>

</HTML>
```

Form Definition

The Acme form has several interesting features. One feature that I'd like to point out is the background. When the form is displayed, this defined bitmap (ACME-BACK.GIF) is sent and displayed in a pattern. The dimensions of ACME-BACK.GIF are 1 pixel high and 1024 pixels wide. Since it is so small, it gets sent and displayed rather quickly. The smart thing is that it is only one pixel high. That's as high as it has to be to give the form the classic look of stationery. The background is defined in the <BODY> statement at the top of the form like so:

```
<BODY BACKGROUND=ACMEBACK.GIF>
```

Another feature is the image that displays "Don't Click," which is Latin for "Click Me Now!" When the user clicks the image, a WAV file is sent. In this case, it is of my favorite cartoon duo, Ren and Stimpy. This is just an example, of course, and you wouldn't really want to subject your users to the disgusting and tasteless sounds of Ren and Stimpy. Or would you?

Notice how the GIF file is transparent. This is done with a public domain command-line GIF utility called GIFTOOL, which is included on the CD-ROM. There isn't any real documentation for this utility but if you type "GIFTOOL -help" at the command line, it will display the command syntax and options.

The image is made into an anchor by incorporating the <IMG> tag within the anchor <A> tag, as follows:

```
<A HREF="SLMONK.WAV"><IMG SRC=DONT.GIF BORDER=0 ALIGN=LEFT HSPACE=20></A>
```

The file SLMONK.WAV is sent when the image is clicked. The SRC=DONT.GIF command in the <IMG> tag defines the image file. The BORDER=0 command defines the image with no border, or no box around the image (this is critical to giving the transparent illusion). The ALIGN=LEFT command places the image on the left-hand side of the form. Finally, the HSPACE=20 command places a little bit of horizontal space between the image and the surrounding text.

All HTML forms start with a <FORM> tag (and end with a </FORM> tag). Here is our <FORM> tag:

```
<FORM ACTION="/cgi-bin/acme.exe" METHOD="POST">
```

The ACTION command defines what happens after the form has been completed. In this case we want to run our CGI program, acme.exe. The second command, METHOD="POST", defines a method performed on the CGI application. This can be either GET, which requests data from the CGI application; or POST, which sends data to the CGI application. In the case of our example, we are sending data to the application, so POST is used.

Field Definitions

The input fields may look complex, but they really are not. The fields themselves are all part of HTML, and are created graphically by the HTTP client. The HTML text just defines the fields; the client actually manages the input.

The ACME.HTM form has 11 text entry fields, and three option (multiple-choice) fields. Defining a field is easy. For example, look at the definition of the first text field:

```
First Name: <INPUT SIZE=25 NAME="FirstName">
```

The <INPUT> tag defines the field. There are two parameters: SIZE=25, which defines the length of the field; and NAME="FirstName", which defines the name of the field. Your Visual Basic CGI application will reference these fields by name.

HTML has a drop-down list input type called SELECT. Select fields are a bit different from text fields, in that there are several selectable options and a default option. Figure 10.3 shows the definition for the first select field. The select field is defined by the <SELECT> tag. Between the <SELECT> tag and its trailer tag, </SELECT>, you can have one or more options, defined with the <OPTION> tag. Whichever option you desire to be the default option you can specify as such with the <OPTION SELECTED> tag. As with the <INPUT> tag, the NAME parameter specifies the name of the field.

The Submit Button

When all the fields are filled in, the user presses the button that says "Register." This button is defined as follows:

```
<INPUT TYPE="submit" VALUE="Register">
```

Just like a text field, the button is defined with an <INPUT> tag. The TYPE="submit" defines the field as a Submit button. When a Submit button is pressed, the action defined in the <FORM> tag is executed, and the CGI application is run. In the case of our Acme form, the application is run with the POST method defined.

Once the CGI application is run, the HTTP server is no longer communicating directly with the client. The CGI application sends any thank you or error messages to the client from this point on. Now, let's take a look at the ACME sample CGI application, which takes the user's data and saves it to an Access database.

Figure 10.3   Definition for the first select field in the Acme demonstration.

```
Operating System: <SELECT NAME="OperatingSystem">
<OPTION>Windows NT
<OPTION>Windows 95
<OPTION>OS/2 Warp
<OPTION SELECTED>Windows 16-Bit
<OPTION>UNIX
<OPTION>Mac
<OPTION>DOS
<OPTION>Other
</SELECT>
```

Hands-On CGI

What follows is a dissection of the elements of the CGI4VB Visual Basic interface. Along the way, we will discuss the sample CGI program ACME.VBP.

CGI4VB.BAS

The only thing you need to add to a VB project to create a CGI application is CGI4VB.BAS. This file includes all the code you need to make a CGI application in VB. Just add a sub- CGI_Main routine and you've got a bare-bones application.

Data is sent back to the server from your CGI application via STDIN and STD-OUT. The CGI4VB.BAS file handles all of this for you. All you really have to do is get the data from the form, process it, and send back HTML text, which will be displayed in the client's web browser.

ACME.BAS: CGI_Main and Inter_Main

The ACME.BAS module contains the code that interacts with the server at the highest level. This is where you process the GET and/or POST methods. Whenever you create a CGI application, you must have a CGI_Main subroutine. CGI_Main is called whenever a GET or POST method is performed on your application. This is where you do your magic, which we will demonstrate in a minute.

Dissecting Sub Main in CGI4VB.BAS

CGI4VB.BAS has a Sub Main, which is to be the startup form (or in this case procedure) for the project. This is the first code that executes. Take a look at Figure 10.4, which shows the code in Sub Main. If the application is executed without any command line arguments, that means that it was probably started directly by the user, in which case the Inter_Main sub is called and the program ends.

Figure 10.4   CGI4VB.BAS—Sub Main listing.

```
Sub Main()

On Error GoTo ErrorRoutine
InitCgi            ' Load environment vars and perform other initialization
GetFormData        ' Read data sent by the server
CGI_Main           ' Process and return data to server

EndPgm:
   End             ' end program                            Continues
```

Figure 10.4   CGI4VB.BAS—Sub Main listing. (Continued)

```
ErrorRoutine:
    sErrorDesc = Err.Description & " Error Number = " & Str$(Err.Number)
    ErrorHandler
    Resume EndPgm
End Sub
```

If command line parameters are specified, the sub InitCgi is called (see Figure 10.5), which grabs all of the CGI variables from the environment. The CGI variables are global variables that contain information such as the HTTP method, the user's IP address, and so forth.

Next, the sub GetFormData is called which reads all of the name/value pairs from the form (in this case, our form's <INPUT> and <SELECT> tags). It places this information in an array called tPair, which you can access to get the data in the form fields.

Figure 10.5   CGI4VB.BAS Sub InitCGI.

```
Sub InitCgi()

hStdIn = GetStdHandle(STD_INPUT_HANDLE)
hStdOut = GetStdHandle(STD_OUTPUT_HANDLE)

sEmail = "YourEmailAddress@Here"

'===============================
' Get the environment variables
'===============================
'
' Environment variables will vary depending on the server.
' Replace any variables below with the ones used by your server.
'
CGI_Accept = Environ("HTTP_ACCEPT")
CGI_AuthType = Environ("AUTH_TYPE")
CGI_ContentLength = Environ("CONTENT_LENGTH")
CGI_ContentType = Environ("CONTENT_TYPE")
CGI_Cookie = Environ("HTTP_COOKIE")
CGI_GatewayInterface = Environ("GATEWAY_INTERFACE")
CGI_PathInfo = Environ("PATH_INFO")
CGI_PathTranslated = Environ("PATH_TRANSLATED")
CGI_QueryString = Environ("QUERY_STRING")
```

Figure 10.5 *Continued.*

```
CGI_Referer = Environ("HTTP_REFERER")
CGI_RemoteAddr = Environ("REMOTE_ADDR")
CGI_RemoteHost = Environ("REMOTE_HOST")
CGI_RemoteIdent = Environ("REMOTE_IDENT")
CGI_RemoteUser = Environ("REMOTE_USER")
CGI_RequestMethod = Environ("REQUEST_METHOD")
CGI_ScriptName = Environ("SCRIPT_NAME")
CGI_ServerSoftware = Environ("SERVER_SOFTWARE")
CGI_ServerName = Environ("SERVER_NAME")
CGI_ServerPort = Environ("SERVER_PORT")
CGI_ServerProtocol = Environ("SERVER_PROTOCOL")
CGI_UserAgent = Environ("HTTP_USER_AGENT")

lContentLength = Val(CGI_ContentLength)     'convert to long
ReDim tPair(0)                              'initialize name/value array

End Sub
```

Let's move on to CGI4VB's Error Handler. The implementation is pretty good. If an error occurs anywhere in the application, the error handler in Sub Main will display the error to the web client and the application will exit. The statement On Error Goto ErrorHandler installs the error handler.

CGI_Main: Where the Magic Happens

Once this data is loaded, the CGI_Main subroutine (in your module) is called. This is where you process the user's input data and display a report in HTML format to the user. This is the real power of CGI4VB, leveraging the world of Visual Basic on the Internet. In this case, we are going to open an access database (ACME.MDB) using the Jet Database Access Objects in Visual Basic and, using an append query, save the user's data.

ACME.MDB should reside in the same directory as the ACME.EXE program. It has one table, CustomerInfo, which has several text fields that are exactly the same size as the fields defined in the form, ACME.HTM.

Retrieving and Saving the Data

Figure 10.6 shows the CGI_Main subroutine. The first thing that happens is a test to see whether the method used to send data is GET or POST. We want to respond only to the POST method. If a POST method was invoked, then we proceed with retrieving the data field values. This is done with the GetCgiValue() function. GetCgiValue returns the data in a field given the name of the field.

Figure 10.6   Sub CGI_Main listing.

```
Sub CGI_Main()

    Dim szFirstName As String
    Dim szLastName As String
    Dim szEmail As String
    Dim szAddress1 As String
    Dim szAddress2 As String
    Dim szAddress3 As String
    Dim szCity As String
    Dim szState As String
    Dim szZip As String
    Dim szHomePhone As String
    Dim szWorkPhone As String
    Dim szOperatingSystem As String
    Dim szPrimaryLanguage As String
    Dim szYears As String

    Dim dbAcme As Database
    Dim szSQL As String
    Dim lRows As Long
    Dim szQuote As String

    szQuote = Chr$(34)

    Select Case CGI_RequestMethod
        Case "POST" '-- A POST method was executed.

            '-- Retrieve the user data
            szFirstName = GetCgiValue("FirstName")
            szLastName = GetCgiValue("LastName")
            szEmail = GetCgiValue("Email")
            szAddress1 = GetCgiValue("Address1")
            szAddress2 = GetCgiValue("Address2")
            szAddress3 = GetCgiValue("Address3")
            szCity = GetCgiValue("City")
            szState = GetCgiValue("State")
            szZip = GetCgiValue("Zip")
            szHomePhone = GetCgiValue("HomePhone")
            szWorkPhone = GetCgiValue("WorkPhone")
            szOperatingSystem = GetCgiValue("OperatingSystem")
```

Figure 10.6 *Continued.*

```
szPrimaryLanguage = GetCgiValue("PrimaryLanguage")
szYears = GetCgiValue("Years")

'-- Open the Access database
Set dbAcme = OpenDatabase(App.Path & "\ACME.MDB")

'-- Create an append query to insert a record.
szSQL = "INSERT INTO CustomerInfo (FirstName, LastName, Email, "
If Len(szAddress1) Then
    szSQL = szSQL & "Address1, "
End If
If Len(szAddress2) Then
    szSQL = szSQL & "Address2, "
End If
If Len(szAddress3) Then
    szSQL = szSQL & "Address3, "
End If
szSQL = szSQL & "City, State, Zip, "
szSQL = szSQL & "HomePhone, WorkPhone, OperatingSystem, "
szSQL = szSQL & "PrimaryLanguage, Years) "
szSQL = szSQL & "VALUES (" & szQuote & szFirstName & szQuote
szSQL = szSQL & ", " & szQuote & szLastName & szQuote & ", "
szSQL = szSQL & szQuote & szEmail & szQuote & ", "
If Len(szAddress1) Then
    szSQL = szSQL & szQuote & szAddress1 & szQuote & ", "
End If
If Len(szAddress2) Then
    szSQL = szSQL & szQuote & szAddress2 & szQuote & ", "
End If
If Len(szAddress3) Then
    szSQL = szSQL & szQuote & szAddress3 & szQuote & ", "
End If
szSQL = szSQL & szQuote & szCity & szQuote & ", " & szQuote
szSQL = szSQL & szState & szQuote & ", " & szQuote & szZip & szQuote
szSQL = szSQL & ", " & szQuote & szHomePhone & szQuote & ", "
szSQL = szSQL & szQuote & szWorkPhone & szQuote & ", " & szQuote
szSQL = szSQL & szOperatingSystem & szQuote & ", " & szQuote
szSQL = szSQL & szPrimaryLanguage & szQuote & ", " & szQuote
szSQL = szSQL & szYears & szQuote & ")"
'MsgBox szSQL
'-- Insert the data
On Error Resume Next
dbAcme.Execute szSQL, dbFailOnError
If Err = 0 Then
```

Continues

Figure 10.6   Sub CGI_Main listing. (Continued)

```
                    '-- The append query worked.
                    SendHeader "Thank You!"
                    Send "<HEAD><CENTER><H1>Thank you for completing our
form!</H1></CENTER>"
                    Send "</HEAD><P><HR SIZE=7><P>"
                    Send "The following information was saved in our database:"
                    Send "<P>"
                    Send "<PRE>"
                    Send "<B>                 Name: </B>" & szFirstName & " " &
szLastName
                    Send "<B>               Email: </B>" & szEmail
                    Send "<B>             Address: </B>" & szAddress1
                    If Len(szAddress2) Then
                        Send "<B>                           </B>" & szAddress2
                    End If
                    If Len(szAddress3) Then
                        Send "<B>                           </B>" & szAddress3
                    End If
                    Send "<B>                           </B>" & szCity & ", " & szState & "
" & szZip
                    Send "<B>       Home Phone: </B>" & szHomePhone
                    Send "<B>       Work Phone: </B>" & szWorkPhone
                    Send "<P>"
                    Send "<B> Operating System: </B>" & szOperatingSystem
                    Send "<B> Primary Language: </B>" & szPrimaryLanguage
                    Send "<B> Years experience: </B>" & szYears
                    Send "</PRE><P><P><HR SIZE=7><P>"
                Else
                    SendHeader "Error saving data"
                    Send "<HEAD><CENTER><H1>Error saving data</H1></CENTER>"
                    Send "</HEAD><P>"
                    Send "There was a problem saving your data to the Acme database. "
                    Send "Error Text: " & Error & "<p>" & "SQL:" & szSQL & "<p>"
                    Send "Contact the system administrator<P>"
                End If

                SendFooter

                '-- Close the database.
                dbAcme.Close

        End Select

End Sub
```

For example, let's say the user entered his first and last name as "John Smith". The following lines of code retrieve the first name and last name from the form:

```
szFirstName = GetCgiValue("FirstName")
szLastName = GetCgiValue("LastName")
```

In this case, szFirstName returns "John" and szLastName is "Smith."

Once we have the raw data from the user, the next step is to open the ACME.MDB database and enter a new record. The OpenDatabase command opens the MDB. *Remember, if there is an error, it will be handled by the universal error handler in Sub Main*. Once the database is open, an append query is defined in the szSQL string variable. I know it looks complex, but it is not. I broke down the creation of this long query into several statements for readability. Basically, an append query has the following format:

```
INSERT INTO TableName (Field1, Field2, Field3) VALUES ("Data1", "Data2", "Data3")
```

The field list (Field1, Field2...) contains the names of the fields. The value list ("Data1", etc.) contains the values to be set. These values must be in the same order as the fields. In other words, the field names and values must correspond to each other and be in the same order. If a field is a text or date field, then its corresponding value must be enclosed in quotes. If there are quotes in the actual data being saved, the query will fail (a seemingly foolish situation, but a situation nonetheless).

Next, the query is executed directly via the EXECUTE Method of the database object. The option dbFailOnError creates a trappable error that occurs if the append query fails. If the query was successful, then an HTML confirmation message is sent to the client. This is done with the Send routine, which simply writes the text to the output file. If the query fails, a failure message is returned to the user.

Sending Data to the Client with the Send Command

When sending HTML to the client, the first two lines must consist of a header. In the case of sending HTML, the header should be sent like so:

```
Send "Content-type: text/html"
Send ""
```

The first line defines the content of the transmission as either HTML or straight text or both. The second line is blank, indicating the end of the header. You can also redirect the output to another HTML page by sending the following lines in place of a header and HTML text:

```
Send "URI: <http://your.link.goes.here.html>"
Send ""
```

where the first line is simply "URI:" followed by the HTML address in arrow brackets. Alternatively, you could use the following syntax to redirect output to another HTML file:

```
Send "Location: http://your.link.goes.here.html"
Send ""
```

Either way, this method lets you create standard response files, which you can simply tell the HTTP server to display to the client.

If you are sending HTML text, as we are in the Acme example, anything goes after the first two lines. You can send HTML directly, you can mix data from the database with the output text, whatever you want to do. You are the Web Master.

In our example, the confirmation message simply repeats back to the client all the data that was entered by the user:

```
Send "Content-type: text/html"
Send ""
Send "<TITLE>Thank You!</TITLE>"
Send "<HEAD><CENTER><H1>Thank you for completing our form!</H1></CENTER>"
Send "</HEAD><P><HR SIZE=7><P>"
Send "The following information was saved in our database:"
...
...
```

The Status Code

The status code is a number returned to the HTTP server from the CGI application. If the program runs and exits normally, a status code of 200 is returned. If an error occurs within the CGI mechanism, special status codes are returned. If a runtime error occurs within your CGI application (such as the append query not working) you can specify a status code of 500, which signifies a runtime error. Do this by sending the following line right at the top of the header:

```
Send "Status: 500 Internal Server Error"
```

Other CGI Options

There are many other alternatives to using CGI to access databases and other programs on the server side. In the next chapter you will learn about Active Server Pages (ASP), Microsoft's built-in alternative to CGI for Internet Information Server. ASP lets you combine VB Script or JavaScript code with HTML to make powerful server-side scripts.

There are also several third-party tools available. For a current list of these technologies, and for more information on CGI, check out the CGI page at Carl & Gary's Visual Basic Home Page: www.cgvb.com/links/lpage.boa?area=CGI.

Epilogue

CGI4VB opens the door to Visual Basic programmers who need to do some quick and dirty server-side programming. You can use CGI4VB.BAS to provide data entry forms, search engines, reports, and much more. In the next chapter, I'll show you how to take advantage of the features of web server, Microsoft's Internet Information Server with Visual Basic.

MICROSOFT INTERNET INFORMATION SERVER

Internet Information Server (IIS) is Microsoft's web and FTP server. IIS comes free with Windows NT Server, and a thinner version of it, called Peer Web Services, comes with NT Workstation. A version for Windows95 users is available separately. This chapter will outline the different technologies available to VB programmers for writing server-side programs that outperform standard CGI methods.

Microsoft's Internet Information Server has many parts. When I first saw version 1.0 (actually a beta), I spent a long weekend exploring it and found it a bit confusing at first. Once I understood the architecture I was blown away, especially when I grasped the importance of the Internet Database Connector (IDC) and the Internet Server API (ISAPI) technologies that were key in version 1.0. I had to go sit in a dark room for nearly an hour to let all the incredible possibilities sink in.

All server programmability in IIS is based on ISAPI, or the Internet Server API. ISAPI was co-developed by Microsoft and Process Software Corporation in 1995 to improve the performance of Windows EXE files used as CGI scripts. In short, ISAPI lets Windows C programmers write their CGI scripts as in-process DLLs. The DLLs are loaded into the same address space as the server, and the entry points are called by their actual address, not by going through an import library and creating a new process. This method is much faster than loading an EXE file, not only because a DLL stays loaded in memory, but also because ISAPI DLLs reside in the same address space as IIS.

All of the other programming technologies in IIS (including IDC and ASP) are ISAPI-based DLLs that extend programmability to VB and other higher-level programmers. A core advantage of this architecture is less redundancy for developers, and we all know that redundancy can be really, really, really, really bad.

This chapter introduces IDC, ASP, and IIS applications. You have to crawl before you can walk, so let's start crawling, shall we?

IDC–The Internet Database Connector

IDC provides a way to create database scripts without doing any real programming, making it easy to access data from web pages. The simplest way to understand the power of this architecture is by comparison with CGI4VB. If you remember from Chapter 10, a user fills out your HTML form and clicks the Submit button. The server runs your VB application and writes the entered data to standard input, passing the data. The VB application then opens a database, executes a query using the specified data, and returns an HTML result string to the server, which passes it back to the user.

However, using IDC, the web server does most of the work. A user fills out your HTML form and clicks the Submit button. The server reads an IDC script (a small text file) that contains an ODBC (Open Database Connectivity) data source, username and password, an SQL query, and the name of an .HTX file (Extended HTML). The server then opens the database and executes the query using the specified data. Finally, the server sends back an HTML response including the resulting data displayed using the HTML Extension file as a template. Got it? If not, don't worry. You will shortly.

Excuse me, but where does Visual Basic fit in? So far, it doesn't. The process never leaves the server! But don't worry, your VB skills aren't becoming obsolete. That's the second half of the story. You can easily integrate VB applications to your server because IDC works smoothly with the ISAPI, as I'll explain later.

Instead of firing up a VB executable to do the database work, the server calls HTTPODBC.DLL (already resident in memory if it has been accessed at least once before) to query the database and return the results. There is no downtime in opening the database because HTTPODBC has its own connection management scheme (Figure 11.1). The power of IDC lies in the use of three types of files:

- *HTM files*. These are standard HTML format files, with no special consideration required except for the fact that they reference an IDC file rather than any other type of CGI script.

- *IDC files*. These Internet Database Connector scripts are small text files that contain at minimum an ODBC data source name, an SQL query, and a reference to an HTX file (see next). By using variables in the query that represent the data passed by the form you can allow users to supply data for the query.

- *HTX files.* At first glance, HTML Extension files look like normal HTML files, but like the IDC file, they contain variables representing data fields. HTML Extension also defines flow control tags so you can return specified results if a certain condition is true, false, or whatever. The HTX file is merely a template—it does not represent the HTML that is sent back to the user. The server uses it to create the final output with the user data.

Figure 11.1 Architecturally sound. The Internet Database Connector is tightly integrated into IIS. Database access occurs from within the server itself using HTTPODBC.DLL to access any ODBC data source.

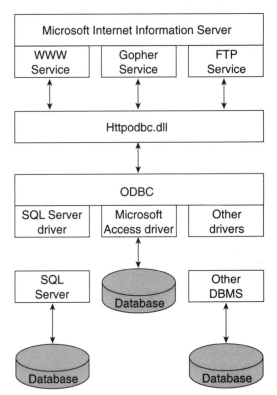

Understanding File Types

Let me give you an example of each one of these file types, beginning with a simple HTML file that runs an IDC script (see Figure 11.2). I've included a screen capture showing how it looks in the browser (see Figure 11.3). The form for the HTML code in Figure 11.2 consists of one field (Search) and a button that runs TEST.IDC in the \scripts directory off of the web server root. Here are the contents of TEST.IDC:

```
Datasource: Biblio
Template: test.htx
SQLStatement:
+SELECT Name, Address FROM Publishers
+WHERE Name Like "%Search%"
```

The Datasource field specifies an ODBC datasource (not the database name), while the Template field specifies an HTML Extension file to be used as the output template, and the SQLStatement field specifies a SQL Query. Although there are a few optional fields, these three fields are required.

Figure 11.2   This sample HTML form accesses an IDC script.

```
<html>
<head>
<title>Sample IDC Form</title>
</head>
<body>
<p>
This is a simple example of using the Database Connector
that queries an ODBC data source called Biblio, an Access
database (BIBLIO.MDB).
<p>
Enter the partial name of a publisher below (ex: "Ran*"
might return "Random House")
<p>
<form action="http://www.mydomain.com/scripts/test.idc" method="POST">
<input name=Search>
<input type=submit value="Query">
</Form>
<p>
</body>
</html>
```

Figure 11.3   A simple HTML form. This form calls the IDC script, TEST.IDC, when the user clicks the Query button.

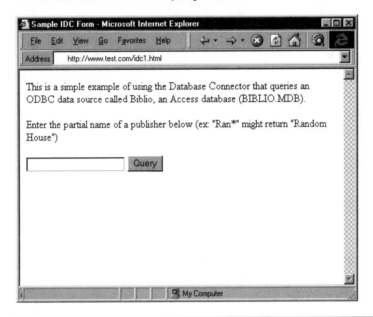

You must have a plus sign in front of each line of the query. When the server reads this IDC file, it opens the ODBC data source called "Biblio" and executes the SQL statement:

```
SELECT Name, Address FROM Publishers
    WHERE Name Like "%Search%"
```

The variable %Search% is replaced with the contents of the Search field on the form when the query is run. You can reference any of the HTML form's fields within your query in this way.

When the data comes back from HTTPODBC.DLL, it is merged with the TEST.HTX file, which looks like this:

```
<html>
<head>
<title>Query Results</title>
</head>
<body>
Here are the results of your query:
<p>
<%begindetail%>
```

```
<pre>
   Company Name: <%Name%>
       Address: <%Address%>
</pre>
<%enddetail%>
</body>
</html>
```

Figure 11.4 shows what the results of this transaction in the web browser might be if the user had entered "A*" for the search term.

 TIP   If you need to access data from a web server either with the ADODB.Connection object or the Internet Database Connecter, you generally use either an ODBC DataSource or an Access file-name to specify the database. Using Access is fine, but if you are using something more powerful like SQL Server or Oracle, you may opt to use an ODBC DataSource. A DataSource is a defini-tion, or a configuration of a database. From the Control Panel on the web server, double-click the ODBC applet. ***Make sure that you create a System DataSource.*** Generally, you enter the name of the server that the database is on, and sometimes you specify an account with which to access the database, as well as the database name. You give the DataSource a name (it could be as simple as the name of the database itself), and use that name to access the database from your web server application.

Remember, the HTX file is a template that the server uses to construct the final HTML output, and it does not represent the code that is actually sent. The <%begindetail%> and <%enddetail%> sections delimit where rows returned from the database will appear in the document. Columns returned from the query are surrounded by <%%>, such as <%Name%> and <%Address%>.

HTML Reserved Words

When writing HTX files you have considerably more control than HTML alone gives you. For example, you can test conditions within the HTX file by using this syntax:

Figure 11.4   Search Results. This is the result of our search on 'A*'.

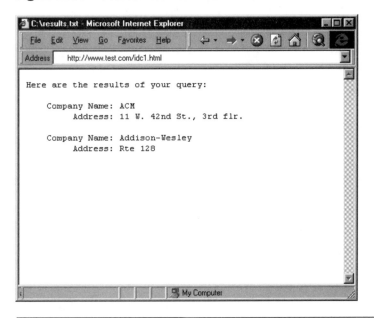

```
<%if condition %>
   HTML text
[<%else%>
   HTML text]
<%endif%>
```

where condition is of the form:

```
value1 operator value2
```

and operator can be one of these:

```
EQ     if value1 equals value2
LT     if value1 is less than value2
GT     if value1 greater than value2
CONTAINS    if any part of value1 contains
    the string value2
```

For example, let's say that you want to return a special message if one of the names returned from the query I explained earlier was "Acme":

```
<%begindetail%>
```

```
<%If Name EQ "Acme"%>
```

```
   <H2>

   Acme is having a sale on all

   size boxes of magnetic

   bird seed!

   </H2><p>

<%EndIf%>

<%enddetail%>
```

The operands value1 and value2 can be column names, one of the built-in variables (CurrentRecord or MaxRecords), an HTTP variable name, or a constant. When used in an <%if%> statement, values are not delimited with <% and %>. The CurrentRecord built-in variable contains the number of times the <%begindetail%> section has been processed. The first time through the <%begindetail%> section, the value is zero. Subsequently, the value of CurrentRecord changes every time another record is fetched from the database. The MaxRecords built-in variable contains the value of the MaxRecords field in the Internet Database Connector file.

You can access parameters from the IDC file in the HTX file by prefixing the name of the parameter with "idc" and a period. For example, if you want to get the actual value the user entered into the Search field on the form, you can do something like this:

```
<%begindetail%>

<pre>

   Company Name: <%Name%>

      Address: <%Address%>

</pre>

<%enddetail%>


<%if CurrentRecord EQ 0%>

   There are no matches with the term, <%idc.Search%>

<%endif%>
```

Several variables can be used in HTML Extension files that give a lot of information about the environment and the web client connected to the server. There are too many to document completely in this chapter, but Table 11.1 shows some of the HTTP variables that can be accessed from within an HTML Extension file. IIS gives you a full CGI header access and more.

Table 11.1   HTTP Variables Used in an HTML Extension (.HTX) File

CONTENT_TYPE	The content type of the information supplied in the body of a POST request.

HTTP_ACCEPT	Special case HTTP header. Values of the Accept: fields are concatenated, separated by ","; for example, if the following lines are part of the HTTP header:
	  accept: */*; q=0.1
	  accept: text/html
	  accept: image/jpeg
	then the HTTP_ACCEPT variable will have a value of:
	/; q=0.1, text/html, image/jpeg.

PATH_INFO	Additional path information, as given by the client. This comprises the trailing part of the URL after the script name but before the query string (if any).
QUERY_STRING	The information thatwhich follows the ? in the URL that referenced this script.
REMOTE_ADDR	The IP address of the client.
REMOTE_HOST	The hostname of the client.
REMOTE_USER	This contains the username supplied by the client and authenticated by the server.
REQUEST_METHOD	The HTTP request method.
SERVER_NAME	The server's hostname (or IP address) as it should appear in self-referencing URLs.

Active Server Pages

Now that you have a sense of how data access works, I'll show you how you can take advantage of the most powerful feature of IIS for VB programmers, Active Server Pages (ASP).

Keep in mind that ASP and OLE (Object Linking and Embedding) Automation makes ISAPI technology available to any object you can write in VB6, as well as any object that could be created with other tools such as VC++. The key to accessing objects from IIS is ASP, Active Server Pages. In an ASP file you can create an invisible object on the server, much like a VB program uses custom controls, and access it using VB Script on the server. Then, merge any data you get back from the objects (or just in your VB code for that matter) with HTML in the

ASP file, and the results are sent to the web browser. For a primer on objects, see Chapter 8, "An Introduction to Objects in Visual Basic."

 NOTE By the way, I hear that there are some places in Silicon Valley where they use more acronyms than real words. The best advice I can offer is not to use your CD-ROM tray as a beverage holder because if you spill H_2O on your CPU your PC will be DOA and you'll be SOL PDQ!

But why use ASP when you can just access data directly using the Internet Database Connector? It's for the same reason there are Access programmers and Visual Basic programmers. They are aimed at people with different skill sets. With the IDC you can read and write to a database with no programming effort. But using VB Script and tapping VB objects via ASP gives you much more capability. What if you need to access other objects to get information that's not in your database? What if you want to send e-mail to someone? There are many reasons for using ASP, and you should evaluate both ASP and IDC, and understand what they can do. This way, you will be prepared to decide what to use when a real-world solution is called for.

Let's start by looking at a very simple ASP page that demonstrates the difference between an ASP page and an HTML page. Look at Figure 11.5

Figure 11.5   TIME.ASP. This ASP page returns the current time on the server.

```
<%
CurTime = Now
%>
<html>
<head>
<title>Time of Day</title>
</head>
<body>
<center>
The current time is <%=CurTime%>
</center>
</body>
</html>
```

You will notice that this looks almost like an HTML file, except for two sections marked with <% and %>. Simply put, anything between <% and %> is considered code. To display the contents of a variable or an expression, use the equal sign.

For example, the following three lines would each display "There are 2 weeks left until my birthday".

```
<%="There are 2 weeks left until my birthday"%>
There are <%="2"%> weeks left until my birthday
There are <%=1 + 1%> weeks left until my birthday
```

As well, this code snippet would also display the same line:

```
<%WeeksLeft = 2%>
There are <%=WeeksLeft%> weeks left until my birthday
```

Figure 11.6 shows a more complex example of an ASP page. This one actually includes a string function. Remember that this code is not running on the client, but on the server.

Figure 11.6   A slightly more complex ASP example.

```
<html>
<head>
<title>ReplaceString Example</title>
</head>
<body>

<%
Function ReplaceString(Orig, Find, Replace)

    Do
        Pos = InStr(LCase(Orig), LCase(Find))
        If Pos Then
            Orig = Left(Orig, Pos - 1) & Replace & _
                Mid(Orig, Pos + Len(Find))
        Else
            Exit Do
        End If
    Loop
    ReplaceString = Orig

End Function
%>                                                  Continues
```

Figure 11.6   A slightly more complex ASP example. *(Continued)*

```
<center>
<H1>ReplaceString Test</H1>
This is a test of the ReplaceString Function.
<p>
<%=ReplaceString("Plesting, plesting, 1.2.3", "pl", "T")%>
<p>
This concludes this test.
</center>
</body>
</html>
```

Note that you can have any combination of code and HTML that you want, and that the code can appear anywhere within the HTML. When the code is run, it is removed from the output. Wherever you see a <%=Expression%> tag, the output of the expression replaces the tag. This lets you use variables, expressions, and functions, etc. wherever you want in your HTML files.

Accessing COM Objects in ASP

COM stands for Component Object Model, and for the sake of simplicity, can be used interchangeably with OLE. Although they are different, you can think of COM and OLE as the same thing. That is, a system by which you can access system-wide objects (those that are available on your machine). Take a look.

```
<%
Set MyObj = Server.CreateObject(<MyClassName>)
%>
```

In the preceding syntax, MyObj is an object created from the class shown as <MyClassName>. For example, if you want to create an object called Book based on the class BookClassObjects.BookClass, it would look like this:

```
<%
Set Book = Server.CreateObject("BookClassObjects.BookClass")
%>
```

Once you have created an object, you can use it in your ASP page just like you would in Visual Basic as if you'd used the New keyword.

Now, why is this important? Because you can create an ActiveX DLL in VB and then access it from your ASP page. The DLL can return back data, which you can then display in the context of an HTML page. Let's try this now.

Hands On

Create a new ActiveX DLL project in VB. The default class module name is Class1. Rename this to vbipTestClass. Edit the class and enter the following code:

```
Public Function RunMe ()
    RunMe = "This text is coming from an object written in VB!"


End Sub
```

Open the Project Properties window from the bottom of the Project menu. Name the project vbipTest.

Now, save and compile the DLL. Next, create a setup program for it using the Package and Deployment Wizard (or if you are using VB5, the Application Setup Wizard). On the web server, stop the web service, install vbipTestClass, restart the web server, and test it by creating and accessing an ASP file with the following two lines:

```
<%Set TestObj = Server.CreateObject("vbipTest.vbipTestClass")%>
Test Message: <%=TestObj.RunMe%>
```

What's going on here? Why is this important? Who the heck cares anyway now that they've resurrected the Volkswagen Beetle? Well, if you walk away from this chapter with any one scrap of practical knowledge, this is probably a good candidate.

The ASP code first instantiates an object called TestObj of the type vbipTestClass from the project named vbipTest. Once the object exists, you can call any of its properties and methods. In this case, we created a single method called RunMe. RunMe is a function that returns a literal string. You can call it anything you like: RunMe, PokeMe, KickMe. It doesn't matter. Also, the function can do anything that VB can do, not just return a string. You can create a function that accepts parameters like FirstName, LastName, etc., save the data to a database, and return a success code.

The second line is back to HTML, since the entire first line is between <% and %>. But, on the second line you see the <%= symbol, which tells ASP to display the results of the expression TestObj.RunMe. Since this function returns the aforementioned literal string, the result of accessing this ASP page in the browser would be:

```
Test Message: This text is coming from an object written in VB!
```

ASP and Database Access

ASP can take advantage of any database engine, but the one most suited for it is ADO (Active Data Objects), which is new to Visual Basic 6.0. ADO is a lean and mean extension of OLE-DB, a core database access set in Windows. With ADO, you can open an ODBC data source, execute SQL statements, and return Recordsets of data. Figure 11.7 shows a sample ASP page that opens a sample database that comes with ASP, accessed by the ADOSamples ODBC data source.

The first line of code (not HTML) creates an ADO connection object. This is all you need to access a database with ADO. Next, the Open method opens the data source, "ADOSamples". If this doesn't work for you, then you probably did not install the samples when you installed IIS with ASP.

The third line executes a SQL statement to return all the records from the Customers table and return the results in an object called rs. Note that there are no data types in ASP (VB Script). You can just pull variables and objects out of thin air, so to speak.

Figure 11.7   Open an ODBC Data source and display data.

```
<html>
<head>
<title>ADO Sample</title>
</head>
<body>
<H1>ADO Sample</H1>
<%
Set Conn = Server.CreateObject("ADODB.Connection")
Conn.Open "ADOSamples"
Set rs = Conn.Execute("SELECT * FROM Customers")
%>
<TABLE CELLPADDING=5>
<%Do Until rs.EOF%>
    <TR>
    <TD><%=rs(1)%></TD>
    <TD><%=rs(4)%></TD>
    </TR>
<%rs.MoveNext%>
<%Loop%>
</TABLE>
</body>
</html>
```

The Open method takes optional parameters that specify a user-name and password required to access the database. Since the database is an MDB file with full access, these parameters are not required.

Next you see HTML that creates a table. In between the <TABLE> and </TABLE> tags is a code loop. The VB code displays the HTML and code results between the Do and Loop repeatedly until the loop is exited. In this example the fields are accessed by number, but you could access them by name if you like.

Processing Input Data from a Form

OK, lets take a look at how you can process forms in ASP. ASP gives you access to several native objects, including the Request object, which returns input data, and the Response object, which lets you reply to the user. Figure 11.8 shows a sample ASP page that displays several fields passed in with a URL using the Request object.

Figure 11.8   Accessing the Request object.

```
<html>
<head>
<title>Request Sample</title>
</head>
<body>
<H1>Request Sample</H1>
Here are a few fields that were passed in to this asp file:
<p>
First Name: <%=Request("FirstName")%><br>
Last Name: <%=Request("LastName")%><br>
Email: <%=Request("Email")%><br>
<p>
You can also access them by field number with the QueryString object:
<p>
<%On Error Resume Next%>
Field #1: <%=Request.QueryString(1)%><br>
Field #2: <%=Request.QueryString(2)%><br>
Field #3: <%=Request.QueryString(3)%><br>
<P>
To test this page, name it test.asp and click below:
<P>
```
Continues

Figure 11.8   Accessing the Request object. *(Continued)*

```
<a
href="test.asp?FirstName=Joe&LastName=Schmoe&Email=JoeSchmoe@withouta.net">test.asp?Fi
rstName=Joe&LastName=Schmoe&Email=JoeSchmoe@withouta.net</a>
</body>
</html>
```

You can test this code by writing it as an ASP file (straight text editing here–sigh) and naming it test.asp. It matters not where you put it, so long as it's in a web directory and you can access it by URL. It will not work as a local file on your machine unless you have installed Peer web services with ASP.

Of course, the request object also returns elements passed from a form just as if they were passed in the URL. Figure 11.9 shows a sample HTML file that accesses the previous asp file, test.asp.

Figure 11.9   Sample Form. This form calls the ASP file, test.asp, and passes three fields.

```
<html>
<head>
<title>Request Sample Form</title>
</head>
<body>
<h1>Sample Form</h1>
<form action=test.asp method=post>

First Name:<br>
<input name=FirstName>
<p>

Last Name:<br>
<input name=LastName>
<p>

Email:<br>
<input name=Email>
<p>

<input type=submit>
```

Figure 11.9   *Continued.*

```
</form>
</body>
</html>
```

Returning Data to the User

Just as the Request object reads data from the URL or calling form, the Response object sends data back to the user. To send HTML or text back to the user, use the Write method, as shown here:

```
Response.Write "<H1>Hello</H1>"
```

Remember that whatever you send ultimately shows up in the web browser. So, if you want to send two lines, you have to separate them with an HTML <BR> or <P> tag. Simply sending a carriage return/linefeed will not separate lines of text in the web browser.

In Figure 11.10, the test.asp file has been modified to save the name and e-mail address in an Access database. Notice how you can return different HTML depending on whether or not an error occurred saving the data.

Figure 11.10   Saving form data in a database and responding with the Response object.

```
<html>
<head>
<%
'-- First, open the database
Set Conn = Server.CreateObject("ADODB.Connection")
Conn.Open "test" '-- Can be any ODBC datasource.

'-- Next, create a SQL string to save the data.
SQL = "INSERT INTO Customers (FirstName, LastName, Email) " & _
    "VALUES ('" & Request("FirstName") & "', " & _
    "'" & Request("LastName") & "', " & _
    "'" & Request("Email") & "')"
On Error Resume Next
Set rs = Conn.Execute(SQL)
If Err Then
    ErrorString = Error
%>
```

Continues

```
    <title>Error Saving Data</title>
    </head>
    <body>
    <h1>Error Saving Data</h1>
    The following error occurred while saving your data:<p>
    <b><%=ErrorString%></b><p>
    Please notify the webmaster immediately.
<%Else%>
    <title>Thank You</title>
    </head>
    <body>
    <h1>Thank you.</h1>
    Your information has been saved.
<%End If%>
</body>
</html>
```

IIS Applications in Visual Basic 6.0

Visual Basic 6.0 introduced a new type of project called the Internet Information Server Application, sometimes referred to as WebClasses. Like ASP and its CGI predecessors, IIS applications let you access data and other processes from the web server, and let you formulate a response. An IIS Application is an ActiveX DLL that has IIS hooks built into it. These hooks let you debug your application in the VB environment, give you access to the ASP objects (Response, Request, etc.), provide state management, let you use template HTML files (like IDC) so you can separate HTML code from server data processing code, and provide other useful tools and benefits.

Technologies evolve. It is for this reason that you may be wondering why not just use IDC, or create an ActiveX DLL. My answer is always, "Go ahead and use whatever works best for you." There is no one way to create a server-side application. I see IIS applications as a logical combination of IDC, ASP, and Visual Basic. You get the template option of IDC, which lets you separate the tasks of VB programming and HTML development. You get the objects of ASP, which simplify just about everything you can do in a server-side application. And, you get the benefits of coding and debugging in VB, which we all know, has the best development environment in the world.

On top of that, you can opt to make your object maintain itself in memory during the entire session. Let me explain. When you first access a WebClass with a web browser, you are starting a session. That session continues until you either close the browser, or move away from the web site. By opting to have the WebClass retain its instance, you tell it not to unload when the user moves from page to page on your web site. This lets you cache data, and maintain properties (like UserID, FirstName, and LastName) that will not reset as the user moves from page to page.

There are really two approaches to developing IIS applications. One is to develop them on the web server machine (not recommended); the other is to set up Peer Web Services and any data connections on your development machine, and then install them on the web server when you are done with the development and debugging process. I recommend the second option. Although you could develop on your web server, why entertain the possibility of messing things up? Therefore, I will assume you are going to use your development machine for the rest of this chapter.

Peer Web Services

You must install the Microsoft Peer Web Services on your development machine before you can create IIS applications. So how do you get that? Well, Peer Web Services comes with the Microsoft Windows NT Option Pack. However, you do not need to run NT to use this. There is a version of Peer Web Services for Windows95, but it still falls under the title of the NT Option Pack. If you are developing on Windows NT 4.0 or Windows95, then read on.

Here is the URL (at the time of this writing) to the Option Pack files on MS's web server:

www.microsoft.com/windows/downloads/contents/updates/nt40ptpk

If this URL has changed since this publication, simply go to www.microsoft.com, hit the Search button, and search for an exact match on "Option Pack." You should find it with no problems. Once you register to download it, you can select which version you want to download (NT4 WS, Server, or 95).

WebClass Designer

Start VB 6.0 and create a new IIS Application. Take a look at Figure 11.11. On the right-hand side of the screen is the Project Explorer. Below the word Project1 is the Designers folder. Open the Designers folder by clicking on the plus sign, and double-click on the word **WebClass1**. This will bring up the Designer for WebClass1.

Figure 11.11   Visual Basic 6.0 WebClass Designer.

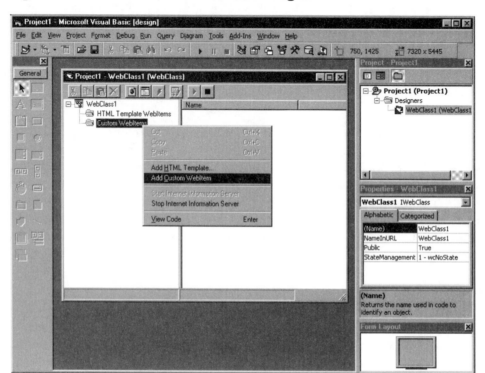

The Designer is sort of like a project explorer custom-made for WebClasses. There is a one-to-one relationship between a Designer and a WebClass object. Notice the StateManagement property. This is where you can set the object to remain loaded throughout a session. The default is no state.

Terminology 101: A WebClass is made up of one or more WebItems. There are two types of WebItems, HTML Template WebItems and Custom WebItems. Both can be used independently.

HTML Template WebItems

An HTML Template is an HTML file from which you can call functions in your WebClass. There are several ways in which you can access code in your WebClass. You can create a tag in your HTML file, which when processed will be replaced with the output of code in the WebClass. You can also create custom User Events, which you can call from HTML. But, the best way to get started is to use the

WebClass designer to "connect" forms and items in your HTML pages to events in your WebItems.

The main idea behind using an HTML template is that your HTML wizard can design the best HTML pages, and you (the developer) can write the best code. So, you can add the HTML pages as templates, and then create hooks into your code where the data should be displayed, thus separating the two jobs.

You can choose to return HTML in your HTML template, or just data. I recommend using as little HTML as possible, so that you remain flexible. If all you need is data, that is, a sentence or two based on the action of the user, just return the text and do all the visual stuff in the HTML page.

Let's take a look at my sample IIS application, which is simply another reincarnation of the old Acme form from projects past. Load Acme.vbp from the \WebClasses folder where you installed the sample code.

When the project loads, double-click on the wcAcme WebClass in the VB Project Explorer, which will show the WebClass Designer for the wcAcme WebClass, as shown in Figure 11.12.

Before I go any further, go ahead and compile this WebClass. When you compile, VB creates an ASP (Active Server Page) that loads the WebClass object. To access the WebClass from a web page, you make a reference to the ASP, not directly to the WebClass, as you might expect.

The wcAcme WebClass has only one WebItem, AcmeForm. If you double-click on this item, you will see the default procedure, Respond, that executes when the WebClass is invoked. In this case it contains three lines of code:

```
Private Sub AcmeForm_Respond()
```

Figure 11.12   wcAcme WebClass.

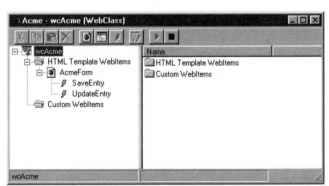

```
    LoadData
AcmeForm.WriteTemplate
Editing = False

End Sub
```

The LoadData function, shown in Figure 11.13, reads data about the user. After the user registers with the Acme form, three cookie values are set: FirstName, LastName, and Email. Cookies are simply text fields written to the user's hard disk with the browser, which can be retrieved by a web server process such as our WebClass.

If the cookie exists, that means this user has already registered, in which case the data is retrieved and placed into the fields in the form. wcAcme sets a Boolean flag called Editing to True, indicating that this is an editing process, and not a registration process. We need to know this so we can use the correct SQL syntax when writing the data to the database.

All of the data variables; FirstName, LastName, Email, and even the rsData Recordset, are defined at the module level, so all functions in this WebClass can access them. Remember, a new WebClass loads for each user request, so you do not have to keep track of multiple users. You can be sure that there is a one-to-one relationship.

Figure 11.13   LoadData loads cookie values and user data.

```
Private Sub LoadData()

    Dim SQL As String

    FirstName = Request.Cookies("FirstName")
    If Len(FirstName) Then
        Editing = True
        LastName = Request.Cookies("LastName")
        Email = Request.Cookies("Email")
        SQL = "SELECT * FROM CustomerInfo WHERE LCASE(FirstName) = '" & _
          LCase$(FirstName) & "' AND LCASE(LastName) = '" & _
          LastName & "' AND LCASE(Email) = '" & LCase$(Email) & "'"
        Set rsData = dbAcme.Execute(SQL, , adCmdText)
        rsData.StayInSync = True
    End If

End Sub
```

Once LoadData is called from AcmeForm_Respond, the next line of code is AcmeForm.WriteTemplate. This tells the WebClass to send the template to the user, which is simply an HTML file with (you guessed it) some specific items that hook it to your WebClass. Our template happens to be our good-old Acme form, with a few changes.

Take a look at the Acme1.htm file in the \WebClasses subfolder of the sample code. Notice at the bottom where there used to be three <SELECT> items, now they seem to have mostly disappeared. Let me explain.

One of the added features of this Acme form over the ASP and CGI versions is that if the user has already filled out a form, all the data that they entered is automatically placed in the fields when they simply go to that form. This is what I was talking about in the last few paragraphs. Now, it is easy to set the value of a text field. There is a VALUE=x portion of an <INPUT> tag that you can use to set the value as well as read it.

However, there is not such a nice way to do this with the <SELECT> tag. For the item that is selected, you must say <OPTION SELECTED>, whereas all other options are simply <OPTION>. So, I had to add logic, effectively moving the SELECT contents to the WebClass.

Custom Tags

That brings me to this business of Custom Tags. Within the HTML template, you can place a tag with a particular defined prefix. When the WebClass reads these tags, it fires an event, in which you can return a string to replace the tag in the template.

The WebItem object has a property called TagPrefix. The default prefix is @WC. Any tags in your HTML Template that start with this prefix are processed at runtime. For each processed tag, the ProcessTag event is fired, where you have an opportunity to replace the tag text based on the tag name.

Take a look at Figure 11.14, which shows the portion of the Acme form containing the <SELECT> tags. Notice the <WC@OperatingSystem> tag. Since our TagPrefix is set to @WC, this tag fires the ProcessTag event in the WebItem called AcmeForm. Based on the selected item, the tag is replaced with the correct HTML code.

Figure 11.14 Using Custom Tags in an HTML Template.

```
<TABLE>
<TR>
<TD>Operating System:</TD>
```
Continues

Figure 11.14   Using Custom Tags in an HTML Template. *(Continued)*

```
<TD>
<SELECT NAME="OperatingSystem">
<WC@OperatingSystem>HTMLTagcontents</WC@OperatingSystem>
</TD>
</TR><TR>
<TD>Primary Language:</TD>
<TD>
<SELECT NAME="PrimaryLanguage">
<WC@PrimaryLanguage>HTMLTagcontents</WC@PrimaryLanguage>
</TD>
</TR><TR>
<TD>Years in Development:</TD>
<TD>
<SELECT NAME="Years">
<WC@Years>HTMLTagcontents</WC@Years>
</TD>
</TR>
</TABLE>
```

Custom Events

WebItems can have custom events that let your code respond to specific actions. To add a custom event, just right-click on your WebItem in the WebClass designer, and select "Add Custom Event." My AcmeForm WebItem has two custom events, SaveEntry and UpdateEntry. SaveEntry is for saving a user's data the first time, and UpdateEntry is used to update an existing record.

In all of these events, you have access to the ASP objects (Request, Response, Server, etc.) so you can reply via "Response.Write" just like I do in SaveEntry and UpdateEntry.

For example, Figure 11.15 shows the portion of SaveEntry where the user's name and e-mail address are saved to cookies, and a response is generated. By using a far-off date, you can extend the cookie's life so it "sticks."

Figure 11.15   Responding with the Response object.

```
Response.Write "<CENTER><H1>Thank You</H1><P>"
Response.Write "Your info has been saved</CENTER>"

Response.Cookies("FirstName").Expires = "January 1, 2037"
```

Figure 11.15 *Continued.*

```
Response.Cookies("FirstName").Secure = False
Response.Cookies("FirstName") = Request("FirstName")

Response.Cookies("LastName").Expires = "January 1, 2037"
Response.Cookies("LastName").Secure = False
Response.Cookies("LastName") = Request("LastName")

Response.Cookies("Email").Expires = "January 1, 2037"
Response.Cookies("Email").Secure = False
Response.Cookies("Email") = Request("Email")
```

Custom WebItems

Besides creating WebItems based on HTML pages, you can also create custom WebItems that are not associated with an HTML page at all. You might choose to do this if your WebClass returns data to processes other than a web browser, such as a standalone application, or if you need to completely separate the HTML development process from the programming process. Whatever your reasons, this option provides more flexibility in your design process. It's also, if I may speak scientifically for a moment, pretty fargin' cool!

Custom WebItems have all the same features that HTML Template WebItems have, without being centered around an HTML file. All output resides within your WebItem.

Testing and Debugging

The debugging features and real-time testing of IIS applications is one of the best reasons to use them. You can set breakpoints in your code with the F9 key, and when you run the project, VB fires up your web browser, and your code stops at the breakpoint. You can take advantage of the best debugging environment known to exist. Simply run your IIS application and VB does the rest.

Let's look at what happens when you compile your WebClass. First, VB creates an ASP file to call your WebClass. Figure 11.16 shows this file.

A moment's thought will make clear what is going on here. First, the code makes sure that the WebClassManager object it needs to reference exists. If not, it creates one. It does this by checking to see that an Application level variable named ~WC~WebClassManager does not exist, or VarType = 0 (uninitialized). Then, it locks the application and again tests to see that this variable is null. If so, then it sets the variable to a new WebClassManager object and unlocks the application.

Figure 11.16   VB Creates an ASP file that calls your WebClass.

```
<%
Response.Buffer=True
Response.Expires=0

If (VarType(Application("~WC~WebClassManager")) = 0) Then
    Application.Lock
    If (VarType(Application("~WC~WebClassManager")) = 0) Then
        Set Application("~WC~WebClassManager") = _
            Server.CreateObject("WebClassRuntime.WebClassManager")
    End If
    Application.UnLock
End If

Application("~WC~WebClassManager").ProcessNoStateWebClass _
    "Acme.wcAcme", _
    Server, _
    Application, _
    Session, _
    Request, _
    Response
%>
```

Once the code knows that the object is there, then it calls the ProcessNoStateWebClass method, and passes all the ASP objects to it. This is where your WebClass code takes over.

Calling WebItems Manually from HTML

When you load an HTML Template, connect forms and items to your WebClass, and save the template, VB makes changes to it so it will call your ASP page instead of whatever it had been calling before. However, If you want to call a WebItem manually from a form or a script, you need to know a few things. Basically, you call the ASP page created by VB, with a few parameters listed in Figure 11.17.

Figure 11.17   URL Parameters for calling WebClass ASP pages.

```
WCI    Identifies the webitem being referenced.
WCE    Tells the webclass the event in the webclass to which this tag corresponds.
When the user selects the element for this tag in the browser, the webclass can read
this notation and determine the event that it should fire.
WCU    (Optional) Serves as a place holder for your existing URL data.
```

Figure 11.18   Form tag from Acme.ASP.

```
<FORM METHOD=POST ACTION = Acme.ASP?WCI=AcmeForm&amp;WCE=
    <WC@Action>HTMLTagcontents</WC@Action>&amp;WCU>
```

So, basically, you call the ASP page, setting WCI to the WebItem name and WCE to the Event name. Figure 11.18 shows the actual form tag from our Acme1.htm form that calls Acme.ASP.

The only thing that might seem strange to you is that the event name specified by WCE is actually a tag. In this case, the event being called is determined by the WebClass. If the user has already filled out the form, then the event gets set to UpdateData (because the user already has a record in the database); otherwise, it is set to SaveData, which creates a new record.

There is much more to creating IIS applications than I can cover in this book, but I believe I have covered enough of the core features to get you started, and that is all I am trying to do here. The online documentation (via MSDN) is essential when creating an IIS application. Press F1 whenever you get into a bind.

Epilogue

At the time of this writing, Microsoft had posted a reference of all the objects in ASP at the following URL: premium.microsoft.com/msdn/library/sdkdoc /iishelp/iis/htm/introobj1orp.htm. Of course, URLs change, and I can't guarantee that this link is still intact. Your best bet for documentation is the Internet Information Server documentation in HTML form that is installed with IIS.

In case you couldn't tell, I'm impressed with the technology in MS Internet Information Server and VB6. These tools make creating a stellar web site a real pleasure. One of my plans is to convert my WorldTRAIN Web site to use IIS Applications so I can have better control over it. WorldTRAIN is my company, which sells Internet-based live training software for Windows (www.worldtrain.com). So much for the curtailing of shameless self-promotion, but hey! This is *my* book!

WRITING CUSTOM WINSOCK CLIENT/SERVER APPLICATIONS

The code used in this chapter will probably prove to be the most useful to you. It was certainly the most fun for me to write. I got to exploit the features of object-oriented Visual Basic to create some code that you can drop into your VB applications to write true client/server systems that use the Internet. If you are not familiar with working with classes and objects, go back and read Chapter 8, "An Introduction to Objects in Visual Basic."

In short, the code presented in this chapter is in two parts. There is a server application that you can use as a starting point for your own server application. The second half of the code is an Internet client object. Yes, that's right, an ActiveX DLL object. You can use Visual Basic, Delphi, Access, or any other COM (Component Object Model) platform to access and communicate with your server application.

The premise here is simple. You create an instance of my cfSocket object in your VB application. The object connects you to a server application via Winsock using a dsSocket or MS Winsock object (see Chapter 9 for more information on these objects). You then send commands and data to the server, and the server returns data back to you. Not only that, but the server can fire an event in your client object (sometimes referred to as PUSH technology). Since it is all written in VB, you can create your own applications that accept custom commands (with data) that you specify. On the Internet server side, you can respond to those commands and data, process them, and send back response codes and data to the client.

Now let me illuminate the possibilities here. You have a web site. You're running Microsoft Internet Information Server. You use Active Server Pages (see Chapter 11) to access your custom Winsock object, which then connects to any machine on the Internet that is running your server application. Now you are effectively routing web page requests from your web server to a machine in another location, which has your data on it.

You could also write your own client/server systems using this method. You have at your disposal everything that the web has, such as the ability to send text and graphics through the Internet, and more. The only thing that's missing is a protocol, and that's exactly what this code gives you.

Remember that when you write your own system you can control both sides, client and server. What if you could define a set of commands that are sent from the client to the server? The server interprets the commands and sends back data. This is exactly the functionality that this code provides—namely the ability to connect to and communicate using commands that you define at a higher level than the sending and receiving of raw data.

The cfSocket ActiveX DLL

cfSocket is an ActiveX DLL written in Visual Basic. As is, it contains enough properties and methods to get you connecting to an Internet server with security, downloading, and uploading files, as well as receiving unsolicited files (those that you do not ask for) and events.

There are two classes in this DLL: cfSockClient and cfData. cfData is a member of cfSockClient. Figure 12.1 shows the hierarchy.

Figure 12.1   The cfSocket class hierarchy.

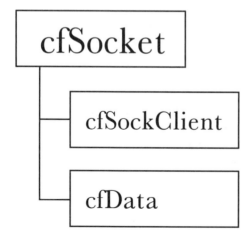

Figure 12.2 The cfData class.

Property	Data Type	Description
Cols	Long	Number of columns
Rows	Long	Number of rows
DataSet()	String	Two-dimensional string property
Method	**Description**	
Resize	Resizes the object given a number of rows and columns	

The cfSockClient class is the interface to your VB application. It contains all of the properties and methods for communicating with the server, including binary file transfers.

The cfData class is a public noncreatable wrapper class for a two-dimensional string array. An object created from the cfData class can be treated like an array and is thus used to hold data transferred between client and server. The definition of this class is shown in Figure 12.2. It acts just like an array, but has the benefit of being a class. The cfSockClient class contains a cfData class member called Data.

It is fitting to explain the cfData class first, since cfData is a member of cfSockClient. cfData is easy to understand since it's just a wrapper for a two-dimensional array. You may find it useful for many other applications, not just Internet programming. In the interest of keeping you awake through all of this, let's jump right into some sample code. Take a look at the code in Figure 12.3.

Figure 12.3 An example use of the cfSockClient class.

```
"-- Create an object from the cfData class
Dim MyData As New cfData

"-- Resize it to 2 rows and 3 columns
MyData.Resize 2, 3

"-- Set row 1, column 1 to "Hello"
MyData.DataSet(1, 1) = "Hello"

"-- Set row 2, column 3 to "Good-bye"
MyData.DataSet(2, 3) = "Good-bye"

"-- Display the contents of row 1, column 1 in the debug window
Debug.Print MyData.DataSet(1, 1)
```

In this example, first a new object (MyData) is created. Next, the Resize method allocates two rows and three columns. Inside the cfData class a two-dimensional string array called Data_Set is created. Here is the code for the Resize method in the cfData class:

```
Public Sub Resize(lRows As Long, lCols As Long)

    On Error Resume Next
    ReDim Data_Set(1 To lRows, 1 To lCols) As String

End Sub
```

The statement On Error Resume Next is used to trap an error in case a zero is passed as a row or a column, or a number too large is passed, meaning that there isn't enough memory. To determine if an error occurred, check the Rows and Cols properties after invoking the Resize method. The Rows and Cols property handlers use the UBound function to retrieve the upper boundaries of the array, which will always give you the correct number. Here is the Get code for the Rows property:

```
Public Property Get Rows() As Long

    On Error Resume Next
    Rows = UBound(Data_Set, 1)

End Property
```

Anytime you read the Rows property this function is called, which gets the upper boundary of the internal Data_Set array's first dimension, or the number of rows.

The Rows and Cols property are both read-only, meaning that you cannot set them yourself. The only way to set the number of rows and columns is with the Resize method.

Figure 12.4 shows cfSockClient, the top-level class. An object of this type represents the client half of a client/server application. Essentially, the client application that makes up the ActiveX DLL consists of the cfSockClient public class, which has a reference to cfWinsockDS (or cfWinsockMS) and the cfData class. Think of cfSockClient like another Winsock control, except that there are higher level commands to communicate real information, not just raw data.

cfSockClient lets you connect with a name and password using the UserName and Password properties. On the server side, you can use the name and password to validate the user against a database, or whatever; simply pass back "OK" to accept the connection and "NO" not to accept it.

Figure 12.4   The cfSockClient class.

Property	Data Type	Description
SendBlockSize	Integer	Largest possible chunk of transmitted data
RecvBlockSize	Integer	Largest possible chunk of received data
CommandTimeout	Integer	Number of seconds before time out when sending commands
Connected	Integer	True if connected, False if not
Data	cfData (class)	See cfData below
DataSize	Long	Maximum size of data packet
DownloadDir	String	Destination path for downloaded files
LocalName	String	Local machine name
LocalDotAddr	String	Local machine IP address
Password	String	Password used to connect to server
ServerName	String	Server machine name
ServerDotAddr	String	Server IP address
ServerPort	Long	Port connected to on server
UserName	String	Username used to connect to server

Method	Description
Connect	Connects you to a server
Disconnect	Disconnects from server
GetFile	Gets a file from the server
SendCommand	Sends a command to the server
SendFile	Sends a file to the server

Event	Description
ReceiveCmd	Fires when a command is received from the server

Once connected you can send data back and forth using the aforementioned cfData class, essentially a two-dimensional array. You can also send and receive files. The client object and the code on the server side sweat the details of managing connections and getting the data across. All you have to do is respond to the commands.

You can send files to the server with the SendFile method, download a file with the GetFile method, and handle the receipt of unsolicited files using the ReceiveCmd event.

But why stop there? The source is included, and I encourage you to expand the code to accommodate your own custom commands. What I consider essential functions are already there: logging on with security, sending and receiving data, and sending and receiving files. Use it as a starting point for your own mega-distributed system. Later in this chapter, I will discuss the built-in ODBC code, which lets you access a database at the Internet server from the client machine using cfSockClient.

The cfSockClient Client/Server Model

Figure 12.5 shows the client/server model used by cfSockClient. On the client side, your Visual Basic application communicates through the cfSockClient COM object, which exists outside of your application. The cfSockClient object contains a cfWinsockDS class, which communicates via Windows Sockets through the network to the server side (see Chapter 9 for more information on the cfWinsockDS and cfWinsockMS classes).

The server application contains the server (CFServer) code, which consists of a form, a cfData class module, and two code modules. The form contains four dsSocket ActiveX controls. You may use the server code as it is. The project runs by itself; there is no need to modify it unless you want to incorporate it into an existing application. If you are starting from scratch, use the CFServer project as a starting point and build it up.

You might be wondering why I chose not to write an OLE server for the Internet server side. I considered it, but decided against it because an OLE server is useful only when more than one application on the local machine is going to use it. Since you normally would not run more than one Internet host application on a single server machine, there is really no need for the extra overhead. You want your server to be as fast as possible to be able to handle lots of clients!

One thing you might want to consider, though, is making it an NT Service. Desaware has an excellent tool called SpyWorks that lets you create an NT service in Visual Basic. Check out their web site at www.desaware.com.

Figure 12.5   The cfSockClient model.

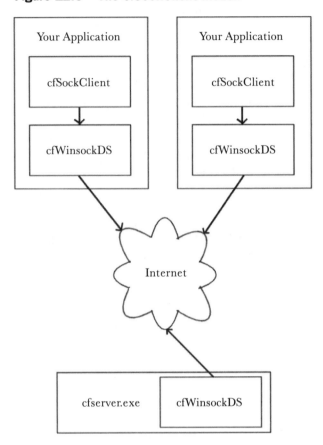

Registering the cfSockClient Object on Your Computer

Before you can use the cfSockClient OLE server, it must be registered. To register it, open the References window by selecting References... from the Project menu. Locate "Carl Franklin's OLE Winsock Client" in the list and check it off. If it is not there, click the Browse button and locate it in the sample code directory as cfSocket\client\cfSocket.dll.

If you are just going to mess around with it and maybe even modify it, you don't have to register it as a DLL. Instead, you can register it as a VB project as it is running. To do this, run a separate instance of VB just for cfSockClient. The project name is cfSocket.vbp. From another instance of VB, select the References menu option from the Tools menu. You will see near the bottom the description "Carl Franklin's OLE Winsock client." Select the checkbox next to it, and you are ready to access cfSockClient from Visual Basic.

Using a cfSockClient Object

Take a look at the code for this hypothetical application. A connection is made using the username "john smith" and the password "password". Once connected, it downloads the daily news file (DailyNews.Txt) from the server's "news" directory and puts it on the Windows Desktop for your reading pleasure. The server does not exist, but all you have to do to bring it to life is run the server code and place the file in a news subdirectory off of the server's path. Figure 12.6 shows an example of this.

Figure 12.6   Hypothetical usage of cfSockClient class to download daily news.

```
"-- Create a cfSockClient object
Dim MyClient As New cfSockClient

"-- Set the Server's name and the app's port number
MyClient.ServerName = "cf.blahbarahmazabbazabba.com"
MyClient.ServerPort = 3000

"-- Specify your username and password
MyClient.UserName = "john smith"
MyClient.Password = "password"

"-- Try to connect by invoking the Connect method.
On Error Resume Next
MyClient.Connect

"-- Could we connect?
If Err Then
    "-- Something went wrong. Display an error.
    MsgBox Error
Else
    "-- We've connected.
    "-- Download the file "DailyNews.Txt" and
    "   put it on the Windows 95 desktop.
    Err = 0
    MyClient.GetFile "\news\DailyNews.Txt", "c:\windows\desktop\DailyNews.Txt"
    "-- Did an error occur?
    If Err Then
```

Figure 12.6   Continued.

```
        MsgBox Error
     End If

     "-- Disconnect from the server
     MyClient.Disconnect
End If
```

You could place this code in the Form_Load of a brand new project and have a complete Internet application. The interface is deceptively simple (that's the idea). The client DLL does the real work. Let's take a look at the code in the cfSockClient project (cfSocket.vbp).

Inside the cfSockClient OLE Server

The cfSockClient project consists of two files:

cfclient.cls.   The cfSockClient class exposed via OLE.

cfdata.cls.   The data class member of cfSockClient.

Take a look at the Class_Initialize event of cfclient.cls, where two WinSock objects are created (Socket1 and Socket2). Socket1 is for communicating commands and data with the server, and Socket2 is for transferring files. Since this object can use both the dsSocket WinSock object or the Microsoft Winsock object, there has to be code to load either, depending on which one you want to use. A Boolean constant named bUsingMS determines which library to use as the Winsock layer. You can change this with the following procedure.

1. Load the References list by selecting "References..." from the Project menu.

2. Uncheck "Carl Franklin's Winsock Object (Dolphin)."

3. Check off "Carl Franklin's Winsock Object (Microsoft)."

4. In the General Declarations section of cfclient.cls, comment the two lines that define Socket1 and Socket2 as New cfWinsockDS, and uncomment the two lines that define Socket1 and Socket2 as New cfWinsockMS.

5. In the same section, change the value of constant bUsingMS to True.

There might be some confusion between the SendBlockSize property and the RecvBlockSize property. The RecvBlockSize property is a direct wrapper for dsSocket's DataSize property, which controls the maximum number of bytes passed to you via Socket2's wsReceive event. If your application has received 20,000 bytes, and the DataSize is 4,000, then the Receive event could fire as few as five times. If the DataSize is 10,000, then it would be possible for the Receive event to fire only twice. DataSize represents only the maximum size of data. The underlying network really decides how big these chunks of data will be. RecvBlockSize has no effect when using the Microsoft Winsock object.

The SendBlockSize property is a setting used within the code of the cfSockClient class. When sending data to the server, SendBlockSize is the size of each transmitted chunk of data. If the Data object is populated with 22,000 bytes of data, and SendBlockSize is set to 4,000, then six chunks will be sent. The first five chunks will be 4,000 bytes, and the last chunk will be 2,000 bytes.

Figure 12.7 shows the declarations section of the cfSockClient class. The variables that are defined as Public are properties that do not require "Get" and "Let" code. In other words, they are just dynamic values. No action has to be taken when they are set or read. The variables that are created with Dim and the error constants are module-level variables, the same as with a form or a code module.

Figure 12.7   cfSockClient declarations section.

```
'-- cfSockClient OLE Class
Option Explicit
'-------------------------------------------------
'CFCLIENT.CLS
'Copyright 1998 by Carl Franklin
'Unauthorized reproduction in any medium of this
'source code is strictly prohibited without written
'permission from the author and John Wiley & Sons.
'-------------------------------------------------


'----------- Public flat Properties and classes -----

'-- The cfData class wraps a 2-dimensional array for easy
'    data transportation
Public Data As New cfData

'-- Maximum size of outgoing packets. (default = 8K)
Public SendBlockSize As Integer

'-- The Server's Port
Public ServerPort As Long
```

Figure 12.7 *Continued.*

```
'-- UserName and Password are used to connect to the server app
'    and are not required to make a socket connection. They are
'    used to identify the client user to the server system. If they
'    are not recognized by the server, the connection will close.
Public UserName As String
Public Password As String

'-- CommandTimeout is the number of seconds to wait after sending
'    a command for a response from the server. The default is 0
'    which means that the client waits forever.
Public CommandTimeout As Long

Public lRows As Long
Public lCols As Long
Public lCurRow As Long
Public lCurCol As Long
Public szLeftOver As String
Public szCmd As String

'-- Custom Event
Event ReceiveCmd(Command As String, Data As cfData)

'------------ Internal Variables -------------------------

'-- Winsock items
'    Change these to cfWinsockMS to use the Microsoft
'    Winsock control. NOTE: You must change the reference
'    to cfWinsockMS. You also need to change
'    the bUsingMS boolean constant to True
Private WithEvents Socket1 As cfWinsockDS
Private WithEvents Socket2 As cfWinsockDS
'Private WithEvents Socket1 As cfWinsockMS
'Private WithEvents Socket2 As cfWinsockMS
'-- Set this to True if using cfWinsockMS
Const bUsingMS As Boolean = False

'-- API Calls
Private Declare Function GetWindowsDirectory Lib "kernel32" _
    Alias "GetWindowsDirectoryA" (ByVal lpBuffer As String, _
    ByVal nSize As Long) As Long

'-- Windows directory
Private szWindowsDir    As String
'-- Host Name (ex: www.worldtrain.com)
```

Continues

Figure 12.7   cfSockClient declarations section. *(Continued)*

```
Private szHostName As String
'-- Internal Dot Address (ex: 199.105.125.50)
Private szDotAddr As String
'-- Internal variable used for communication
'   between the object and the form.
Private m_CommandReturned As Boolean
'-- Set to True to print out debug messages
Private m_DebugMode      As Boolean
'-- Set to the FileNumber of the file
'   being received.
Private m_GetFileNum     As Integer
'-- Connect Flag
Private m_Connected      As Boolean


'------------ Error Private Constants ----------------------------

'-- No address was specified when attempting to connect to the server
Private Const ERR_NOADDRESS = 1
'-- No port was specified when attempting to connect to the server
Private Const ERR_NOPORT = 2
'-- The username and password were not accepted by the host. Connection closed.
Private Const ERR_BADUSERPASS = 3
'-- An invalid row or column was specified when accessing the DataSet property
Private Const ERR_INVALID_ROWCOL = 4
'-- A timeout occurred when sending a command to the server.
Private Const ERR_COMMAND_TIMEOUT = 5
'-- General Winsock error
Private Const ERR_WINSOCK = 7
'-- An error occurred while sending the file
Private Const ERR_SENDFILE = 8
'-- An attempt to make a data connection failed
Private Const ERR_BADDATACONNECTION = 9
'-- Unexpected empty file
Private Const ERR_ZEROBYTEFILE = 10
'-- Problem while receiving file
Private Const ERR_GETFILE = 11
```

The statement, **Public Data As New cfData** makes the Data object a dependent of the cfSockClient object. Figure 12.8 shows an example of how to access the Data object.

Figure 12.8   Accessing the Data object of a cfSockClient class.

```
'-- Create a new cfSockClient object
Dim MyClient As New cfSockClient

'-- Allocate one row and one column in the cfData member
MyClient.Data.Resize 1, 1

'-- Assign a string to this field
MyClient.Data.DataSet(1,1) =   "Hello There"
```

Initialization

When the cfSockClient object is created the Class_Initialize procedure executes. This is where the default values are set. Figure 12.9 shows this code.

Figure 12.9   cfSockClient initialization code.

```
Private Sub Class_Initialize()

    Dim lLen       As Long
    Dim szBuffer   As String

    If bUsingMS = True Then
        Set Socket1 = CreateObject("cfWinsockMSClass.cfWinsockMS")
        Set Socket2 = CreateObject("cfWinsockMSClass.cfWinsockMS")
    Else
        Set Socket1 = CreateObject("cfWinsockDSClass.cfWinsockDS")
        Set Socket2 = CreateObject("cfWinsockDSClass.cfWinsockDS")
    End If
    Socket1.LineMode = False
    Socket2.LineMode = False

    '-- Lower these values to 1000 if you have
    '   trouble sending and receiving.
    RecvBlockSize = 8192
    SendBlockSize = 8192
    CommandTimeout = 15

    szBuffer = Space$(200)
    lLen = GetWindowsDirectory(szBuffer, Len(szBuffer))
    If lLen Then
        szWindowsDir = Left$(szBuffer, lLen)
```

Continues

Figure 12.9   cfSockClient initialization code. (*Continued*)

```
    End If

    'DownloadDir = szWindowsDir & "\desktop"

    m_DebugMode = True

End Sub
```

Connecting to the Server

The Connect method connects to the server, the address and port of which must be specified in the ServerName or ServerDotAddr and ServerPort properties. Figure 12.10 shows the code for the Connect method.

Figure 12.10   The Connect method of the cfSockClient class.

```
Public Sub Connect()
'-- This function connects to a cfSock Server application

    Dim szAddress    As String

    '-- Name specified?
    If Len(szHostName) = 0 Then
        If Len(szDotAddr) = 0 Then
            '-- Neither type of address specified. Error out.
            Err.Raise vbObjectError + ERR_NOADDRESS, App.EXEName, _
             "The server's host name or dot address was not " _
             "specified when trying to connect."
            Exit Sub
        Else
            szAddress = szDotAddr
        End If
    Else
        szAddress = szHostName
    End If

    '-- Port specified?
    If ServerPort = 0 Then
        '-- No port specified. Error out.
        Err.Raise vbObjectError + ERR_NOPORT, App.EXEName, _
```

Figure 12.10   *Continued.*

```
            "The server's port was not specified when trying to connect."
        Exit Sub
    End If

    '-- Attempt to connect.
    If Socket1.SocketConnect(ServerPort, szAddress, (CommandTimeout)) Then
        Err.Raise vbObjectError + ERR_WINSOCK, App.EXEName, _
        "Winsock Error" & Str$(Err) & ": " & Error
        Exit Sub
    End If

    '-- Verify the username and password. The server may or may not be
    '   using security. If not, then any values are accepted.
    Data.Resize 1, 2
    Data.DataSet(1, 1) = UserName
    Data.DataSet(1, 2) = Password

    SendCommand "LOGIN"

    If Data.DataSet(1, 1) = "NO" Then
        '-- The user was not allowed access to the system.
        Err.Raise vbObjectError + ERR_BADUSERPASS, App.EXEName, _
        "Your username and password were not accepted by the host." & _
        "Access denied."
    End If

End Sub
```

The first two blocks of code (shown separately in Figure 12.11) verify that the port is specified, and that either a remote name or IP address is specified. If one of these conditions are not met, either the NO_ADDRESS or NO_PORT errors are returned.

Figure 12.11   Connect method. The server name and port number are verified.

```
'-- Name specified?
    If Len(szHostName) = 0 Then
        If Len(szDotAddr) = 0 Then
            '-- Neither type of address specified. Error out.
            Err.Raise vbObjectError + ERR_NOADDRESS, App.EXEName, _
            "The server's host name or dot address was not " _
```

Continues

```
            "specified when trying to connect."
        Exit Sub
    Else
        szAddress = szDotAddr
    End If
Else
    szAddress = szHostName
End If

'-- Port specified?
If ServerPort = 0 Then
    '-- No port specified. Error out.
    Err.Raise vbObjectError + ERR_NOPORT, App.EXEName, _
     "The server's port was not specified when trying to connect."
    Exit Sub
End If
```

Next, an attempt is made to connect to the server by calling SocketConnect. If the connection is not made then cfSockClient raises an error. Errors are handled by the standard Err object. To trap errors, use On Error Resume Next when calling Connect.

The next block of code (shown separately in Figure 12.12) is a good first example of sending a command with data to the server. The LOGIN command, as defined by both client and server, logs the client into the server system. Optionally, the server can verify the client and refuse connection if the UserName and/or Password are invalid. The UserName and Password specified here exist only for access to your server. If you wish to grant access to everyone, you do not need to specify them. The LOGIN command accepts one row and two columns of data, namely the UserName and Password.

Figure 12.12   Sending the LOGIN command to the Internet server.

```
'-- Verify the username and password. The server may or may not be
    '   using security. If not, then any values are accepted.
    Data.Resize 1, 2
    Data.DataSet(1, 1) = UserName
    Data.DataSet(1, 2) = Password
    SendCommand "LOGIN"
```

Figure 12.13   Testing to see if the server refused your connection.

```
If Data.DataSet(1, 1) = "NO" Then
        '-- The user was not allowed access to the system.
        Err.Raise vbObjectError + ERR_BADUSERPASS, App.EXEName, _
         "Your username and password were not accepted by the host." & _
         "Access denied."
    End If
```

To set this data before sending the command, the Resize method is invoked, and the strings are assigned to the DataSet array property. SendCommand is an internal routine that actually sends the command and the data. We'll look at this routine shortly.

After the SendCommand routine returns, the Data object will be filled and sized with the data sent back from the server, if any. If the connection is refused by the server, then the server will send back the word "NO"; otherwise it will send "OK." Either way, the data is sent in one row and one column. A simple test for the word "NO" determines if we have permission or not. This little piece of code is broken out in Figure 12.13.

Sending Data to the Server

SendCommand is a method of the cfSockClient class. It lets you send a command to the server along with a two-dimensional array of data via the Data object member. This is where the real data transfer protocol is at work. Figure 12.14 shows the SendCommand Method.

Figure 12.14   The SendCommand property of the cfSockClient class.

```
Public Sub SendCommand(ThisCommand As String)
'-- The SendCommand method sends a command string along with the contents
'    of the Data object to the server.

    Dim DoneTime
    Dim szSendMe As String
    Dim lCol As Long
    Dim lRow As Long

    lRows = 0
    lCols = 0                                               Continues
```

```
lCurRow = 0
lCurCol = 0
szLeftOver = ""
szCmd = ""

'-- Convert the command to uppercase
ThisCommand = UCase$(ThisCommand)

'-- What command is being issued? (for documentation only)
Select Case ThisCommand
    Case "LOGIN"
        '-- 1,1 = Username
        '   2,1 = Password
    Case "SENDFILE"
        '-- 1,1 = File Name (sans path)
        '   2,1 = File Size (in bytes)
        '   3,1 = File Type
        '           0 = Binary (default)
        '          -1 = Text (one line per row)
        '   4,1 through ?,1 = Data
    Case "GETFILE"
        '-- 1,1 = File Name (full path)
        '   2,1 = File Type
        '           0 = Binary (default)
        '          -1 = Text (one line per row)
End Select

'-- Set the internal flag for returned command.
m_CommandReturned = False

'-- Generate the string(s) to send

'-- The header consists of the command, followed by the number of rows
'   and number of columns in the data set.
szSendMe = Format$(ThisCommand, "@@@@@@@@@@") & _
 Format$(Trim$(Str$(Data.Rows)), "@@@@@") & _
 Format$(Trim$(Str$(Data.Cols)), "@@@@@")

'-- For each field or cell, send the size of the field (5) followed by
'   the data itself.
For lRow = 1 To Data.Rows
    For lCol = 1 To Data.Cols
        szSendMe = szSendMe _
```

Figure 12.14 *Continued.*

```
                & Format$(LTrim$(Str$(Len(Data.DataSet(lRow, lCol))))), "@@@@@") _
                & Data.DataSet(lRow, lCol)
            Next
            '-- If the string is getting too big, send what we've got
            If Len(szSendMe) >= SendBlockSize Then
                If m_DebugMode Then
                    Debug.Print "Sending" & Str$(Len(szSendMe)) & " bytes"
                End If
                Socket1.SendData szSendMe
                szSendMe = ""
            End If
        Next


        '-- If there is data to send, send it.
        If Len(szSendMe) Then
            If m_DebugMode Then
                Debug.Print "Sending" & Str$(Len(szSendMe)) & " bytes"
            End If
            Socket1.SendData szSendMe
            szSendMe = ""
        End If


        '-- At what time do we timeout?
        If CommandTimeout Then
            DoneTime = DateAdd("s", CommandTimeout, Now)
        End If


        '-- Wait until you get a response or timeout one or the other.
        Do
            DoEvents
            '-- Are we supposed to check for timeout?
            If CommandTimeout Then
                '-- Check for timeout
                If Now >= DoneTime Then
                    '-- Time's up. Error out.
                    Err.Raise vbObjectError + ERR_COMMAND_TIMEOUT, _
                     App.EXEName, "A command was sent to the server, " & _
                     "but a response was not received in time."
                    Exit Do
                End If
            End If
        Loop Until m_CommandReturned
End Sub
```

The first thing that happens in SendCommand is that the command is converted to uppercase. Then a Select Case statement is executed. This Select Case is really for documentation, but it's nice to have if you need to do any special processing at the OLE server before a command and data are sent.

The variable m_CommandReturned is set True in the Socket1_wsReceive event after a response is received from the server and data has been collected. In this portion of the code, the m_CommandReturned variable is set to False.

```
'-- Set the internal flag for returned command.
m_CommandReturned = False
```

At this point, the data is prepared to be sent to the server. All the data is copied into a string variable, szSendMe, and sent to the server. The data is sent in chunks, the size of which is determined by the SendBlockSize property. The default size for one block of data sent is 8192 bytes.

Next, a 20-character header is created, formatted as follows:

Command	10 chars
Rows	5 chars
Columns	5 chars

The Rows and Columns values are the number of rows and columns in the Data.DataSet array that will be sent. The variable szSendMe is used to create the string to be sent. First it is initialized as the header as follows:

```
'-- Generate the string(s) to send

'-- The header consists of the command, followed by the number of rows
'   and number of columns in the data set.
szSendMe = Format$(ThisCommand, "@@@@@@@@@@") & _
  Format$(Trim$(Str$(Data.Rows)), "@@@@@") & _
  Format$(Trim$(Str$(Data.Cols)), "@@@@@")
```

Notice the Format$ function. Format$ is a powerful string function in Visual Basic that performs a variety of string formatting tasks. The first argument is the string to format, and the second is a "format string." The at-sign character represents a space. The Format$ statement is essentially padding a string to a number of spaces. The result of the previous code might look like this:

```
Data:       LOGIN    4    2
            --------------------
Position:   12345678901234567890
```

The first ten characters are the command, LOGIN. Characters 11 through 15 represent the number of rows being sent. Characters 16 through 20 represent the number of columns. It might seem like I am beating a dead horse, but I want to be clear about how the protocol works.

After the header is created, the data is added to the string. For each field (array element) added, first a five-byte string length is added, then the data. This makes it easy for the server to interpret the incoming data and place it appropriately in its own cfData class object, which you will then access with your server application.

For example, let's say you are sending a command called GETNEWS that gets a specific text file containing news on a particular subject. There is one row and two columns of attached data. The first column is six characters, and describes the type of news (daily or weekly) and the second column is fifteen characters and defines the area of interest (politics or entertainment). Here is a breakdown of the data that will be sent:

```
Description      Length    Data
--------------------------------------
Command            10     GETNEWS
Rows                5           1
Columns             5           2
Length of (1,1)     5           6
Data in (1,1)       6       DAILY
Length of (1,2)     5          15
Data in (1,2)      15    POLITICS

Total Bytes.......51
```

Since the data is left-padded with spaces, the actual complete 51-byte string sent would look like this:

```
Data:   GETNEWS   1   2   6    DAILY  15  POLITICS
        -------------------------------------------------
Position:  12345678901234567890123456789012345678901234567890
```

Figure 12.15 shows the code that assembles and sends the data. Note that when the buffer gets too big, as defined by the SendBlockSize property, the data is sent and the buffer cleared.

The data is assembled by a loop within a loop. The outside For/Next loop sets lRow from one to the number of rows, and the inside For/Next loop sets lCol from one to the number of columns. Each field is sent prefaced by a five-byte length. In

Figure 12.15 Assembling and sending data (SendCommand).

```
'-- For each field or cell, send the size of the field (5) followed by
'    the data itself.
   For lRow = 1 To Data.Rows
      For lCol = 1 To Data.Cols
         szSendMe = szSendMe _
         & Format$(LTrim$(Str$(Len(Data.DataSet(lRow, lCol)))), "@@@@@") _
         & Data.DataSet(lRow, lCol)
      Next
      '-- If the string is getting too big, send what we've got
      If Len(szSendMe) >= SendBlockSize Then
         If m_DebugMode Then
            Debug.Print "Sending" & Str$(Len(szSendMe)) & " bytes"
         End If
         Socket1.SendData szSendMe
         szSendMe = ""
      End If
   Next

   '-- If there is data to send, send it.
   If Len(szSendMe) Then
      If m_DebugMode Then
         Debug.Print "Sending" & Str$(Len(szSendMe)) & " bytes"
      End If
      Socket1.SendData szSendMe
      szSendMe = ""
   End If
```

other words: For each field, the first five bytes indicate the number of bytes of data that follow for that field.

The routine that actually sends the data to the server is the SendData method of the cfWinsockDS (or cfWinsockMS) object. The only reason you need a SendData routine is to catch and resolve the errors that may occur when trying to send data. The only real error (other than losing your connection) to be concerned with is the Winsock 1.1 error 21035, or Operation Would Block. This occurs when the underlying network is busy sending other data, and cannot send your data right away. Blocking, as it is called, is what happens when an application goes into a tight loop waiting for the availability of some other process; in doing so it locks up the system. For more information on the SendData routine, see Chapter 9, "Using the cfInternet Objects."

The final portion of the SendCommand routine, shown in Figure 12.16, waits for a response from the server, as signified by the m_CommandReturned variable being set to True.

Now let's look at what happens elsewhere while we are in this loop after sending the command, waiting for a response.

Receiving Data from the Server

After the client has sent the server a command, the server will send back a response. Even if there is no data required by the server's response, the server sends a header anyway just to notify the client that it received and processed the command.

When either the cfSockClient class or any other OLE client invokes the SendCommand method, the command and data are sent to the server, and then data is passed back to the client from the server. Socket1 object receives this data. Figure 12.17 shows the wsReceive event procedure of this object.

Figure 12.16   SendCommand waits for a server response.

```
'-- At what time do we timeout?
If CommandTimeout Then
    DoneTime = DateAdd("s", CommandTimeout, Now)
End If


'-- Wait until you get a response or timeout one or the other.
Do
    DoEvents
    '-- Are we supposed to check for timeout?
    If CommandTimeout Then
        '-- Check for timeout
        If Now >= DoneTime Then
            '-- Time's up. Error out.
            Err.Raise vbObjectError + ERR_COMMAND_TIMEOUT, _
            App.EXEName, "A command was sent to the server, " & _
            "but a response was not received in time."
            Exit Do
        End If
    End If
Loop Until m_CommandReturned
```

Figure 12.17   cfSockClient processes raw data in Socket1_wsReceive.

```
Private Sub Socket1_wsReceive(ReceiveData As String)

    Dim lRow As Long
    Dim lCol As Long
    Dim nLenField As Integer

    '-- Append the leftover data (if any) to the buffer passed in.
    ReceiveData = szLeftOver & ReceiveData

    '-- If this is a response from the server, the first 15
    '    bytes will be "REPLYFROMSERVER", followed by 5 bytes
    '    for the number of rows and five bytes for the number
    '    of columns, followed by the field data by row, then
    '    column. For each field, the length of the field followed
    '    by a space and then the data itself is sent.
    If Len(szCmd$) = 0 Then
        If Len(ReceiveData) >= 25 Then
            szCmd = Trim$(Left$(ReceiveData, 15))

            '-- szCmd will be "REPLYFROMSERVER" if this is a
            '    response to a client command,
            '    otherwise it is an unsolicited command.

            '-- This is the header. Extract the number of
            '    rows and columns, and redim the Data_Set array.
            lRows = Val(Mid$(ReceiveData, 16, 5))
            lCols = Val(Mid$(ReceiveData, 21, 5))
            lCurRow = 1
            lCurCol = 1
            If lRows Then
                Data.Resize lRows, lCols
            Else
                Set Data = Nothing
            End If
            '-- Trim the header from the received data.
            ReceiveData = Mid$(ReceiveData, 26)
            szLeftOver = ""
        End If
    End If

    '-- Has the header been received?
    If lRows Then
        '-- Have we not processed all the fields?
```

Figure 12.17 *Continued.*

```
If lCurRow <= lRows Then
    '-- Step through the data
    For lRow = lCurRow To lRows
        For lCol = lCurCol To lCols
            '-- Is there enough data to get the next field size?
            If Len(ReceiveData) < 5 Then
                '-- No. Save the remaining data and scoot.
                lCurRow = lRow
                lCurCol = lCol
                szLeftOver = ReceiveData
                Exit Sub
            Else
                '-- Get the length of the next field (5 chars)
                nLenField = Val(Left$(ReceiveData, 5))
                '-- Are we missing any characters?
                If Len(ReceiveData) < 5 + nLenField Then
                    '-- Yep. Save the remaining data and exit.
                    lCurRow = lRow
                    lCurCol = lCol
                    szLeftOver = ReceiveData
                    Exit Sub
                Else
                    '-- Read the data into the Data_Set array
                    Data.DataSet(lRow, lCol) = _
                      Mid$(ReceiveData, 6, nLenField)
                    '-- Is there any more data here?
                    If Len(ReceiveData) > 5 + nLenField Then
                        '-- Is this NOT the last field of
                        '   the last column?
                        If (lRow < lRows) Or (lCol < lCols) Then
                            '-- Trim this data off the left of
                            '   ReceiveData
                            ReceiveData = Mid$(ReceiveData, _
                             6 + nLenField)
                            If m_DebugMode Then
                                Debug.Print "Field Read"
                            End If
                        Else
                            '-- This is the last field, yet there is
                            '   more data. This may be indicative of
                            '   corrupted string space or a problem
                            '   at the data level of the network.
                            ReceiveData = ""
```

Continues

```
                                      If m_DebugMode Then
                                          Debug.Print "Last Field processed"
                                      End If
                                  End If
                          Else
                              '-- Is this NOT the last field of the
                              '   last column?
                              If (lRow < lRows) Or (lCol < lCols) Then
                                  '-- There is no data left in the
                                  '   buffer, so exit. the Static
                                  '   variables will keep the position.
                                  If lRow < lRows Then
                                      If lCol < lCols Then
                                          lCurCol = lCol + 1
                                          lCurRow = lRow
                                      Else
                                          lCurCol = 1
                                          lCurRow = lRow + 1
                                      End If
                                  Else
                                      lCurCol = lCol + 1
                                      lCurRow = lRow
                                  End If
                                  szLeftOver = ""
                                  If m_DebugMode Then
                                      Debug.Print "Holding the position"
                                      Debug.Print "saving leftovers "
                                  End If
                                  Exit Sub
                              End If
                          End If
                      End If
                  End If
              Next
          Next

      If lRow = lRows + 1 Then
          If szCmd <> "REPLYFROMSERVER" Then
              '-- This is an unsolicited command.
              '   Fire the Command method
              '   at the OLE Client application.
              RaiseEvent ReceiveCmd(szCmd, Data)
```

Figure 12.17 *Continued.*

```
            End If

            '-- Zero all the static variables.
            lCurRow = 0
            lCurCol = 0
            lRows = 0
            lCols = 0
            szLeftOver = ""
            szCmd = ""

            '-- Done.
            m_CommandReturned = True
        End If
    End If
Else
    '-- Some unidentified data was received.. print it in
    '   the debug window if in design mode.
    If m_DebugMode Then
        Debug.Print ReceiveData
    End If
End If

End Sub
```

This is perhaps the second most complex piece of code in the cfSock library, the first most complex being the equivalent Receive event on the server side. Let's break down what is happening here. First of all, this event is called any time the client receives any type of data from the server. This is the entry point into the client object for data from the server. The RecvBlockSize property (which is actually dsSocket's DataSize property) determines the maximum number of bytes that the ReceiveData variable can possibly be. The underlying network determines the actual size for each chunk of data that comes up the stack, but RecvBlockSize is the maximum size that cfSockClient receives at any given time.

Since the server's response including data can be larger than the amount of data able to be passed into the wsReceive event, multiple Receive events may and often do occur. The trick is, then, to identify the data as it comes in so it can be processed properly. The only task in the wsReceive event is to get the raw data stream into the Data object, the cfData subordinate class of the cfSockClient class that holds data.

You will always be faced with the task of interpreting received data, even if you are not using the cfSockClient class, and you are writing your own Internet protocol with cfWinsock or some other communications device. This task is the essence of communications programming, since no other task is quite as important. Sending is easy. It's receiving and processing data that is the most critical. Think about it. If you could rely only on your ears for sensory input, and they were so damaged that life to you sounded like sideband bleedover on a 40-channel CB radio or the teacher in Charlie Brown's math class, you would not be able to communicate at all. But I digress.

The first thing the code does is to determine whether this is a new response from the server or data from the current response. When the server sends a response, the first 15 characters are REPLYFROMSERVER. If we receive this, then the first 25 bytes of data will be the header, which is defined as follows.

```
Description             Length  Data
----------------------------------------
Header ID                  15   REPLYFROMSERVER
Rows                        5   ?
Columns                     5   ?
```

If a command (szCmd) has not yet been received, meaning that the client is ready to accept a new command from the server, and the ReceiveData is at least 25 bytes, then the data being passed to Socket1_wsReceive is the command. The first task is to identify the command and break down the header. First, the number of rows and the number of columns are stored in two Static long integer variables, lRows and lCols. When you define a local variable as static its value is retained when the routine is exited, but it exists only within the local procedure. So, once lCols and lRows are set, their values remain until set to zero. Two other static long integer variables, lCurRow and lCurCol hold the next row and column to be read. These are initialized to 1 (the first row and column) when the header is received. Next, the Data object member is resized to the number of rows and columns, and the header is trimmed from the left of the received data string.

I purposely skipped over the top line, which references the szLeftOver variable. I'll discuss that in a moment or two.

The second (bigger) block of code is the meat of the procedure. After determining that the header has been received and there are still fields of data to be read, the remaining fields are extracted and placed into the Data object. This is done in a manner similar to the way the client sends data to the server, by using a loop within a loop.

The variables lRow and lCol (singular) are the current row and column being read, starting from where the reading last left off. Starting with the current row and column, the loops iterate through all rows and columns being received. If at any time there is not enough data left in the ReceiveData string to determine either the length of the next field, or the field itself, the remaining data is saved off in the szLeftOver variable, a static local string variable. The next time the wsReceive event is fired, szLeftOver is tacked onto the beginning of ReceiveData at the top of the procedure.

After all of the data has been received and put in the Data object, the static variables are zeroed, or returned to their default values, and the global flag m_CommandReturned is set to True. If you remember, in the SendCommand method, after the client sends a command to the server, it waits in a loop calling DoEvents waiting for m_CommandReturned to equal True or a timeout to occur, one or the other. This is where the m_CommandReturned flag is set, indicating that the command has been processed by the server, and that a response has been received that may or may not include data. You can tell this, of course, by reading the Rows and Cols properties of the client's Data object.

The Debug Flag

You shouldn't need to debug my code, but in case you really want to see what's happening in this code, you can set the global variable, m_DebugMode equal to True in the Class_Initialize event. When you run cfSockClient in the Visual Basic environment, debug messages will print in the debug window during operation.

Sending a File to the Server

To send a file to the server, use the SendFile method. SendFile is a wrapper for the SendCommand method in which you specify the local filename and a transfer mode. SendFile places the name of the file into the Data Object and sends the SENDFILE command, which tells the server to prepare for a file transfer. The server sends back a port number for cfSockClient to connect to and send the file data. cfSockClient closes the port after sending the file.

Figure 12.18 shows you how to send a file.

Figure 12.18   The SendFile method.

```
'-- Assuming you are connected already!
On Error Resume Next
cfSocket.SendFile "C:\WINDOWS\WINLOGO.BMP"
If Err Then                                        Continues
```

Figure 12.18   The SendFile method. *(Continued)*

```
    MsgBox Error, vbExclamation, App.Title
End If

Public Sub SendFile(szFileName As String)
'-- Sends a file

    Dim szAddress       As String
    Dim szTemp          As String
    Dim szFileTitle     As String

    Dim nFileNum        As Integer
    Dim nRemainder      As Integer
    Dim nConnectError   As Integer

    Dim lCounter        As Long
    Dim lIndex          As Long
    Dim lNumBlocks      As Long
    Dim lFileSize       As Long
    Dim lPort           As Long
    Dim Address         As String

    On Error GoTo SendFileError

    '-- Send the SENDFILE Command to tell the server
    '    we want to send a file.

    '    1,1 = File Name (sans path)
    '    2,1 = Target Directory (optional)
    '    3,1 = File Size
    szFileTitle = szJustTheFileName(szFileName)
    Data.Resize 3, 1
    Data.DataSet(1, 1) = szFileTitle
    Data.DataSet(2, 1) = ""
    Data.DataSet(3, 1) = Trim$(Str$(FileLen(szFileName)))

    SendCommand "SENDFILE"

    If Data.Rows Then
        If Data.DataSet(1, 1) <> "OK" Then
            Err.Raise vbObjectError + ERR_SENDFILE, App.EXEName, _
              Data.DataSet(1, 1)
            Exit Sub
        End If
```

Figure 12.18 *Continued.*

```
End If

'-- Connect to the new port for the data connection
If bUsingMS = True Then
    Address = Socket1.Control.RemoteHostIP
Else
    Address = Socket1.Control.RemoteDotAddr
End If
If Socket2.SocketConnect(Val(Data.DataSet(2, 1)), Address, 15) Then
    Err.Raise vbObjectError + ERR_BADDATACONNECTION, App.EXEName, _
      "Could Not Make Data Connection"
    Exit Sub
End If

'-- Open the file
nFileNum = FreeFile
Open szFileName For Binary As nFileNum

'-- Get the size information
lFileSize = LOF(nFileNum)
If lFileSize = 0 Then
    Close nFileNum
    Err.Raise vbObjectError + ERR_ZEROBYTEFILE, App.EXEName, _
      "Zero byte file"
    Exit Sub
End If

lNumBlocks = lFileSize \ SendBlockSize
nRemainder = lFileSize Mod SendBlockSize

'-- Send the data
For lIndex = 1 To lNumBlocks
    szTemp = Space$(SendBlockSize)
    Get #nFileNum, , szTemp
    Socket2.SendData szTemp
Next
If nRemainder Then
    szTemp = Space$(nRemainder)
    Get #nFileNum, , szTemp
    Socket2.SendData szTemp
End If

'-- Close the file
```

Continues

Figure 12.18   The SendFile method. _(Continued)_

```
    Close nFileNum

    '-- Close the socket
    Socket2.Disconnect

    Exit Sub

SendFileError:

    'On Error Resume Next
    '-- Raise the error here
    Close nFileNum
    Socket2.Disconnect
    Exit Sub

End Sub
```

The first thing that happens is the SENDFILE command is sent to the server with three fields. The first field is the file name with no path information. This will be the name of the file written on the server. The second parameter is an optional path on the server where the file should be stored, and the third parameter is the size of the file in bytes. This is used on the server to display file transfer status information. I will discuss what happens on the server side shortly.

If the server has a problem opening the file for writing on the server, or any other error, it will return a single row with one column containing the error message. If there was no problem, then the first row, column 1 contains OK and the second row, column 1 contains a port number. cfSockClient then connects to the server on the designated port. This is called the data connection. To keep things easy and straightforward, a separate data connection is used for sending and receiving files. Once the data connection is established, the local file is opened, and the file is sent through the data connection in chunks, the size of which is set with the SendBlockSize property (the default size is 8,192 bytes). The number of chunks is determined by dividing the total size of the file by the block size. Using the Mod operator you can determine the size of the last block, which is always less than the block size (or zero, if the file size is an even multiple of the block size).

Once the file has been completely sent, the local file is closed, the data connection is disconnected, and the routine exits.

Receiving a File from the Server

To receive a file from the server, use the GetFile method. GetFile is a wrapper for the SendCommand property which takes two arguments, the remote filename to send and the local file name to save. Here is a sample use of the GetFile Method:

```
On Error Resume Next
cfSocket.GetFile "\bin\files\myfile.zip", "c:\windows\desktop\myfile.zip"
If Err Then
    MsgBox Error, vbInformation
End IF
```

The remote filename is relative to the server. That is, \bin\files\myfile.zip is a reference to a file on the server, not the client. The second argument specifies a local file name. Figure 12.19 shows the GetFile method.

Figure 12.19   The GetFile method.

```
Public Sub GetFile(szFileName As String, szSaveFileName As String)

    Dim Address As String

    If Len(szSaveFileName) = 0 Then
        Err.Raise vbObjectError + ERR_GETFILE, App.EXEName, _
          "No destination file specified"
        Exit Sub
    End If


    '-- Send the GETFILE command.
    '   1,1 = File Name
    Data.Resize 1, 1
    Data.DataSet(1, 1) = szFileName
    SendCommand "GETFILE"
    If Data.Rows >= 2 Then
        If Data.DataSet(1, 1) <> "OK" Then
            Err.Raise vbObjectError + ERR_GETFILE, App.EXEName, _
              Data.DataSet(2, 2)
            Exit Sub
        End If
    Else
        Err.Raise vbObjectError + ERR_GETFILE, App.EXEName, _
          "Server did not specify a socket for the data connection"
        Exit Sub
    End If
```

Continues

Figure 12.19   The GetFile method. *(Continued)*

```
'-- Open the file
m_GetFileNum = FreeFile
Open szSaveFileName For Binary As m_GetFileNum

'-- Connect to the new port for the data connection
If bUsingMS = True Then
    Address = Socket1.Control.RemoteHostIP
Else
    Address = Socket1.Control.RemoteDotAddr
End If
If Socket2.SocketConnect(Val(Data.DataSet(2, 1)), Address, 15) Then
    m_GetFileNum = 0
    Close m_GetFileNum
    Err.Raise vbObjectError + ERR_BADDATACONNECTION, App.EXEName, _
      "Could Not Make Data Connection"
    Exit Sub
End If

'-- Send a "Start" byte
Socket2.SendData vbCrLf

'-- Wait until the file has been received
Do
    DoEvents
Loop Until m_GetFileNum = 0

End Sub
```

After verifying that a local filename was specified cfSockClient prepares to send the GETFILE command to the server application. Internally, the GETFILE command (not the method) accepts only one parameter, the server filename. Just as with the SendFile method, GetFile makes a data connection to the port that is passed back from the server in Data(2,1). However, GetFile interacts with the Socket2 object, which actually receives the file.

After the data connection is made with Socket2, the local file is opened, and a carriage return/linefeed is sent on the data connection to tell the server to start sending the file. At that point, the code goes into a loop until m_GetFileNum (the file number of the received file) is set to zero, which happens either when the data connection is closed or an error occurs. Figure 12.20 shows the Socket2_wsReceive event, which saves the file data to disk.

Figure 12.20   Socket2 receives file data.

```
Private Sub Socket2_wsReceive(ReceiveData As String)

    If m_GetFileNum Then
        Put #m_GetFileNum, , ReceiveData
    End If

End Sub
```

Once the file has been sent, the server closes the data connection. Figure 12.21 shows the Socket2_wsClose event, in which the received file is closed. The m_GetFileNum variable is set to zero, and the loop at the bottom of the GetFile method exits.

The CFServer Application

CFServer, shown in Figure 12.22, is an easily modifiable application that I wrote to compliment the cfSockClient object. There are only two options on the main screen: The port number to listen to and the download directory, where received files are stored. Pressing the Start button starts the server service. Pressing the Pause button causes the server to stop accepting new connections. When the server is paused, the Pause button's Caption says Resume, and pressing it will resume the service. Pressing Stop will close all connections and cause the server to refuse any new connections.

Figure 12.21   The received file is written to disk when the data connection closes.

```
Private Sub Socket2_wsClose(ErrorCode As Integer, ErrorDesc As String)

    If m_GetFileNum Then
        Close m_GetFileNum
        m_GetFileNum = 0
    End If

    If ErrorCode Then
        Err.Raise vbObjectError + ERR_WINSOCK, App.EXEName, _
            "Socket2 Error" & Str$(ErrorCode) & ": " & ErrorDesc
    End If

End Sub
```

Figure 12.22   The CFServer application.

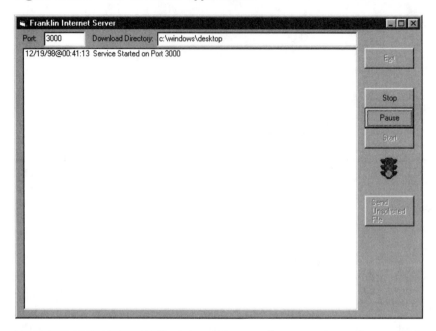

The internal mechanism for communicating with cfSockClient objects is exactly the same as within the cfSockClient class, except that code has been added to handle the requirements of multiple simultaneous connections.

Easy To Modify

When modifying the server, you really only have to be concerned with one internal subroutine, ProcessCommand, which is shown in Figure 12.23.

Figure 12.23 CFServer's ProcessCommand routine in the server application.

```
Sub ProcessCommand(Index As Integer, szCmd As String, Data As cfData)
'-- This is where server commands are processed and data
'    is sent back to the server. If no data is to be sent, then
'    one row and one column is sent with the data set to "ACK"

'-- To add a new command to the "repertoire", simply perform a select
'    case on the command string, use the data in the Data object,
```

Figure 12.23 *Continued.*

```
'   do your thing, and set the return data in the Data object.

    Dim szUsername  As String
    Dim szPassword  As String
    Dim szDir       As String
    Dim szTargetDir As String

    Dim nCtrlIndex  As Integer
    Dim nThere      As Integer
    Dim nFileNum    As Integer
    Dim lIndex      As Integer
    Dim nIndex      As Integer


    ReDim szSQLData(1 To 1, 1 To 1) As String

    DisplayMessage szCmd & " " & Status(Index).szDotAddress

    Select Case szCmd
        Case "LOGIN"
            '-- Do an optional security check here
            szUsername = Data.DataSet(1, 1)
            szPassword = Data.DataSet(1, 2)

        '-- Do security check against a user database right here ----

            '-- Send back "OK" if logged in, or "NO" if not logged in.
            Data.Resize 1, 1
            Data.DataSet(1, 1) = "OK"

            Status(Index).szUsername = szUsername
            Status(Index).szPassword = szPassword

            DisplayMessage szUsername & " logged in."

        Case "SENDFILE"
            '-- Is the data connection already in use?
            If Status(Index).DataAction Then
                Data.Resize 1, 1
                Data.DataSet(1, 1) = "Data Connection In Use"
                Exit Sub
            End If

            '-- Was a target directory specified?
```

Continues

Figure 12.23   CFServer's ProcessCommand routine in the server application.
(Continued)

```
szTargetDir = Data.DataSet(2, 1)
If Len(szTargetDir) Then
    '-- See if the directory exists.
    szDir = Dir$(szTargetDir, vbDirectory)
    If Len(szDir) Then
        Do
            If GetAttr(szDir) And vbDirectory Then
                If szDir <> "." And szDir <> ".." Then
                    nThere = True
                    Exit Do
                End If
            Else
                Exit Do
            End If
            szDir = Dir$()
        Loop
        If Not nThere Then
            '-- The directory does not exist.
            Data.Resize 1, 1
            Data.DataSet(1, 1) = "Cannot create file on server"
            Exit Sub
        End If
    Else
        '-- The directory does not exist.
        Data.Resize 1, 1
        Data.DataSet(1, 1) = "Cannot create file on server"
        Exit Sub
    End If
End If

On Error Resume Next
'-- Load the data answer and data connection Sockets controls
'   for the file xfer and tell the answer socket to listen
Load frmServer.dssData(Index)
Load frmServer.dssDataAnswer(Index)
Status(Index).DataAction = DATA_ACTION_CLIENT_TO_SERVER
frmServer.dssDataAnswer(Index).Action = SOCK_ACTION_LISTEN

'-- Save the path and filename of the file to be received.
If Len(szTargetDir) = 0 Then
    szTargetDir = frmServer.txtDownloadDir
End If
```

Figure 12.23 *Continued.*

```
            If Right(szTargetDir, 1) <> "\" Then
                szTargetDir = szTargetDir & "\"
            End If
            Status(Index).szFileName = szTargetDir & Data.DataSet(1, 1)
            Status(Index).FileSize = Val(Data.DataSet(3, 1))

            '-- Send back the OK, with the port number
            Data.Resize 2, 1
            Data.DataSet(1, 1) = "OK"
            Data.DataSet(2, 1) = _
              Trim$(Str$(frmServer.dssDataAnswer(Index).LocalPort))

        Case "GETFILE"
            '-- Does the file exist?
            If Len(Dir$(Data.DataSet(1, 1))) = 0 Then
                Data.Resize 1, 1
                Data.DataSet(1, 1) = "File Not Found"
                Exit Sub
            End If

            On Error Resume Next
            '-- Load the data answer and data connection Sockets controls
            '   for the file xfer and tell the answer socket to listen
            Load frmServer.dssData(Index)
            Load frmServer.dssDataAnswer(Index)

            On Error GoTo 0

            Status(Index).szFileName = Data.DataSet(1, 1)
            Status(Index).FileSize = FileLen(Data.DataSet(1, 1))
            Status(Index).DataAction = DATA_ACTION_SERVER_TO_CLIENT
            frmServer.dssDataAnswer(Index).Action = SOCK_ACTION_LISTEN

            '-- Send back the OK, with the port number
            Data.Resize 2, 1
            Data.DataSet(1, 1) = "OK"
            Data.DataSet(2, 1) = _
              Trim$(Str$(frmServer.dssDataAnswer(Index).LocalPort))

    End Select

End Sub
```

The ProcessCommand routine is called after the command and data have been properly received and before the Data object is sent back to the client. In this routine it is your job to take any action and then set the contents of the Data object to whatever you want to send back to the client. The process of sending the response is done by the SendCommandAndData routine in CFSERVER.BAS.

Take a look at the part of ProcessCommand that handles a LOGIN command. When cfSockClient sends you a LOGIN command, data element (1,1) is the username, and element (1,2) is the password. In ProcessCommand you can do a security check with the username and password. If the user checks out OK, set Data.DataSet(1,1) to OK; otherwise set it to NO.

That brings up the topic of authentication. This is the point at which you should identify and authenticate the client. You can do this buy checking their username and password against a database of registered users. You might also want to write an entry in a log file. A simple text file will do, or you can opt to create a log in a database. So long as there is a record of the user logging on, or failing to authenticate.

 You can create your own custom commands in the same way. You don't need to modify the cfSockClient object, just the server. Your actual client application will send the appropriate commands to the server using cfSockClient. Got it?

Receiving Unsolicited Commands from the Server

As I outlined in Chapter 8, "An Introduction to Objects in Visual Basic," when you use the WithEvents keywords to create an Object variable, VB gives you access to the object's events. The cfSockClient object has an event called ReceiveCmd, which is fired when the server sends a command to the client. I have implemented a command that tells the client to download a file, but you could easily use this to allow clients to interact with each other or for any other situation when the server needs to notify the client.

Figure 12.24 shows the ReceiveCmd event. You can, and should, add your own callback commands as needed.

Figure 12.24   The ReceiveCmd Event allows the server to "push" commands and data to your application.

```
Private Sub cfSock_ReceiveCmd(Command As String, Data As cfSocket.cfData)

    Dim szFilePath  As String
    Dim szFileName  As String

    Select Case Command
    Case "PUSHFILE" '-- The server is telling you to download a file.
        '-- Obviously, you should change the destination path to
        '   your liking.
        szFilePath = szWindowsDir & "\desktop\"
        '-- Get the file name
        szFileName = Data.DataSet(1, 1)
        '-- Get the file.
        On Error Resume Next
        cfSock.GetFile szFileName, szFilePath & _
          szJustTheFileName(szFileName)
        '-- Display confirmation
        If Err = 0 Then
            MsgBox "You have received an unsolicited file from the server."
        Else
            MsgBox Err.Description
        End If
    End Select

End Sub
```

This code from cfsDemo.vbp is set up to act on the PUSHFILE command. When the server wants to send your application a file, it sends the PUSHFILE command to cfSockClient. When cfSockClient receives any command that is not a REPLYFROMSERVER command it fires the Command event in your object, passing the command string and Data object.

In the case of PUSHFILE, the server sends the name of a file on the server. The code simply calls the cfSockClient.GetFile method to retrieve the file.

I wholeheartedly encourage you to take advantage of this technique to write applications in which the server can initiate a conversation just like the client. There are numerous applications for such a system.

Some other ideas: You can use the event to notify e-mail clients when they have mail so that the client doesn't have to poll for this information taking up valuable processor time. You can write a chat server, where clients communicate with each other. In general, you can free the client from having to poll for data, making your system extremely efficient.

Remote Data Access

One of the benefits of having this kind of framework in Visual Basic is that you can easily make your ODBC datasources (or any other data access source) accessible via the Internet. The CFServer application connects to a local ODBC datasource. cfSockClient connects to CFServer (with password protection, of course) and sends a SQL query. The server receives the query and queries the datasource. The resulting data set is then returned to your application through cfSockClient.

Using the event procedure outlined in the previous section, you can write code on the server to update all clients when the data they are viewing has changed. This is especially important in network-based client/server applications where the latest data must be accessible at all times.

My remote ODBC code uses the cfSockClient object and an enhanced version of the CFServer application. In that regard, you already know how it works if you read this chapter. The ODBCServ project looks exactly like the Server project, except that it uses a modified version of cfserver.bas, called odbcsrv.bas. This file contains an extended ProcessCommand procedure. The ODBCServ project also includes declares for the ODBC API, which is used to talk to the database. There are a couple of new commands added to ProcessCommand: ODBC_OPEN, ODBC_QUERY, and ODBC_CLOSE.

ODBC_OPEN

This command opens a data source on the server. Just as with opening a local database, there are three arguments:

```
Argument:              Example:
-----------------------------------------------------------------------

Datasource Name        MyDataSource
User ID                John Smith
Password               higgledy-piggledy

'-- Allocate memory for five arguments
cfSock.Data.Resize 3, 1

'-- These variables are specified by the user
```

```
cfSock.Data.DataSet(1, 1) = szDataSource
cfSock.Data.DataSet(2, 1) = szUserID
cfSock.Data.DataSet(3, 1) = szPassword

cfSock.SendCommand "ODBC_OPEN"

If cfSock.Data(1, 1) = "NO" Then
    MsgBox "Could not connect to remote data source", _
      vbInformation
Else
    '-- Success! Save the hdbc (preferably to a global
    '   long integer)
    glhdbc = Val(cfSock.Data.DataSet(1, 1))
End If
```

On the server side, my code uses the ODBC API directly. The routines were originally developed by Andrew J. Brust (abrust@progsys.com) and Michael Love Graves (72240.1123@compuserve.com). You could easily rewrite the code to use Active Data Objects (ADO) or any other database engine, since the routines for opening, querying, and closing the data source are so clearly defined. At the time of this original writing, this direct ODBC method was the fastest way to access an ODBC database, the next fastest method being Remote Data Objects. Figure 12.25 shows the ProcessCommand routine in odbcserv.bas. Nowadays, ADO represents the smartest and fastest way to access a database.

Figure 12.25   ODBCServ contains a modified ProcessCommand routine to handle database requests.

```
Sub ProcessCommand(Index As Integer, szCmd As String, Data As cfData)
'-- This is where server commands are processed and data
'   is sent back to the server. If no data is to be sent, then
'   one row and one column is sent with the data set to "ACK"

'-- To add a new command to the "repertoire", simply perform a select
'   case on the command string, use the data in the Data object, do your
'   thing, and set the return data in the Data object.

    Dim szUsername      As String
    Dim szPassword      As String
    Dim szDir    As String
    Dim szTargetDir     As String
```

Continues

```
Dim nCtrlIndex        As Integer
Dim nThere  As Integer
Dim nFileNum As Integer
Dim lIndex  As Integer
Dim nIndex  As Integer

'-- ODBC variables
Dim szRemotePwd As String
Dim szDataSource As String
Dim szUserID As String
Dim szPwd As String
Dim nIndex As Integer
Dim ldbc As Long
Dim szQuery As String
Dim szReturn As String
Dim nRows As Integer
Dim nColumns As Integer
Dim nRow As Integer
Dim nColumn As Integer
Dim nSentHeader As Integer
Dim nDummy As Integer

ReDim szSQLData(1 To 1, 1 To 1) As String
DisplayMessage szCmd & " " & Status(Index).szDotAddress

Select Case szCmd
    Case "LOGIN"
        '-- Do an optional security check here
        szUsername = Data.DataSet(1, 1)
        szPassword = Data.DataSet(1, 2)

    '-- Do security check against a user database right here ----

        '-- Send back "OK" if logged in, or "NO" if not logged in.
        Data.Resize 2, 1
        Data.DataSet(1, 1) = "OK"

        Status(Index).szUsername = szUsername
        Status(Index).szPassword = szPassword

        DisplayMessage szUsername & " logged in."
```

Figure 12.25 *Continued.*

```
Case "SENDFILE"
      '-- Is the data connection already in use?
      If Status(Index).DataAction Then
          Data.Resize 1, 1
          Data.DataSet(1, 1) = "Data Connection In Use"
          Exit Sub
      End If

      '-- Was a target directory specified?
      szTargetDir = Data.DataSet(2, 1)
      If Len(szTargetDir) Then
          '-- See if the directory exists.
          szDir = Dir$(szTargetDir, vbDirectory)
          If Len(szDir) Then
              Do
                  If GetAttr(szDir) And vbDirectory Then
                      If szDir <> "." And szDir <> ".." Then
                          nThere = True
                          Exit Do
                      End If
                  Else
                      Exit Do
                  End If
                  szDir = Dir$()
              Loop
              If Not nThere Then
                  '-- The directory does not exist.
                  Data.Resize 1, 1
                  Data.DataSet(1, 1) = "Cannot create file on server"
                  Exit Sub
              End If
          Else
              '-- The directory does not exist.
              Data.Resize 1, 1
              Data.DataSet(1, 1) = "Cannot create file on server"
              Exit Sub
          End If
      End If

      On Error Resume Next
      '-- Load the data answer and data connection Sockets controls
      '   for the file xfer and tell the answer socket to listen
      Load frmServer.dssData(Index)
```

Continues

```
            Load frmServer.dssDataAnswer(Index)
            Status(Index).DataAction = DATA_ACTION_CLIENT_TO_SERVER
            frmServer.dssDataAnswer(Index).Action = SOCK_ACTION_LISTEN

            '-- Save the path and filename of the file to be received.
            If Len(szTargetDir) = 0 Then
                szTargetDir = frmServer.txtDownloadDir
            End If
            If Right(szTargetDir, 1) <> "\" Then
                szTargetDir = szTargetDir & "\"
            End If
            Status(Index).szFileName = szTargetDir & Data.DataSet(1, 1)
            Status(Index).FileSize = Val(Data.DataSet(3, 1))

            '-- Send back the OK, with the port number
            Data.Resize 2, 1
            Data.DataSet(1, 1) = "OK"
            Data.DataSet(2, 1) = _
              Trim$(Str$(frmServer.dssDataAnswer(Index).LocalPort))

    Case "GETFILE"
            '-- Does the file exist?
            If Len(Dir$(Data.DataSet(1, 1))) = 0 Then
                Data.Resize 1, 1
                Data.DataSet(1, 1) = "File Not Found"
                Exit Sub
            End If
            On Error Resume Next
            '-- Load the data answer and data connection Sockets controls
            '   for the file xfer and tell the answer socket to listen
            Load frmServer.dssData(Index)
            Load frmServer.dssDataAnswer(Index)

            On Error GoTo 0

            Status(Index).szFileName = Data.DataSet(1, 1)
            Status(Index).FileSize = FileLen(Data.DataSet(1, 1))
            Status(Index).DataAction = DATA_ACTION_SERVER_TO_CLIENT
            frmServer.dssDataAnswer(Index).Action = SOCK_ACTION_LISTEN

            '-- Send back the OK, with the port number
            Data.Resize 2, 1
```

Figure 12.25 *Continued.*

```
     Data.DataSet(1, 1) = "OK"
   Data.DataSet(2, 1) = _
      Trim$(Str$(frmServer.dssDataAnswer(Index).LocalPort))

Case "ODBC_OPEN"    '-- Open ODBC Database

   szDataSource = Data.DataSet(1, 1)
   szUserID = Data.DataSet(1, 2)
   szPwd = Data.DataSet(1, 3)

   For nIndex = 1 To nNumDataSources
      If UCase$(typDataSource(nIndex).szDataSource) = _
       UCase$(szDataSource) Then
          '-- The datasource exists!
          Exit For
      End If
   Next

   '-- Prepare to send confirmation
   Data.Resize 1, 1
   If nIndex = nNumDataSources + 1 Then
       '-- No Match Found. Open a new connection.
       If OpenODBCDataBase(szDataSource, szUserID, szPwd) = 0 Then
           '-- Could not open database.. failure
           Data.DataSet(1, 1) = "NO"
       Else
           '-- Successfully opened the database.
           nIndex = nNumDataSources
           '-- Return the hdbc of the open datasource
           Data.DataSet(1, 1) = Str$(typDataSource(nIndex).hdbc)
       End If
   Else
       '-- Added this Socket connection to the existing database.
       typDataSource(nIndex).nNumConnections = _
          typDataSource(nIndex).nNumConnections + 1
       '-- Return the hdbc of the open datasource
       Data.DataSet(1, 1) = Str$(typDataSource(nIndex).hdbc)
   End If

Case "ODBC_QUERY"    '-- Remote Query

   '-- Is this database currently open and available?
   ldbc = Val(Data.DataSet(1, 1))
```

Continues

Figure 12.25   ODBCServ contains a modified ProcessCommand routine to handle database requests. *(Continued)*

```
            For nIndex = 1 To nNumDataSources
                If ldbc = typDataSource(nIndex).hdbc Then
                    Exit For
                End If
        Next
        If nIndex = nNumDataSources + 1 Then
            '-- No it is not. Send back an error
            Data.Resize 1, 1
            Data.DataSet(1, 1) = "NO"
        Else
            '-- Get the query and call it.
            szQuery = Data.DataSet(2, 1)

            If Len(szQuery) Then
                nRows = LoadArray(szSQLData(), nIndex, _
                    szQuery, nColumns)

                If nRows Then
                    '-- Send back the query results
                    Data.Resize (nRows + 3), (nColumns)
                    Data.DataSet(1, 1) = "OK"
                    Data.DataSet(2, 1) = Val(nRows)
                    Data.DataSet(3, 1) = Val(nColumns)

                    For nRow = 1 To nRows
                        For nColumn = 1 To nColumns
                            '-- Send each field's size and then the
                            data itself
                            Data.DataSet(nRow + 3, (nColumn)) = _
                                szSQLData(nColumn, nRow)
                        Next
                    Next
                Else
                    Data.Resize 1, 1
                    Data.DataSet(1, 1) = "NO"
                End If
            Else
                Data.Resize 1, 1
                Data.DataSet(1, 1) = "NO"
            End If
        End If
```

Figure 12.25 *Continued.*

```
        Case "ODBC_CLOSE"    '-- Close Database
            ldbc = Val(Data.DataSet(1, 1))
            For nIndex = 1 To nNumDataSources
                If ldbc = typDataSource(nIndex).hdbc Then
                    typDataSource(nIndex).nNumConnections = _
                        typDataSource(nIndex).nNumConnections - 1
                    If typDataSource(nIndex).nNumConnections <= 0 Then
                        nDummy = DisconnectFromDataSource(ldbc, _
                            typDataSource(nIndex).hstmt)
                        If nNumDataSources > 1 Then
                          '-- Copy the last entry to this entry, and delete
                          '   the last entry
                          typDataSource(nIndex).hdbc = _
                              typDataSource(nNumDataSources).hdbc
                          typDataSource(nIndex).hstmt = _
                              typDataSource(nNumDataSources).hstmt
                          typDataSource(nIndex).szDataSource = _
                              typDataSource(nNumDataSources).szDataSource
                          typDataSource(nIndex).nNumConnections = _
                              typDataSource(nNumDataSources).nNumConnections
                          nNumDataSources = nNumDataSources - 1
                        ReDim typDataSource(1 To nNumDataSources) As _
                        DataSourceType
                          Else
                              Erase typDataSource
                          End If
                    End If
                    Exit For
                End If
            Next

    End Select

End Sub
```

The server has to keep track of connections to the ODBC database. It manages these connections with an array (typDataSource) of a user-defined type called DataSourceType, as follows.

```
Type DataSourceType
    hdbc            As Long
```

```
    hstmt           As Long

    szDataSource    As String

    nNumConnections As Integer
End Type
```

hdbc and hstmt are the database and statement handles returned by ODBC that identify a connection to a datasource. szDataSource is the name of the datasource, and nNumConnections is the number of current Winsock connections to the datasource.

When the server receives an ODBC_OPEN command, the code first determines whether it needs to open a new connection. First it looks through the Global typDataSource() array to see if the data source is currently open. If it is, it looks at the number of currently connected Winsock clients for that data source. If the datasource is opened or an existing connection is used successfully, the server returns the hdbc of the datasource, a handle that the client must use for all queries and for closing the datasource.

ODBC_QUERY

This command sends a SQL query to the server, which in turn queries the datasource and returns the resultant data set. There are two arguments, the ODBC handle and SQL query:

```
Argument:             Example:
-----------------------------------------------------------------------

hdbc<long integer returned from ODBC_OPEN>
Query   SELECT * FROM Customer
```

To send a query to an open database, follow the example in Figure 12.26.

Figure 12.26   Sending a query with ODBC_QUERY.

```
'-- Allocate memory for two arguments
cfSock.Data.Resize 2, 1

'-- The first parameter is the return value of
'   ODBC_OPEN, the hdbc that identifies an open
'   datasource connection.
cfSock.Data.DataSet(1, 1) = Str$(glhdbc)

'-- Create a query and select it into the second row
```

Figure 12.26 *Continued.*

```
szQuery = "SELECT * FROM Customer"
cfSock.Data.DataSet(2, 1) = szQuery

'-- Send the query command
cfSock.SendCommand "ODBC_QUERY"

If cfSock.Data(1, 1) = "NO" Then
    MsgBox "Could not query the remote data source", _
      vbInformation
Else
    '-- Success! We have results
    '   Display in the debug window.
    For nRow = 1 to cfSock.Data.Rows
        For nColumn = 1 to cfSock.Data.Cols
            Debug.Print cfSock.Data.DataSet(nRow, nColumn), ", ";
        Next
        '-- Advance the line
        Debug.Print
    Next
End If
```

If the query fails on the server, the Data object will have the word "NO" in row 1, column 1, otherwise it contains the resultant data set.

ODBC_CLOSE

ODBC_CLOSE closes a previously opened ODBC connection. In general, you do not need to close a connection; by simply disconnecting, you will close it. You should close the connection only if you are done with the database but still wish to remain connected for other reasons.

ODBC_CLOSE takes one argument, the hdbc that was returned from ODBC_OPEN that identifies the datasource connection.

```
Argument:               Example:
----------------------------------------------------------------------

hdbc<long integer returned from ODBC_OPEN>
```

Here is an example of how to close a data source:

```
'-- Allocate memory for one argument
cfSock.Data.Resize 2, 1
```

```
'-- The only parameter is the return value of
'   ODBC_OPEN, the hdbc that identifies an open
'   datasource connection.
cfSock.Data.DataSet(1, 1) = Str$(glhdbc)

'-- Send the close command
cfSock.SendCommand "ODBC_CLOSE"

If cfSock.Data(1, 1) = "NO" Then
    MsgBox "Could not close the remote data source", _
        vbInformation
Else
    '-- Success! The connection is closed.
End If
```

ODBCTest: A Sample ODBC Client Application

ODBCTest, shown in Figure 12.27, is a small program that connects to ODBCServ
with cfSockClient. ODBCTest lets the user fill in the datasource name, User ID,

---

**Figure 12.27   ODBCTest uses cfSockClient to connect to an ODBC datasource
on the server.**

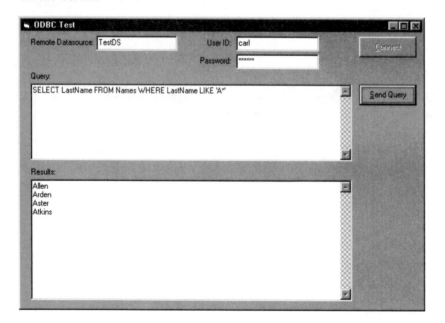

---

and password, and select read-only or exclusive mode. Once connected, ODBCTest lets you submit a query to CFServer. The results are displayed for the user as they come back from the server.

Epilogue

Well, this was the last chapter of the first revision of this book. When I first wrote it, my daughter was four months old and she was sitting up on the desk looking at my monitor as I typed. Now she is three. She can drag and drop, read the words Cat and Dog, blow a solid F on the trumpet, and converse at length on just about any topic. It still blows me away that we can do such amazing things with technology. I wonder what things will be like when she turns 30.

Anything is possible now. Visual Basic 6.0 and the Internet represent countless possibilities. The real problem we all face now is learning how to find the time in our lives to do all the things we want to do, and write all the code we want to write.

Please make sure you visit my web site for issues surrounding this book. The URL is: carl.franklins.net/vbip

I hope this book has helped to lift up a few rocks so you can see and understand the murky details of Internet programming. I certainly have learned a lot in the course of its writing. So until the next chapter, do good things and keep in touch.

NNTP COMMAND REFERENCE

The following is a listing of both standard and draft NNTP commands. Draft commands are those that do not appear in RFC 977 as of this writing. These commands are indicated with an asterisk. You may find that some servers implement only some of them and not others. This is to be expected.

NNTP Commands (ARTICLE)

Command: ARTICLE

Description: Requests the retrieval of a specific article's header and text.

Usage: ARTICLE [<ArticleNumber | MessageID>] <CRLF>

Parameters: ArticleNumber is the number of an article in the current newsgroup. MessageID is the Message ID of an article in the current newsgroup.

Examples:

```
SendData dsSocket1, "ARTICLE 1123" & vbCrlf
SendData dsSocket1, "ARTICLE <133970@netcom.com>" & vbCrlf
```

Comments: There are three ways to use the ARTICLE Command:

1. ARTICLE

2. ARTICLE <Article Number>

3. ARTICLE <Message-ID>

You can select the current article header and text by not specifying an argument.

You can select a specific article by specifying its article number or message-ID as an argument. If either is specified, the current article pointer is updated to the specified article and the header and text are returned.

A blank line (CR/LF) separates the header from the text of the message.

A period on a line by itself indicates the end of the article text.

Return Values (bold indicates success):

- **220 <article #> <msg-ID> Article retrieved—head and body follow**
- **221 <article #> <msg-ID> Article retrieved—head follows**
- **222 <article #> <msg-ID> Article retrieved—body follows**
- **223 <article #> <msg-ID> Article retrieved—request text separately**
- 412 No newsgroup has been selected
- 420 No current article has been selected
- 423 No such article number in this group
- 430 No such article found

NNTP Commands (AUTHINFO *)

Command: AUTHINFO *

Description: Used to identify a specific entity to the server using a simple username/password combination.

Usage: AUTHINFO USER <Username> <CRLF>

AUTHINFO PASS <Password> <CRLF>

Parameters: Username and Password are the user's username and password required for authorization purposes.

Examples:

```
'-- Send your name and password to the server in response to a 480 reply code.
SendData dsSocket1, "AUTHINFO USER JohnSmith" & vbCrlf
SendData dsSocket1, "AUTHINFO PASS MyPassword" & vbCrlf
```

Comments: Sometimes authorization is required to access an NNTP server or a specific command.

When authorization is required, the server will send a 480 response requesting authorization from the client. The client must enter AUTHINFO USER followed by the username. Once sent, the server will cache the username and send a 381 response requesting the password associated with that username. The client must then enter AUTHINFO PASS followed by the password for the username. The server will then check the authentication database to see if the username/password combination is valid.

If the combination is valid, the server will return a 281 response. The client should then retry the original command to which the server responded with the 480 response. The command should then be processed by the server normally. If the combination is not valid, the server will return a 502 response.

Clients must provide authentication when requested by the server. It is possible that some implementations will accept authentication information at the beginning of a session, but this was not the original intent of the specification. If a client attempts to reauthenticate, the server may return a 482 response indicating that the new authentication data is rejected by the server.

The 482 code will also be returned when the AUTHINFO commands are not entered in the correct sequence (like two AUTHINFO USERs in a row, or AUTHINFO PASS preceding AUTHINFO USER).

When authentication succeeds, the server will create an e-mail address for the client from the username supplied in the AUTHINFO USER command and the hostname generated by a reverse lookup on the IP address of the client. If the reverse lookup fails, the IP address, represented in dotted-quad format, will be used. Once authenticated, the server will generate a Sender: line using the e-mail address provided by authentication if it does not match the client-supplied From: line. Additionally, the server should log the event, including the e-mail address. This will provide a means by which subsequent statistics generation can associate newsgroup references with unique entities—not necessarily by name.

This is not a standard command as of this writing.

Return Values (bold indicates success):

- **281 Authentication accepted**
- **381 More authentication information required**
- **480 Authentication required**

- 482 Authentication rejected
- 502 No permission

NNTP Commands (AUTHINFO SIMPLE *)

Command: AUTHINFO SIMPLE *

Description: Used to identify a specific entity to the server using a simple username/password combination.

Usage: AUTHINFO SIMPLE <CRLF>

(Wait for 350 response)

<Username> <Password> <CRLF>

Parameters: Username and Password are the user's username and password required for authorization purposes.

Examples:

```
'-- Send the command in response to a 450 reply code.
SendData dsSocket1, "AUTHINFO SIMPLE" & vbCrlf

'-- Then, after receiving a 350 response.. send the username and password
SendData dsSocket1, "JohnSmith MyPassword" & vbCrlf
```

Comments: AUTHINFO SIMPLE was part of the proposed NNTP V2 specification and is implemented in some servers and clients. It is a refinement of the original AUTHINFO and provides the same basic functionality, but the sequence of commands is much simpler.

When authorization is required, the server sends a 450 response requesting authorization from the client. The client must enter AUTHINFO SIMPLE. If the server will accept this form of authentication, the server responds with a 350 response. The client must then send the username followed by one or more space characters followed by the password. If accepted, the server returns a 250 response and the client should then retry the original command to which the server responded with the 451 response. The command should then be processed by the server normally. If the combination is not valid, the server will return a 452 response.

The response codes used here were part of the NNTP V2 specification and are violations of RFC 977. It is recommended that this command not be implemented, but use either or both of the other forms of AUTHINFO if such functionality is required.

This is not a standard command as of this writing.

Return Values (bold indicates success):

- Authorization accepted
- Continue with authorization sequence
- Authorization required for this command
- Authorization rejected

NNTP Commands (AUTHINFO GENERIC *)

Command: AUTHINFO GENERIC *

Description: Used to identify a specific entity to the server using a simple username/password combination.

Usage: AUTHINFO GENERIC <Arg1> [<Arg2>...] <CRLF>

Parameters: Username and Password are the user's username and password required for authorization purposes.

Example:

```
'-- Send the command in response to a 380 reply code.
SendData dsSocket1, "AUTHINFO GENERIC" & vbCrlf
```

Comments: AUTHINFO GENERIC is used to identify a specific entity to the server using arbitrary authentication or identification protocols. The desired protocol is indicated by the authenticator parameter, and any number of parameters can be passed to the authenticator.

When authorization is required, the server will send a 380 response requesting authorization from the client. The client should enter AUTHINFO GENERIC followed by the authenticator name, and the arguments if any. The authenticator and arguments must not contain the sequence "..".

The server will attempt to engage the server end authenticator; similarly, the client should engage the client end authenticator. The server end authenticator will then initiate authentication using the NNTP sockets (if appropriate for that authentication protocol), using the protocol specified by the authenticator name. These authentication protocols are not included in this document, but are similar in structure to those referenced in RFC 1731[7] for the IMAP-4 protocol.

If the server returns 501, this means that the authenticator invocation was syntactically incorrect, or that AUTHINFO GENERIC is not supported. The client should retry using the AUTHINFO USER command.

If the requested authenticator capability is not found or there is some other unspecified server program error, the server returns the 503 response code.

The authenticators converse using their protocol until complete.

If the authentication succeeds, the server authenticator will terminate with a 281, and the client can continue by reissuing the command that prompted the 380. If the authentication fails, the server will respond with a 502.

The client must provide authentication when requested by the server. The server may request authentication at any time. Servers may request authentication more than once during a single session.

When the server authenticator completes, it provides to the server (by a mechanism herein undefined) the e-mail address of the user, and potentially what the user is allowed to access. Once authenticated, the server shall generate a Sender: line using the e-mail address provided by the authenticator if it does not match the user-supplied From: line.

Additionally, the server should log the event, including the user's authenticated e-mail address (if available). This will provide a means by which subsequent statistics generation can associate newsgroup references with unique entities—not necessarily by name.

This is not a standard command as of this writing.

Return Values (bold indicates success):

- **281 Authentication succeeded**
- **380 Authentication required**
- 501 Command not supported or Command syntax error
- 502 No permission
- 503 Program error, function not performed
- **nnn Authenticator-specific protocol**

NNTP Commands (DATE *)

Command: DATE *

Description: Returns the current date and time from the server's perspective.

Usage: DATE <CRLF>

Parameters: None.

Example:

```
'-- Send the command in response to a 380 reply code.
SendData dsSocket1, "DATE" & vbCrlf
```

Comments: At the time this command was discussed (1991–1992), the Network Time Protocol (NTP) was not yet in wide use and there was also some concern that small systems might not be able to make effective use of NTP.

This command returns a one-line response code of 111 followed by the GMT (Grenwich Mean Time) date and time on the server in the form YYYYMMDDhhmmss.

This is not a standard command as of this writing.

Return Values (bold indicates success):

- **111 YYYYMMDDhhmmss**

NNTP Commands (GROUP)

Command: GROUP

Description: Selects a Usenet newsgroup by name.

Usage: GROUP <Newsgroup> <CRLF>

Parameters: Newsgroup is the name of a Usenet newsgroup.

Example:

```
SendData dsSocket1, "Group alt.winsock.programming" & vbCrLF
```

Comments: If the newsgroup exists on the server, the return value indicates the estimated (very important) number of articles available, the first article number, and the last article number in the group. The name of the group is also returned but you don't need this unless you send several GROUP commands at the same time and must identify the newsgroup for each set of statistics.

Return Values (bold indicates success):

- 211 n f l s group selected

  n = Estimated number of articles in group

  f = First article number in the group

  l = Last article number in the group

  s = Name of the group
- 411 No such newsgroup

NNTP Commands (HELP)

Command: HELP

Description: Requests a list of supported NNTP commands.

Usage: HELP <CRLF>

Parameters: Newsgroup is the name of a Usenet newsgroup.

Example:

```
SendData dsSocket1, "HELP" & vbCrLf
```

Comments: If you really want to know if the server supports the commands you intend to send it, you can query the server with the **HELP** command. The only situation in which I can see this as being useful is for commands that are in the process of being implemented as standards and not supported on all systems. However, it's just as easy to receive an error code and report "function not available" to the user, or some such nonsense.

Return Values (bold indicates success):

- 100 Help text follows

NNTP Commands (IHAVE)

Command: IHAVE

Description: Informs the server that a particular article exists locally. The server reply instructs either to send the article or not to send the article.

Usage: IHAVE <Message-ID> <CRLF>

Parameters: Message-ID is the message-id of a local Usenet article.

Example:

```
SendData dsSocket1, "IHAVE 192401@domain.com" & vbCrLf
```

Comments: The IHAVE message is for use mainly for server-to-server communication. Its sole purpose is to move existing articles throughout the network. If you are not planning to write an NNTP server, you can ignore this command.

In a perfect world you will receive a 335 reply immediately after sending this command. You should then send the article in the format defined in RFC 850 (at the time of this writing). You will then either receive a 235 reply indicating success or a 400 series error reply indicating failure. Be aware that just because you receive a 235 reply does not mean the server will post and/or forward the article.

It has become acceptable for NNTP servers to send a 235 reply immediately, no matter what, and decide later if the article is appropriate for posting. This behavior will probably change with the next NNTP RFC after 977.

Return Values (bold indicates success):

- **235 Article transferred ok**
- 335 Send article to be transferred. End with <CR-LF>.<CR-LF>
- 435 Article not wanted—do not send it
- 436 Transfer failed—try again later
- 437 Article rejected—do not try again
- 480 Transfer permission denied

NNTP Commands (LAST)

Command: LAST

Description: Moves the current article pointer to the previous article in the current newsgroup. The previous article is the article previous to the current article.

Usage: LAST <CRLF>

Parameters: None.

Example:

```
SendData dsSocket1, "LAST" & vbCrLF
```

Comments: If the current article is the first article in the newsgroup an error code is returned and the current article stays selected.

Return Values (bold indicates success):

- **223 <article #> <msg-ID> Article retrieved—request text separately**
- 412 No newsgroup selected
- 420 No current article has been selected
- 422 No previous article in this group

NNTP Commands (LIST)

Command: LIST

Description: Returns a list of valid newsgroups, as well as other associated information.

Usage: LIST <CRLF>

Parameters: None.

Example:

```
'-- This example does the same as sending just the LIST command.
SendData dsSocket1, "LIST" & vbCrlf
```

Comments: Each newsgroup is sent as a line of text in the following format:

group last first p

group is the name of the newsgroup

last is the number of the last known article currently in that newsgroup

first is the number of the first article currently in the newsgroup

p is either y or n indicating whether posting to this newsgroup is allowed

Note that posting may still be prohibited to a client even though the LIST command indicates that posting is permitted to a particular newsgroup. See the POST command for an explanation of client prohibitions. The posting flag exists for each newsgroup because some newsgroups are moderated or are digests, and therefore cannot be posted to; that is, articles posted to them must be mailed to a moderator who will post them for the submitter. This is independent of the posting permission granted to a client by the NNTP server.

Please note that an empty list (i.e., the text body returned by this command consists only of the terminating period) is a possible valid response, and indicates that there are currently no valid newsgroups.

Return Values (bold indicates success):

- **215 List of newsgroups follows**

  The server sends a period on a line by itself to indicate the end of file.

  No error is ever returned. If there are no newsgroups, an empty list will be returned.

NNTP Commands (LIST ACTIVE *)

Command: LIST ACTIVE *

Description: Returns a list of valid newsgroups. If specified, limits the list to a particular pattern of newsgroup.

Usage: LIST ACTIVE [<Wildmat String>] <CRLF>

Parameters: None.

Examples:

```
'-- This example does the same as sending just the LIST command.
SendData dsSocket1, "LIST ACTIVE" & vbCrlf


'-- This example tells the server to only list those newsgroups that begin
'   with comp.lang.basic
SendData dsSocket1, "LIST ACTIVE comp.lang.basic*" & vbCrlf
```

Comments: LIST ACTIVE does exactly the same thing as the LIST command, except that you can specify a newsgroup pattern. If no pattern is specified the result is the same as if you were to send just a LIST command.

This is not a standard command as of this writing.

Return Values (bold indicates success):

- **215 List of newsgroups follows**

  The server sends a period on a line by itself to indicate the end of file.

  No error is ever returned. If there are no newsgroups, an empty list will be returned.

NNTP Commands (LIST ACTIVE.TIMES *)

Command: LIST ACTIVE.TIMES *

Description: Returns the contents of the active.times file, which contains information about who created a particular newsgroup and when.

Usage: LIST ACTIVE.TIMES <CRLF>

Parameters: None.

Example:

```
SendData dsSocket1, "LIST ACTIVE.TIMES" & vbCrlf
```

Comments: The active.times file is only maintained by some news transports systems.

If nothing is matched an empty list is returned, not an error.

This is not a standard command as of this writing.

Return Values (bold indicates success):

- **215 Information follows**

   The format of this information generally includes three fields. The first field is the name of the newsgroup. The second is the time when this group was created on this newsserver measured in seconds since January 1, 1970. The third is the e-mail address of the entity that created the newsgroup.

   The server sends a period on a line by itself to indicate the end of file.

- 503 Data is not available

NNTP Commands (LIST DISTRIBUTIONS *)

Command: LIST DISTRIBUTIONS *

Description: Returns the contents of the distributions file, which contains a list of valid values for the Distributions: line in a news article header, and what each value means.

Usage: LIST DISTRIBUTIONS <CRLF>

Parameters: None.

Example:

```
SendData dsSocket1, "LIST DISTRIBUTIONS" & vbCrlf
```

Comments: The distributions file is only maintained by some news transport systems.

If nothing is matched an empty list is returned, not an error.

This is not a standard command as of this writing.

Return Values (bold indicates success):

- **215 Information follows**

  Each line contains two fields, the value and a short explanation on the meaning of the value. The server sends a period on a line by itself to indicate the end of file.

- 503 Data is not available

NNTP Commands (LIST DISTRIB.PATS *)

Command: LIST DISTRIB.PATS *

Description: Returns the contents of the distrib.pats file, which contains default values for the Distribution: line in a news article header when posting to particular newsgroups.

Usage: LIST DISTRIB.PATS <CRLF>

Parameters: None.

Example:

```
SendData dsSocket1, "LIST DISTRIB.PATS" & vbCrlf
```

Comments: The distrib.pats file is only maintained by some news transport systems.

This information could be used to provide a default value for the Distribution: line in the header when posting an article.

The information returned involves three fields separated by colons. The first column is a weight. The second is a group name or a pattern that can be used to match a group name in the wildmat format. The third is the value of the Distribution: line that should be used when the group name matches and the weight value is the highest. All this processing is done by the newsposting client and not by the server itself. The server just provides this information to the client for it to use or ignore as it chooses.

If nothing is matched an empty list is returned, not an error.

This is not a standard command as of this writing.

Return Values (bold indicates success):

- **215 Information follows**

  The information returned involves three fields separated by colons. The first column is a weight. The second is a group name or a pattern that can be used to match a group name in the wildmat format. The third is the value of the Distribution: line that should be used when the group name matches and the weight value is the highest.

  The server sends a period on a line by itself to indicate the end of file.

- 503 Data is not available

NNTP Commands (LIST NEWSGROUPS *)

Command: LIST NEWSGROUPS *

Description: Returns the contents of the newsgroups file, which contains the name and a short description of each active newsgroup.

Usage: LIST NEWSGROUPS [<Wildmat String>] <CRLF>

Parameters: None.

Examples:

```
'-- This example tells the server to display info about all newsgroups
SendData dsSocket1, "LIST NEWSGROUPS" & vbCrlf


'-- This example tells the server to display info about only those newsgroups
'    that begin with "comp.lang"
SendData dsSocket1, "LIST NEWSGROUPS comp.lang*" & vbCrlf
```

Comments: The newsgroups file is only maintained by some news transport systems.

If the optional matching parameter is specified, the list is limited to only the groups that match the pattern (no matching is done on the group descriptions). Specifying a single group is usually very efficient for the server, and multiple groups may be specified by using wildmat patterns (similar to file globbing), not regular expressions.

When the optional parameter is specified, this command is equivalent to the XGTITLE* command, though the response codes are different.

If nothing is matched an empty list is returned, not an error.

This is not a standard command as of this writing.

Return Values (bold indicates success):

- **215 Information follows**

  Each line in the file contains two fields, the newsgroup name and a short explanation of the purpose of the newsgroup.

  The server sends a period on a line by itself to indicate the end of file.

- 503 Data is not available

NNTP Commands (LIST OVERVIEW.FMT *)

Command: LIST OVERVIEW.FMT *

Description: Returns the contents of the overview.fmt file, which contains the order in which header information is stored in the overview databases for each newsgroup.

Usage: LIST OVERVIEW.FMT <CRLF>

Parameters: None.

Example:

```
SendData dsSocket1, "LIST OVERVIEW.FMT" & vbCrlf
```

Comments: The overview.fmt file is only maintained by some news transport systems.

If the header has the word "full" (without quotes) after the colon, the header's name is prepended to its field in the output returned by the server.

If nothing is matched an empty list is returned, not an error.

This is not a standard command as of this writing.

Return Values (bold indicates success):

- **215 Information follows**

  The article header fields are displayed one line at a time in the order in which they are stored in the overview database.

  The server sends a period on a line by itself to indicate the end of file.

- 503 Data is not available

NNTP Commands (LIST SUBSCRIPTIONS *)

Command: LIST SUBSCRIPTIONS *

Description: Returns a default subscription list for new users of the server.

Usage: LIST SUBSCRIPTIONS <CRLF>

Parameters: None.

Example:

```
SendData dsSocket1, "LIST SUBSCRIPTIONS" & vbCrlf
```

Comments: The order of groups is significant.

This is not a standard command as of this writing.

Return Values (bold indicates success):

- **215 Information follows**

  The server sends a period on a line by itself to indicate the end of transmission.

- 503 Data is not available

NNTP Commands (LISTGROUP *)

Command: LISTGROUP *

Description: Returns a listing of all the article numbers in the currently selected newsgroup or a specified newsgroup.

Usage: LISTGROUP [<Group Name>] <CRLF>

Parameters: Group Name is an optional parameter. It specifies the name of a newsgroup. If not specified, article numbers for the currently selected newsgroup are returned.

Examples:

```
'-- Asks for a listing of all article numbers in the currently selected group
SendData dsSocket1, "LISTGROUP" & vbCrlf

'-- Asks for a listing of all article numbers in comp.lang.basic.visual
SendData dsSocket1, "LISTGROUP comp.lang.basic.visual.misc" & vbCrlf
```

Comments: A list of newsgroups may be obtained from the LIST command.

When a valid group is selected by means of this command, the internally maintained "current article pointer" is set to the first article in the group. If an invalid group is specified, the previously selected group and article remain selected. If an empty newsgroup is selected, the "current article pointer" is in an indeterminate state and should not be used.

The name of the newsgroup is case insensitive. It must otherwise match a newsgroup obtained from the LIST command or an error will result.

Return Values (bold indicates success):

- **211 List of article numbers follows**

  The server sends a period on a line by itself to indicate the end of transmission.

- 412 Not currently in newsgroup

- 502 No permission

NNTP Commands (MODE READER *)

Command: MODE READER *

Description: Used by the client to indicate to the server that it is a newsreading client.

Usage: MODE READER <CRLF>

Parameters: None.

Example:

```
SendData dsSocket1, "MODE READER" & vbCrlf
```

Comments: Some implementations make use of this information to reconfigure themselves for better performance in responding to news-reader commands. Some servers require a MODE command before allowing access at all.

The command MODE QUERY is also used sometimes in place of MODE READER. MODE QUERY means exactly the same thing.

Return Values (bold indicates success):

- **200 Hello, you can post**

  Indicates that posting is allowed.

- **201 Hello, you can't post**

Indicates that posting is not allowed.

NNTP Commands (NEWGROUPS)

Command: NEWGROUPS

Description: Retrieves all the newsgroups that were created after a specified point in time.

Usage: NEWGROUPS <yymmdd> <hhmmss> [GMT] [<distributions>]

Parameters: The date is specified as six digits in the format YYMMDD, where YY is the last two digits of the year, MM is the two digits of the month (with leading zero, if appropriate), and DD is the day of the month (with leading zero, if appropriate). The closest century is assumed as part of the year (i.e., 86 specifies 1986, 30 specifies 2030, 99 is 1999, 00 is 2000). The time is specified as six digits HHMMSS with HH being hours on the 24-hour clock, MM minutes 00–59, and SS seconds 00–59. The time is assumed to be in the server's timezone unless the token "GMT" appears, in which case both time and date are evaluated at the 0 meridian. You can use the DATE command to determine the date and time relative to the server. The optional parameter "distributions" is a list of distribution groups, enclosed in angle brackets. If specified, the distribution portion of a new newsgroup (e.g., 'net' in 'net.wombat') will be examined for a match with the distribution categories listed, and only those new newsgroups that match will be listed. If more than one distribution group is to be listed, they must be separated by commas within the angle brackets.

Example:

```
'-- Returns all newsgroups created since March 1, 1995
'   at exactly 8 PM
SendData dsSocket1, "NEWGROUPS 950301 200000" & vbCrlf
```

Comments: Note that an empty list (i.e., the text body returned by this command consists only of the terminating period) is a possible valid response, and indicates that there are currently no new newsgroups.

Return Values (bold indicates success):

- **231 List of new newsgroups follows**

  Each line in the file contains two fields, the newsgroup name and a short explanation of the purpose of the newsgroup.

The server sends a period on a line by itself to indicate the end of file.

NNTP Commands (NEWNEWS)

Command: NEWNEWS

Description: Retrieves all articles in a specified newsgroup that were created after a specified point in time.

Usage: NEWNEWS <newsgroup> <yymmdd> <hhmmss> [GMT] [<distributions>]

Parameters: The date is specified as six digits in the format YYMMDD, where YY is the last two digits of the year, MM is the two digits of the month (with leading zero, if appropriate), and DD is the day of the month (with leading zero, if appropriate). The closest century is assumed as part of the year (i.e., 86 specifies 1986, 30 specifies 2030, 99 is 1999, 00 is 2000). The time is specified as six digits HHMMSS with HH being hours on the 24-hour clock, MM minutes 00–59, and SS seconds 00–59. The time is assumed to be in the server's timezone unless the token "GMT" appears, in which case both time and date are evaluated at the 0 meridian. You can use the DATE command to determine the date and time relative to the server. The optional parameter "distributions" is a list of distribution groups, enclosed in angle brackets. If specified, the distribution portion of a new newsgroup (e.g., 'net' in 'net.wombat') will be examined for a match with the distribution categories listed, and only those new newsgroups that match will be listed. If more than one distribution group is to be listed, they must be separated by commas within the angle brackets.

Example:

```
'-- Returns all new articles in rec.audio.pro since March 1, 1995
'    at exactly 8 PM
SendData dsSocket1, "NEWNEWS rec.audio.pro 950301 200000" & vbCrlf
```

Comments: A newsgroup name containing an asterisk (*) may be specified to broaden the article search to some or all newsgroups. The asterisk will be extended to match any part of a newsgroup name (e.g., net.micro* will match net.micro.wombat, net.micro.apple, etc.). Thus if only an asterisk is given as the newsgroup name, all newsgroups will be searched for new news.

Note that the asterisk (*) expansion is a general replacement; in particular, the specification of, for example, net.*.unix should be correctly expanded to embrace names such as net.wombat.unix and net.whocares.unix.

Conversely, if no asterisk appears in a given newsgroup name, only the specified newsgroup will be searched for new articles. Newsgroup names must be chosen from those returned in the listing of available groups. Multiple newsgroup names (including an asterisk) may be specified in this command, separated by a comma. No comma shall appear after the last newsgroup in the list. (Implementors are cautioned to keep the 512 character command length limit in mind.)

The exclamation point (!) may be used to negate a match. This can be used to selectively omit certain newsgroups from an otherwise larger list. For example, a newsgroups specification of net.*,mod.*,!mod.map.* would specify that all net.<anything> and all mod.<anything> *except* mod.map.<anything> newsgroup names would be matched. If used, the exclamation point must appear as the first character of the given news-group name or pattern.

Note: An empty list (i.e., the text body returned by this command consists only of the terminating period) is a possible valid response, and indicates that there are currently no new newsgroups.

Return Values (bold indicates success):

- **230 List of new articles by message-ID follows**

    The server sends a list of Message-IDs followed by a period on a line by itself.

NNTP Commands (POST)

Command: POST

Description: Requests permission to post a new article.

Usage: POST <CRLF>

Parameters: None.

Examples:

```
'-- Request permission to post an article
SendData dsSocket1, "POST" & vbCrlf

'-- After receiving a 340 reply...
```

```
SendData dsSocket1, "From: Carl Franklin <carlf@apexsc.com>"& vbCrlf _
    & "Newsgroup: alt.winsock.programming" & vbCrlf _
    & "Subject: This is a test post" & vbCrlf _
    & vbCrlf _
    & "Hello, this was a posted from a VB program!" & vbCrlf _
    & "." & vbCrlf
```

Comments: After the initial connection to the server is made, the server sends a 200 reply if posting is allowed and 201 reply if not.

After sending the POST command, you will either receive a 340 reply, granting permission to post the article, or a 440 reply denying permission. If you receive a 340 reply then you should immediately send your post.

When posting, there are only three header fields required:

From	Your name and e-mail address
Newsgroup	Newsgroup to post to
Subject	The subject of the article

The subject line is followed by a blank line and that is followed by your article text. End your post with a period on a line by itself.

Return Values (bold indicates success):

- **340 Send your post**
- 440 Do not post

NNTP Commands (XGTITLE *)

Command: XGTITLE *

Description: Retrieves newsgroup descriptions for specific newsgroups.

Usage: XGTITLE [<Wildmat String>] <CRLF>

Parameters: The optional wildmat string argument specifies a newsgroup pattern such as comp.lang.basic.*, alt.b*, or comp.binaries.s?? When not specified, data for the currently selected newsgroup is returned.

Examples:

```
'-- Asks for a description of the current newsgroup
SendData dsSocket1, "XGTITLE" & vbCrlf

'-- Asks for a description of all newsgroups that begin with "comp.lang"
SendData dsSocket1, "XGTITLE comp.lang*" & vbCrlf
```

Comments: XGTITLE and LIST NEWSGROUP provide the same functionality, but just return different response codes.

If the optional matching parameter is specified, the list is limited to only the groups that match the pattern (no matching is done on the group descriptions). Specifying a single group is usually very efficient for the server, and multiple groups may be specified by using wildmat patterns (similar to file globbing), not regular expressions.

If nothing is matched an empty list is returned, not an error.

This extension first appeared in ANU-NEWS, an NNTP implementation for DEC's VMS.

This is not a standard command as of this writing.

Return Values (bold indicates success):

- **282 List of groups and descriptions follows**

    Each line in the file contains two fields, the newsgroup name and a short description of the newsgroup.

    The server sends a period on a line by itself to indicate the end of transmission.

- 412 Not currently in newsgroup

- 502 No permission

NNTP Commands (XHDR *)

Command: XHDR *

Description: Retrieves specific header lines from specific articles.

Usage: XHDR <Header> [<Range>|<Message-ID>] <CRLF>

Parameters: Header is the name of a header line (e.g., subject). See RFC 1036 for a list of valid header lines.

The second parameter is optional. This can be either a range of message numbers or a valid Message ID.

The optional range argument may be any of the following:

1. An article number (e.g., 100)

2. An article number followed by a dash to indicate all following (e.g., 100–)

3. An article number followed by a dash and another article number (e.g., 100–105)

If the second parameter is not specified, then information from the current article is displayed.

Examples:

```
'-- Requests the Subject of the current article
SendData dsSocket1, "XHDR subject" & vbCrlf

'-- Requests the email address of article 100's sender
SendData dsSocket1, "XHDR from 100" & vbCrlf

'-- Requests the number of lines in articles from 1 to 100
SendData dsSocket1, "XHDR lines 1-100" & vbCrlf

'-- Requests the date of article with message-id <87623@baz.UUCP>
SendData dsSocket1, "XHDR date <87623@baz.UUCP>" & vbCrlf
```

Comments: The range and message-ID arguments are mutually exclusive.

The XHDR command has been available in the UNIX reference implementation from its first release. However, until now, it has only been documented in the source for the server.

This is not a standard command as of this writing.

Return Values (bold indicates success):

- **221 Header follows**

  The server sends a period on a line by itself to indicate the end of transmission.
- 412 No newsgroup current selected
- 420 No current article selected
- 430 No such article exists
- 502 No permission

NNTP Commands (XINDEX *)

Command: XINDEX *

Description: Retrieves an index file in the format of originally created for use by the UNIX TIN newsreader.

Usage: XINDEX <Newsgroup> <CRLF>

Parameters: Newsgroup is the name of a newsgroup. If not specified, then index file for the current newsgroup is returned.

Examples:

```
'-- Requests the index file for the current newsgroup
SendData dsSocket1, "XINDEX" & vbCrlf

'-- Requests the index file for comp.lang.basic.visual.misc
SendData dsSocket1, "XINDEX comp.lang.basic.visual.misc" & vbCrlf
```

Comments: A list of valid newsgroups may be obtained from the LIST command.

When a valid group is selected by means of this command, the internally maintained "current article pointer" is set to the first article in the group. If an invalid group is specified, the previously selected group and article remain selected. If an empty newsgroup is selected, the "current article pointer" is in an indeterminate state and should not be used.

The format of the tin-style index file is discussed in the documentation for the TIN newsreader. Since more recent versions of TIN support the news overview (NOV) format, it is recommended that this extension become historic and no longer be used in current servers or future implementations.

This is not a standard command as of this writing.

Return Values (bold indicates success):

- **218 Tin-style index follows**

  The server sends a period on a line by itself to indicate the end of file.

- 418 No tin-style index is available for this newsgroup

NNTP Commands (XOVER *)

Command: XOVER *

Description: Returns reference information about the specified article(s).

Usage: XOVER <Range> <CRLF>

Parameters: Range may be any of the following:

1. An article number (e.g., 100)

2. An article number followed by a dash to indicate all following (e.g., 100–)

3. An article number followed by a dash and another article number (e.g., 100–105)

If no argument is specified, the information for the current article is returned.

Examples:

```
'-- Returns information about article #120
SendData dsSocket1, "XOVER 120" & vbCrlf

'-- Returns information about all articles starting from 145
SendData dsSocket1, "XOVER 145-" & vbCrlf

'-- Returns information about articles from 100 to 200
SendData dsSocket1, "XOVER 100-200" & vbCrlf
```

Comments: This is not a standard command as of this writing.

Return Values (bold indicates success):

- **282 XOVER Information follows**

  Each line consists of the article number, followed by reference overview information separated by a tab character. Generally these fields are as follows:

  Message Number

  Subject

  From

  Date

  Message-ID

  Bytes

  Lines

  The server sends a period on a line by itself to indicate the end of transmission.

- 412 No newsgroup currently selected

- 420 No article(s) selected

- 502 No permission

NNTP Commands (XPAT *)

Command: XPAT *

Description: Retrieves specific headers from specific articles in the current newsgroup given one or more search patterns.

Usage: XPAT <Header> <Range|Message-ID> <Wildmat String> [<Wildmat String>] <CRLF>

Parameters: Header is the name of a header line (e.g., subject). See RFC 1036 for a list of valid header lines. The second parameter is either a range of message numbers or a valid Message ID. Range may be any of the following:

1. An article number (e.g., 100)

2. An article number followed by a dash to indicate all following (e.g., 100–)

3. An article number followed by a dash and another article number (e.g., 100–105)

At least one wildmat string is required. This argument selects a search pattern for the header line being selected. Additional patterns can follow separated by a space.

Examples:

```
'-- Searches all articles starting with 100 and returns all articles
'    where the subject line begins with "RE:"
SendData dsSocket1, "XPAT Subject 100- RE:*" & vbCrlf

'-- Searches all articles from 100 to 200 and returns all articles
'    where the email address contains netcom.com
SendData dsSocket1, "XPAT From 100-200 *netcom.com*" & vbCrlf
```

Comments: The range and message-id arguments are mutually exclusive.

This is not a standard command as of this writing.

Return Values (bold indicates success):

• 221 Header follows

   Each line consists of the article number, followed by each of the headers in the overview database for that article separated by a tab character.

The server sends a period on a line by itself to indicate the end of transmission.

- 430 No such article

NNTP Commands (XTHREAD *)

Command: XTHREAD *

Description: Retrieves threading information in a format originally created for use by the UNIX TRN newsreader.

Usage: XTHREAD [DBINIT|THREAD] <CRLF>

Parameters: The optional parameter is either DBINIT or THREAD. XTHREAD DBINIT may be issued prior to entering any groups to see if a thread database exists. If it does, the database's byte order and version number are returned as binary data. If no parameter is given, XTHREAD THREAD is assumed.

Examples:

```
SendData dsSocket1,"XTHREAD" & vbCrlf

SendData dsSocket1, "XTHREAD DBINIT THREAD" & vbCrlf

SendData dsSocket1, "XTHREAD DBINIT" & vbCrlf
```

Comments: This is not a standard command as of this writing.

Return Values (bold indicates success):

- **288 Binary data to follow**

  The format of the trn-style thread format is discussed in the documentation for the TRN newsreader. Since more recent versions of TRN support the news overview (NOV) format, it is recommended that this extension become historic and no longer be used in current servers or future implementations.

- 412 No newsgroup currently selected
- 502 No permission
- 503 Program error, function not performed

SMTP COMMAND LISTING

T he following listing of standard Simple Mail Transfer Protocol commands is adapted from RFC #821 by Jonathan B. Postel.

SMTP Commands (DATA)

Command: DATA

Description: Requests permission to send message data.

Usage: DATA <CRLF>

Parameters: None.

Example:

```
'-- Sends the DATA command
SendSMTPCommand dsSocket1, "DATA"
```

Comments: After sending a DATA command, you will receive a 354 reply from the server, which means "Go ahead and send." You then send the message data followed by a period on a line by itself, after which you will receive a 250 reply from the server.

Return Values (bold indicates success):

*   354 Send data

    Sender sends message data followed by a period on a line by itself, after which the sender receives a 250 reply.

- 421 <domain> Service not available, closing transmission channel
- 451 Requested action aborted: error in processing
- 452 Requested action not taken: insufficient system storage
- 500 Syntax error, command unrecognized
- 501 Syntax error in parameters or arguments
- 503 Bad sequence of commands
- 552 Requested mail action aborted: exceeded storage allocation
- 554 Transaction failed

SMTP Commands (EXPAND)

Command: EXPN

Description: Asks the SMTP server to verify a mailing list and returns a membership listing.

Usage: EXPN <list name> <CRLF>

Parameters: <list name> is the name of a mailing list.

Example:

```
'-- Sends the EXPN command
SendSMTPCommand dsSocket1, "EXPN admin"
```

Comments: <list name> is the name of a mailing list. For example, "admin" is generally a mailing list on most networks. Sometimes a mailing list is referred to as an *alias*.

Return Values (bold indicates success):

- **250 OK**

  The server sends a list of members each beginning with a 250 code. There is no period at the end of this list.
- 421 <domain> Service not available, closing transmission channel
- 500 Syntax error, command unrecognized
- 501 Syntax error in parameters or arguments
- 502 Command not implemented
- 504 Command parameter not implemented
- 550 Requested action not taken: mailbox unavailable

SMTP Commands (HELLO)

Command: HELLO

Description: Initiates a mail transaction, identifies the sender to the receiver, and tells the server to reset state tables and buffers.

Usage: HELO <sender's domain> <CRLF>

Parameters: The sender's domain is specified as the portion of your e-mail address following the @ sign (e.g., the domain of santa@north-pole.com is northpole.com).

Example:

```
'-- Sends the HELLO command
SendSMTPCommand dsSocket1, "HELO northpole.com"
```

Comments: You should always send the HELLO command after receiving the first 220 reply upon connection.

Return Values (bold indicates success):

- **250 OK**
- 421 <domain> Service not available, closing transmission channel
- 500 Syntax error, command unrecognized
- 501 Syntax error in parameters or arguments
- 504 Command parameter not implemented

SMTP Commands (HELP)

Command: HELP

Description: Asks the server for helpful information.

Usage: HELP <CRLF>

Parameters: None.

Example:

```
'-- Sends the HELP command
SendSMTPCommand dsSocket1, "HELP"
```

Comments: HELP usually returns a list of supported commands, but there is no standard format for help messages, since they are really meant to be read by a human user. You can usually get an explanation of any supported command by sending HELP followed by the name of the command. Therefore, if you want to determine if a system supports a command, for example SOML, you can send "HELP SOML." If you get back a 211 or 214 you know the command is supported. If not, you will get back an error reply.

Return Values (bold indicates success):

- **211 System status, or system help reply**
- **214 Help message**
- 421 <domain> Service not available, closing transmission channel
- 500 Syntax error, command unrecognized
- 501 Syntax error in parameters or arguments
- 502 Command not implemented
- 504 Command parameter not implemented

SMTP Commands (MAIL)

Command: MAIL

Description: Initiates a mail transaction and tells the server to reset state tables and buffers.

Usage: MAIL FROM: <sender's email address> <CRLF>

Parameters: The sender's e-mail address is specified as a complete e-mail address between angle brackets (e.g., <santa@northpole.com>).

Example:

```
'-- Sends the MAIL command
SendSMTPCommand dsSocket1, "MAIL FROM: <santa@northpole.com>"
```

Return Values (bold indicates success):

- **250 OK**
- 421 <domain> Service not available, closing transmission channel
- 451 Requested action aborted: error in processing
- 452 Requested action not taken: insufficient system storage
- 500 Syntax error, command unrecognized
- 501 Syntax error in parameters or arguments
- 552 Requested mail action aborted: exceeded storage allocation

SMTP Commands (NOOP)

Command: NOOP

Description: Does nothing but request a positive reply from the server.

Usage: NOOP <CRLF>

Parameters: None.

Example:

```
'-- Sends the NOOP command
SendSMTPCommand dsSocket1, "NOOP"
```

Comments: If you receive a 250 reply then you have successfully established communication with the server. If nothing comes back then you could be disconnected, or the server could be extremely busy (unlikely).

Using NOOP is a good way to see if you are still talking successfully with the server. If your application has been idle for a while, for example, you may want to establish a clear line of communication before continuing.

Return Values (bold indicates success):

- **250 OK**
- 421 <domain> Service not available, closing transmission channel
- 500 Syntax error, command unrecognized

SMTP Commands (QUIT)

Command: QUIT

Description: Tells the receiver of this command to close the connection and terminate the transaction.

Usage: QUIT <CRLF>

Parameters: None.

Examples:

```
'-- Sends the QUIT command
SendSMTPCommand dsSocket1, "QUIT"
```

Return Values (bold indicates success):

- **211 System status, or system help reply**

  The server returns a signoff message.

- 500 Syntax error, command unrecognized

SMTP Commands (RECIPIENT)

Command: RECIPIENT

Description: Gives a forward-path identifying one recipient. Used in creating a new mail message.

Usage: RCPT <receiver's e-mail address> <CRLF>

Parameters: The receiver's e-mail address is specified as a complete e-mail address between angle brackets (e.g., <santa@northpole.com>).

Examples:

```
'-- Sends the RECIPIENT command
SendSMTPCommand dsSocket1, "RCPT TO: <jaque@southpole.com>"
```

Comments: RCPT.

Return Values (bold indicates success):

- **250 OK**
- **251 User not local; will forward to <forward-path>**
- 421 <domain> Service not available, closing transmission channel
- 450 Requested mail action not taken: mailbox unavailable
- 451 Requested action aborted: error in processing
- 452 Requested action not taken: insufficient system storage
- 500 Syntax error, command unrecognized
- 501 Syntax error in parameters or arguments
- 503 Bad sequence of commands
- 550 Requested action not taken: mailbox unavailable
- 551 User not local; please try <forward-path>
- 552 Requested mail action aborted: exceeded storage allocation
- 553 Requested action not taken: mailbox name not allowed

SMTP Commands (RESET)

Command: RESET

Description: Resets the server and aborts the current mail transaction.

Usage: RSET <CRLF>

Parameters: None.

Example:

```
'-- Sends the RESET command
SendSMTPCommand dsSocket1, "RSET"
```

Comments: Any time you encounter an error and wish to abort the current transaction or start over you should first send a RESET command and wait for a 250 reply.

Return Values (bold indicates success):

- **250 OK**
- 421 <domain> Service not available, closing transmission channel
- 500 Syntax error, command unrecognized
- 501 Syntax error in parameters or arguments
- 504 Command parameter not implemented

SMTP Commands (SEND and MAIL)

Command: SEND and MAIL

Description: Sends a message directly to the recipient and also places the message in the recipient's mailbox.

Usage: SAML FROM: <sender's e-mail address> <CRLF>

Parameters: The sender's e-mail address is specified as a complete e-mail address between angle brackets (e.g., <santa@northpole.com>).

Example:

```
'-- Sends the SEND AND MAIL command
SendSMTPCommand dsSocket1, "SAML FROM: <santa@northpole.com>"
```

Comments: When you SEND (as opposed to MAIL) a message, the message is delivered directly to the user's terminal if the user indeed *has* a terminal and is logged on. SENDing is really only appropriate for terminal-based UNIX shell systems and does not apply throughout the enterprise.

SAML (Send And Mail) performs both a SEND and a MAIL command.

Return Values (bold indicates success):

- **250 OK**

- 421 <domain> Service not available, closing transmission channel
- 451 Requested action aborted: error in processing
- 452 Requested action not taken: insufficient system storage
- 500 Syntax error, command unrecognized
- 501 Syntax error in parameters or arguments
- 502 Command not implemented
- 552 Requested mail action aborted: exceeded storage allocation

SMTP Commands (SEND)

Command: SEND

Description: Sends a message directly to the recipient.

Usage: SEND FROM: <sender's e-mail address> <CRLF>

Parameters: The sender's e-mail address is specified as a complete e-mail address between angle brackets (e.g., <santa@northpole.com>).

Example:

```
'-- Sends the SEND command
SendSMTPCommand dsSocket1, "SEND FROM: <santa@northpole.com>"
```

Comments: When you SEND (as opposed to MAIL) a message, the message is delivered directly to the user's terminal if the user indeed *has* a terminal and is logged on. SENDing is really only appropriate for terminal-based UNIX shell systems and does not apply throughout the enterprise.

Return Values (bold indicates success):

- **250 OK**
- 421 <domain> Service not available, closing transmission channel
- 451 Requested action aborted: error in processing
- 452 Requested action not taken: insufficient system storage
- 500 Syntax error, command unrecognized
- 501 Syntax error in parameters or arguments
- 502 Command not implemented
- 552 Requested mail action aborted: exceeded storage allocation

SMTP Commands (SEND or MAIL)

Command: SEND or MAIL

Description: Sends a message directly to the recipient and places the message in the recipient's mailbox only if there is a problem sending to the terminal.

Usage: SOML FROM: <sender's e-mail address> <CRLF>

Parameters: The sender's e-mail address is specified as a complete e-mail address between angle brackets (e.g., <santa@northpole.com>).

Example:

```
'-- Sends the SEND OR MAIL command
SendSMTPCommand dsSocket1, "SOML FROM: <santa@northpole.com>"
```

Comments: When you SEND (as opposed to MAIL) a message, the message is delivered directly to the user's terminal if the user indeed *has* a terminal and is logged on. SENDing is really only appropriate for terminal-based UNIX shell systems and does not apply throughout the enterprise.

SOML (Send Or Mail) performs a SEND command and performs a MAIL command only if there is a problem with SEND.

Return Values (bold indicates success):

- **250 OK**
- 421 <domain> Service not available, closing transmission channel
- 451 Requested action aborted: error in processing
- 452 Requested action not taken: insufficient system storage
- 500 Syntax error, command unrecognized
- 501 Syntax error in parameters or arguments
- 502 Command not implemented
- 552 Requested mail action aborted: exceeded storage allocation

SMTP Commands (TURN)

Command: TURN

Description: Instructs the receiver to switch sender/receiver roles. If a sender receives a TURN command, he or she must become a receiver, and vice versa.

Usage: TURN <CRLF>

Parameters: None.

Example:

```
'-- Sends the TURN command
SendSMTPCommand dsSocket1, "TURN"
```

Comments: When you connect to an SMTP server and send a TURN command, your process becomes the receiver and the other side becomes the sender of commands. This situation should never present itself when performing the task of sending e-mail. I quote from RFC 821 by Jon Postel:

> *Please note that this command is optional. It would not normally be used in situations where the transmission channel is TCP. However, when the cost of establishing the transmission channel is high, this command may be quite useful. For example, this command may be useful in supporting be mail exchange using the public switched telephone system as a transmission channel, especially if some hosts poll other hosts for mail exchanges.*

For Windows TCP/IP-based networks, therefore, you shouldn't have to worry about this command at all.

Return Values (bold indicates success):

- **250 OK**
- 500 Syntax error, command unrecognized
- 502 Command not implemented
- 503 Bad sequence of commands

SMTP Commands (VRFY)

Command: VRFY

Description: Asks the SMTP server to verify an e-mail address.

Usage: VRFY carlf <CRLF>

Parameters: The sender's e-mail address is specified as a complete e-mail address between angle brackets (e.g., <santa@northpole.com>).

Example:

```
'-- Sends the SEND OR MAIL command
SendSMTPCommand dsSocket1, "SOML FROM: <santa@northpole.com>"
```

Return Values (bold indicates success):

- **250 OK**
- **251 User not local; will forward to \<forward-path\>**
- 421 \<domain\> Service not available, closing transmission channel
- 500 Syntax error, command unrecognized
- 501 Syntax error in parameters or arguments
- 502 Command not implemented
- 504 Command parameter not implemented
- 550 Requested action not taken; mailbox unavailable
- 551 User not local; please try \<forward-path\>
- 553 Requested action not taken; mailbox name not allowed

POP3 COMMAND LISTING

C

The following listing of standard Post Office Protocol 3 commands is adapted from RFC #1725 by J. Myers.

POP3 Commands (DELE)

Command: DELE (DELETE)

Description: Deletes a message from the mailbox.

Usage: DELE <Message Number> <CRLF>

Parameters: <Message Number> identifies a message currently in the mailbox.

Example:

```
'-- Sends the DELETE command
SendPOP3Command dsSocket1, "DELE 1"
```

Comments: DELE can be issued only in the TRANSACTION state.

The POP3 server marks the message as deleted. Any future references to the message-number associated with the deleted message in a POP3 command generates an error. The POP3 server does not actually delete the message until the POP3 session enters the UPDATE state.

Return Values (bold indicates success):

- **+OK Message deleted**

- -ERR No such message

POP3 Commands (LIST)

Command: LIST

Description: Returns the header of a specified message (or all messages).

Usage: LIST [<Message Number>] <CRLF>

Parameters: <Message Number> is an optional argument that identifies a message currently in the mailbox. If not given then the server returns header lines for all available messages.

Example:

```
'-- Sends the LIST command
SendPOP3Command dsSocket1, "LIST 1"
```

Comments: LIST may be given only in the TRANSACTION state.

After the initial +OK, for each message in the maildrop, the POP3 server responds with a line containing information for that message. This line is also called a "scan listing" for that message.

A scan listing consists of the message-number of the message, followed by a single space and the exact size of the message in bytes.

Messages marked as deleted are not listed.

Return Values (bold indicates success):

- **+OK Scan listing follows**

  <Message Number> <space> <message size (bytes)>

- -ERR No such message

POP3 Commands (NOOP)

Command: NOOP

Description: This command does nothing but invoke an +OK response from the server.

Usage: NOOP <CRLF>

Parameters: None.

Example:

```
'-- Sends the NOOP command
SendPOP3Command dsSocket1, "NOOP"
```

Return Values (bold indicates success):

- **+OK**

POP3 Commands (PASS)

Command: PASS

Description: Specifies a password for access to the POP3 server.

Usage: PASS <password> <CRLF>

Parameters: <password> is the user's password. The username is specified with the USER command, which is issued prior to the PASS command.

Example:

```
'-- Specify the USER name
SendPOPCommand dsSocket1, "USER jsmith"
'-- Wait for an +OK response here.
'-- Specify the PASS name
SendPOPCommand dsSocket1, "PASS MyPassword"
```

Comments: PASS may be given only in the AUTHORIZATION state after a successful USER command.

Since the PASS command has exactly one argument, a POP3 server may treat spaces in the argument as part of the password, instead of as argument separators.

Return Values (bold indicates success):

- **+OK Maildrop locked and ready**
- -ERR Invalid password
- -ERR Unable to lock maildrop

POP3 Commands (QUIT)

Command: QUIT

Description: Logs off of the POP3 server.

Usage: QUIT <CRLF>

Parameters: None.

Example:

```
'-- Sends the QUIT command
SendPOP3Command dsSocket1, "QUIT"
```

Comments: You should send the QUIT command prior to logging off. One advantage to sending a QUIT command as opposed to simply closing the socket is that the POP3 server closes the connection, which results in a Close event (when using dsSOCK). You can simply put your exit code in the Close event.

Return Values (bold indicates success):

- **+OK**

POP3 Commands (RETR)

Command: RETR (RETRIEVE)

Description: Retrieves a message from the mailbox.

Usage: RETR <Message Number> <CRLF>

Parameters: <Message Number> identifies a message currently in the mailbox.

Example:

```
'--Retrieve the first message in the mailbox
SendPOP3Command dsSocket1, "RETR 1"
```

Comments: RETR may be given only in the TRANSACTION state.

If you get an +OK back from the server, the server will send the message one line at a time ending with a period on a line by itself.

Return Values (bold indicates success):

- **+OK Message follows**
- -ERR No such message

POP3 Commands (RSET)

Command: RSET

Description: Resets the mailbox to its state prior to your connection.

Usage: RSET <CRLF>

Parameters: None.

Example:

```
'-- Resets the mailbox
SendPOP3Command dsSocket1, "RSET"
```

Comments: RSET may be given only in the TRANSACTION state.

If any messages have been marked as deleted by the POP3 server, they are unmarked.

Return Values (bold indicates success):

- **OK**

POP3 Commands (STAT)

Command: STAT

Description: Returns a single line, called a "drop listing," from the server containing information for the maildrop.

Usage: STAT <CRLF>

Parameters: None.

Example:

```
'-- Sends the STAT command
SendPOP3Command dsSocket1, "STAT"
```

Comments: STAT may be given only in the TRANSACTION state.

The positive response consists of "+OK" followed by a single space, the number of messages in the maildrop, a single space, and the size of the maildrop in bytes.

Messages marked as deleted are not counted in either total.

Return Values (bold indicates success):

- **OK <space> <message count> <space> <total bytes>**

  <message count> is the number of messages available.

  <total bytes> is the total size of all messages combined in bytes.

POP3 Commands (TOP *)

Command: TOP

Description: Returns the header lines and a given number of lines of the message body for a given message.

Usage: TOP <Message Number> <Number Of Lines> <CRLF>

Parameters:

1. <Message Number> identifies a message currently in the mailbox.

2. <Number Of Lines> is the (maximum) number of lines to return from the top of the message.

Example:

```
'-- Retrieve the header and top 10 lines of message 1
SendPOP3Command dsSocket1, "TOP 1 10"

'-- The POP3 server sends the headers of the message, a blank line,
'-- and the first 10 lines of the body of the message>
```

Comments: TOP may be given only in the TRANSACTION state.

TOP is not implemented in all POP3 implementations.

If the POP3 server issues a positive response, then the response given is multiline.

After the initial +OK, the POP3 server sends the headers of the message, the blank line separating the headers from the body, and then the number of lines indicated message's body.

If the number of lines requested by the POP3 client is greater than the number of lines in the body, then the POP3 server sends the entire message.

Return Values (bold indicates success):

- **+OK Top of message follows**

  The server sends the header lines followed by a blank line followed by the top *x* number of lines of the message body all ending with a period on a line by itself.

- -ERR No such message

POP3 Commands (UIDL *)

Command: UIDL (Unique ID Listing)

Description: Returns a "unique ID listing" for a given message (or all messages).

Usage: UIDL [<Message Number>] <CRLF>

Parameters: <Message Number> is an optional argument that identifies a message currently in the mailbox. If not given then the server returns header lines for all available messages.

Example:

```
'-- Get a Unique ID Listing for all messages
SendPOP3Command dsSocket1, "UIDL"
```

Comments: UIDL may be given only in the TRANSACTION state.

A unique-ID listing consists of the message-number of the message followed by a single space and the unique-ID of the message.

The unique-ID of a message is an arbitrary server-determined string, consisting of characters in the range 0×21 to 0×7E, which uniquely identifies a message within a maildrop and which persists across sessions. The server never reuses a unique-ID in a given maildrop for as long as the entity using the unique-ID exists.

If no argument is given the server returns an -OK reply followed by a list of unique-IDs for (one for each current message) all ending with a period on a line by itself.

Return Values (bold indicates success):

- **+OK Unique-ID listing follows**

   <message number> <space> <unique-ID>

- -ERR No such message

POP3 Commands (USER)

Command: USER

Description: Specifies the username required to log onto the POP3 server.

Usage: USER <username> <CRLF>

Parameters: <username> is the name of the user logging on.

Example:

```
'-- Specify the USER name
SendPOPCommand dsSocket1, "USER jsmith"
'-- Wait for an +OK response here.
'-- Specify the PASS name
SendPOPCommand dsSocket1, "PASS MyPassword"
```

Comments: The USER command is immediately followed by the PASS command.

Return Values (bold indicates success):

- **+OK Name is a valid mailbox**
- -ERR Never heard of mailbox name

FTP COMMAND LISTING

D

T he following listing of standard File Transfer Protocol commands is adapted from RFC #929 by Postel and Reynolds.

FTP Commands (ABOR)

Command: ABOR (Abort)

Description: Tells the server to abort the previous FTP service command and any associated transfer of data.

Usage: ABOR <CRLF>

Parameters: None.

Example:

```
SendData dsSocket1, "ABOR" & vbCrlf
```

Comments: The abort command may require "special action" to force recognition by the server (see RFC 959 for details). No action is to be taken if the previous command has been completed (including data transfer). The control connection is not to be closed by the server, but the data connection must be closed.

There are two cases for the server upon receipt of this command: (1) the FTP service command was already completed, or (2) the FTP service command is still in progress.

In the first case, the server closes the data connection (if it is open) and responds with a 226 reply, indicating that the abort command was successfully processed.

In the second case, the server aborts the FTP service in progress and closes the data connection, returning a 426 reply to indicate that the service request terminated abnormally. The server then sends a 226 reply, indicating that the abort command was successfully processed.

Return Values (bold indicates success):

- 225 Data connection open; no transfer in progress
- **226 Closing data connection; Requested file action successful**
- 421 Service not available, closing control connection

    This may be a reply to any command if the service knows it must shut down.

- 426 Connection closed; transfer aborted
- 500 Syntax error, command unrecognized

    This may include errors such as command line too long.

- 501 Syntax error in parameters or arguments
- 502 Command not implemented.

FTP Commands (ACCT)

Command: ACCT (Account)

Description: Specifies the user's account information. This command should be sent only after receiving a 332 code after sending a PASS command.

Usage: ACCT <Account > <CRLF>

Parameters: Account is the user's account, which may be additionally required to access certain services.

Example:

```
SendData dsSocket1, "ACCT N322s" & vbCrlf
```

Comments: When account information is required for login, the response to a successful PASS command is reply code 332. On the other hand, if account information is *not* required for login, the reply to a successful PASS command is 230; and if the account information is needed for a command issued later in the dialogue, the server returns a 332 or 532 reply depending on whether it stores (pending receipt of the ACCT command) or discards the command, respectively.

Return Values (bold indicates success):

- 202 Command not implemented, superfluous at this site
- **230 User logged in, proceed**
- 421 Service not available, closing control connection

    This may be a reply to any command if the service knows it must shut down.

- 500 Syntax error, command unrecognized

    This may include errors such as command line too long.

- 501 Syntax error in parameters or arguments
- 502 Command not implemented
- 503 Bad sequence of commands
- 530 Not logged in

FTP Commands (ALLO)

Command: ALLO (Allocate)

Description: Allocates x number of bytes on the server before a file is sent.

Usage: ALLO <NumBytes> [<MaxSize>] <CRLF>

Parameters: NumBytes is an integer representing the number of bytes (using the logical byte size) of storage to be reserved for the file. MaxSize is an optional maximum record or page size when using record or page data structures.

Example:

```
SendData dsSocket1, "ALLO 3000 128" & vbCrlf
```

Comments: This command may be required by some servers to reserve sufficient storage to accommodate the new file to be transferred. For files sent with record or page structure a maximum record or page size (in logical bytes) might also be necessary; this is indicated by a decimal integer in a second argument field of the command. This second argument is optional, but when present should be separated from the first by the three ASCII characters <SP> R <SP>. This command is followed by a STORe or APPEnd command. The ALLO command should be treated as a NOOP (no operation) by those servers that do not require that the maximum size of the file be declared beforehand, and those servers interested in only the maximum record or page size should accept a dummy value in the first argument and ignore it.

Return Values (bold indicates success):

- **200 Command okay**
- **202 Command not implemented, superfluous at this site**
- 421 Service not available, closing control connection

  This may be a reply to any command if the service knows it must shut down.
- 500 Syntax error, command unrecognized

  This may include errors such as command line too long.
- 501 Syntax error in parameters or arguments
- 504 Command not implemented for that parameter
- 530 Not logged in

FTP Commands (APPE)

Command: APPE (Append with create)

Description: Prepares the server to receive a file and instructs it to append the data to the specified filename, or create the specified file if it does not already exist.

Usage: APPE <FileName> <CRLF>

Parameters: FileName is a fully qualified path and filename at the server site.

Example:

```
SendData dsSocket1, "APPE " & szFileName & vbCrlf
```

Return Values (bold indicates success):

- 110 Restart marker reply

In this case, the text is exact and not left to the particular implementation; it must read:

MARK yyyy = mmmm

where yyyy is User-process data stream marker, and mmmm server's equivalent marker (note the spaces between markers and "=").

- 125 Data connection already open; transfer starting
- 150 File status okay; about to open data connection
- 226 Closing data connection; the requested file action was successful
- 250 Requested file action okay, completed
- 421 Service not available, closing control connection

  This may be a reply to any command if the service knows it must shut down.
- 425 Can't open data connection
- 426 Connection closed; transfer aborted
- 450 Requested file action not taken; file unavailable (e.g., file busy)
- 451 Requested action aborted: local error in processing
- 452 Requested action not taken; insufficient storage space in system
- 500 Syntax error, command unrecognized

  This may include errors such as command line too long.
- 501 Syntax error in parameters or arguments
- 502 Command not implemented
- 530 Not logged in
- 532 Need account for storing files
- 550 Requested action not taken; file unavailable (e.g., file not found, no access)
- 551 Requested action aborted: page type unknown
- 552 Requested file action aborted; exceeded storage allocation (for current directory or dataset)
- 553 Requested action not taken; filename not allowed

FTP Commands (CDUP)

Command: CDUP (Change to Parent Directory)

Description: Changes the current directory to the root of the remote file system without altering login, accounting information, or transfer parameters.

Usage: CDUP <CRLF>

Parameters: None.

Example:

```
SendData dsSocket1, "CDUP" & vbCrlf
```

Comments: The CDUP command changes to the parent directory. The MS-DOS equivalent of the command is cd \. This command was created to accommodate the different operating systems that incorporate FTP.

Return Values (bold indicates success):

- **250 Requested file action okay, completed**
- 421 Service not available, closing control connection

  This may be a reply to any command if the service knows it must shut down.

- 500 Syntax error, command unrecognized

  This may include errors such as command line too long.

- 501 Syntax error in parameters or arguments
- 502 Command not implemented
- 530 Not logged in
- 550 Requested action not taken; file unavailable (e.g., file not found, no access)

FTP Commands (CWD)

Command: CWD (Change Working Directory)

Description: Changes the current directory to the specified path of the remote file system without altering login, accounting information, or transfer parameters.

Usage: CWD <Path> <CRLF>

Parameters: Path is a working directory on the remote system.

Example:

```
SendData dsSocket1, "CWD /pub/cgvb/uploads" & vbCrlf
```

Return Values (bold indicates success):

- **250 Requested file action okay, completed**
- 421 Service not available, closing control connection

  This may be a reply to any command if the service knows it must shut down.

- 500 Syntax error, command unrecognized

  This may include errors such as command line too long.

- 501 Syntax error in parameters or arguments
- 502 Command not implemented
- 530 Not logged in
- 550 Requested action not taken; file unavailable (e.g., file not found, no access)

FTP Commands (DELE)

Command: DELE (Delete)

Description: Causes the file specified in the pathname to be deleted at the server site.

Usage: DELE <FileName> <CRLF>

Parameters: FileName is a fully qualified path and filename on the server side.

Example:

```
SendData dsSocket1, "DELE temp.fil" & vbCrlf
```

Comments: If an extra level of protection is desired (such as a "Do you really wish to delete this file?" option), it should be provided by the client software.

Return Values (bold indicates success):

- **250 Requested file action okay, completed**
- 421 Service not available, closing control connection

This may be a reply to any command if the service knows it must shut down.

- 450 Requested file action not taken; file unavailable (e.g., file busy)
- 500 Syntax error, command unrecognized

  This may include errors such as command line too long.

- 501 Syntax error in parameters or arguments
- 502 Command not implemented
- 530 Not logged in
- 550 Requested action not taken; file unavailable (e.g., file not found, no access)

FTP Commands (HELP)

Command: HELP (Help)

Description: Causes the server to send helpful information regarding its implementation status over the control connection to the client.

Usage: HELP [<Topic>] <CRLF>

Parameters: Topic is an optional command or other argument concerning which help text is requested.

Example:

```
SendData dsSocket1, "HELP" & vbCrlf
```

Comments: HELP may take an argument (e.g., any command name) and return more specific information as a response. The reply is type 211 or 214. It is suggested that HELP be allowed before entering a USER command. The server may use this reply to specify site-dependent parameters, e.g., in response to HELP SITE.

Return Values (bold indicates success):

- 211 System status, or system help reply
- 214 Help message

  Describes how to use the server or the meaning of a particular non-standard command. This reply is useful only to the user as there is no standard format for help messages.

- 421 Service not available, closing control connection

This may be a reply to any command if the service knows it must shut down.

- 500 Syntax error, command unrecognized

  This may include errors such as command line too long.

- 501 Syntax error in parameters or arguments

- 502 Command not implemented

FTP Commands (LIST)

Command: LIST (List)

Description: Causes a list to be sent from the server to the client.

Usage: LIST [<PathName>] <CRLF>

Parameters: PathName is a valid path and filespec on the server system.

Example:

```
SendData dsSocket1, "LIST /pub/*.*" & vbCrlf
```

Comments: If the pathname specifies a directory or other group of files, the server should transfer a list of files in the specified directory. If the pathname specifies a file then the server should send current information on the file. A null argument implies the user's current working or default directory. The data transfer is over the data connection in type ASCII or type EBCDIC (the user must ensure that the type is appropriately ASCII or EBCDIC).

Since the information on a file may vary widely from system to system, this information may be hard to use automatically in a program, but may be quite useful to a human user.

Return Values (bold indicates success):

- **125 Data connection already open; transfer starting**

- **150 File status okay; about to open data connection**

- **226 Closing data connection; requested file action successful (for example, file transfer or file abort)**

- **250 Requested file action okay, completed**

- 421 Service not available, closing control connection

This may be a reply to any command if the service knows it must shut down.

- 425 Can't open data connection
- 426 Connection closed; transfer aborted
- 450 Requested file action not taken; file unavailable (e.g., file busy)
- 451 Requested action aborted: local error in processing
- 500 Syntax error, command unrecognized

  This may include errors such as command line too long.

- 501 Syntax error in parameters or arguments
- 502 Command not implemented
- 530 Not logged in

FTP Commands (MKD)

Command: MKD (Make Directory)

Description: Causes the directory specified in the pathname to be created as a directory (if the pathname is absolute) or as a subdirectory of the current working directory (if the pathname is relative).

Usage: MKD <Path> <CRLF>

Parameters: Path is a valid path on the server side.

Example:

```
SendData dsSocket1, "MKD /users/johnsmith" & vbCrlf
```

Return Values (bold indicates success):

- 257 "PATHNAME" created
- 421 Service not available, closing control connection

  This may be a reply to any command if the service knows it must shut down.

- 500 Syntax error, command unrecognized

  This may include errors such as command line too long.

- 501 Syntax error in parameters or arguments
- 502 Command not implemented

- 530 Not logged in
- 550 Requested action not taken; file unavailable (e.g., file not found, no access)

FTP Commands (MODE)

Command: MODE (Transfer Mode)

Description: Specifies the transfer mode.

Usage: STRU <Mode> <CRLF>

Parameters: Mode is one of the following ASCII values:

S—Stream (Default)

B—Block

C—Compressed

Example:

```
SendData dsSocket1, "STRU B" & vbCrlf
```

Return Values (bold indicates success):

- **200 Command okay**
- 421 Service not available, closing control connection

    This may be a reply to any command if the service knows it must shut down.

- 500 Syntax error, command unrecognized

    This may include errors such as command line too long.

- 501 Syntax error in parameters or arguments
- 504 Command not implemented for that parameter
- 530 Not logged in

FTP Commands (NLST)

Command: NLST (Name List)

Description: Causes a directory listing to be sent from server to client.

Usage: NLST [<PathName>] <CRLF>

Parameters: PathName is a valid path and filespec on the server system.

Example:

```
SendData dsSocket1, "NLST /pub/cgvb" & vbCrlf
```

Comments: The pathname should specify a directory or other system-specific file group descriptor; a null argument implies the current directory. The server will return a stream of names of files and no other information. The data will be transferred in ASCII or EBCDIC type over the data connection as valid pathname strings separated by <CRLF> or <NL> (again the user must ensure that the *type* is correct.)

NLST is intended to return information that can be used by a program to further process the files automatically; for example, in the implementation of a "multiple get" function.

Return Values (bold indicates success):

- **125 Data connection already open; transfer starting**
- **150 File status okay; about to open data connection**
- **226 Closing data connection; requested file action successful (for example, file transfer or file abort)**
- **250 Requested file action okay, completed**
- 421 Service not available, closing control connection

   This may be a reply to any command if the service knows it must shut down.

- 425 Can't open data connection
- 426 Connection closed; transfer aborted
- 450 Requested file action not taken; file unavailable (e.g., file busy)
- 451 Requested action aborted: local error in processing
- 500 Syntax error, command unrecognized

   This may include errors such as command line too long.

- 501 Syntax error in parameters or arguments
- 502 Command not implemented
- 530 Not logged in

FTP Commands (NOOP)

Command: NOOP (NOOP)

Description: This is a nonaction command. It does nothing.

Usage: NOOP <CRLF>

Parameters: None.

Example:

```
SendData dsSocket1, "NOOP" & vbCrlf
```

Comments: NOOP does not affect any parameters or previously entered commands. It specifies no action except for the server to send an OK reply.

Return Values (bold indicates success):

- **200 Command okay**
- 421 Service not available, closing control connection

  This may be a reply to any command if the service knows it must shut down.

- 500 Syntax error, command unrecognized

FTP Commands (PASS)

Command: PASS (Password)

Description: Sends the user's password to the remote system. Use after a USER command.

Usage: PASS <Password> <CRLF>

Parameters: Password is the password of the registered user as specified by the USER command.

Example:

```
SendData dsSocket1, "PASS mypassword" & vbCrlf
```

Comments: The USER command is sent immediately after connecting to an FTP server on port 21 after receiving a line that starts with the code 220, indicating that the server is ready for you to send it USER and PASS commands to log into the FTP server.

The PASS command should immediately follow the USER command.

If you have an account on the FTP server, you can specify your username and password. If you would like to log in anonymously, specify "anonymous" for the username and your e-mail address for the password.

Return Values (bold indicates success):

- 202 Command not implemented, superfluous at this site
- **230 User logged in**
- 332 Need account for login (see ACCT command)
- 421 Service not available, closing control connection

  This may be a reply to any command if the service knows it must shut down.

- 500 Syntax error, command unrecognized

  This may include errors such as command line too long.

- 501 Syntax error in parameters or arguments
- 530 Not logged in

FTP Commands (PASV)

Command: PASV (Passive)

Description: Tells the server to listen for a data connection on a non-standard port.

Usage: PASV <CRLF>

Parameters: This command requests the server-DTP to "listen" on a data port (which is not its default data port) and to wait for a connection rather than initiate one upon receipt of a transfer command. The response to this command includes the host and port address on which this server is listening.

Example:

```
SendData dsSocket1, "PASV" & vbCrlf
```

Return Values (bold indicates success):

- **227 Entering Passive Mode (h1,h2,h3,h4,p1,p2)**

  The return value includes a HOST-PORT specification for the data port to be used in data connection. The argument is the concatenation of a 32-bit Internet host address and a 16-bit TCP port address. This address information is broken into 8-bit fields and the value of each field is transmitted as a decimal number (in character string representation). h1 is the high-order byte of the Internet host address and p1 is the high-order byte of the port.

- 421 Service not available, closing control connection

  This may be a reply to any command if the service knows it must shut down.

- 500 Syntax error, command unrecognized

  This may include errors such as command line too long.

- 501 Syntax error in parameters or arguments
- 502 Command not implemented
- 530 Not logged in

FTP Commands (PORT)

Command: PORT (Data Port)

Description: Specifies an IP address and local port for a data connection.

Usage: PORT <Socket> <CRLF>

Parameters: Socket is a HOST-PORT specification for the data port to be used in data connection. There are defaults for both the user and server data ports, and under normal circumstances this command and its reply are not needed. If this command is used, the argument is the concatenation of a 32-bit Internet host address and a 16-bit TCP port address. This address information is broken into 8-bit fields and the value of each field is transmitted as a decimal number (in character string representation). The fields are separated by commas. A port command would be:

PORT h1,h2,h3,h4,p1,p2

where h1 is the high-order byte of the Internet host address and p1 is the high-order byte of the local port.

Example:

```
SendData dsSocket1, "199,199,199,0,33,1" & vbCrlf
```

Return Values (bold indicates success):

- **200 Command OK**
- 421 Service not available, closing control connection

This may be a reply to any command if the service knows it must shut down.

- 500 Syntax error, command unrecognized

  This may include errors such as command line too long.

- 501 Syntax error in parameters or arguments
- 530 Not logged in

FTP Commands (PWD)

Command: PWD (Print Working Directory)

Description: Causes the name of the current working directory to be returned in the reply.

Usage: PWD <CRLF>

Parameters: None.

Example:

```
SendData dsSocket1, "PWD" & vbCrlf
```

Return Values (bold indicates success):

- 257 "PATHNAME" returned
- 421 Service not available, closing control connection

  This may be a reply to any command if the service knows it must shut down.

- 500 Syntax error, command unrecognized

  This may include errors such as command line too long.

- 501 Syntax error in parameters or arguments
- 502 Command not implemented
- 550 Requested action not taken; file unavailable (e.g., file not found, no access)

FTP Commands (QUIT)

Command: QUIT (Logout)

Description: Terminates the connection.

Usage: QUIT <CRLF>

Parameters: None.

Example:

```
SendData dsSocket1, "QUIT" & vbCrlf
```

Comments: QUIT terminates the USER and if file transfer is not in progress, the server closes the control connection. If file transfer is in progress, the connection will remain open for result response and the server will then close it. If the user-process is transferring files for several USERs but does not wish to close and then reopen connections for each, then the REIN command should be used instead of QUIT.

An unexpected close on the control connection will cause the server to take the effective action of an abort (ABOR) and a logout (QUIT).

Return Values (bold indicates success):

- **221 Service closing control connection**
- 500 Syntax error, command unrecognized

FTP Commands (REIN)

Command: REIN (Reinitialize)

Description: Terminates a user.

Usage: REIN <CRLF>

Parameters: None.

Example:

```
SendData dsSocket1, "REIN" & vbCrlf
```

Comments: REIN flushes all I/O and account information, except to allow any transfer in progress to be completed. All parameters are reset to the default settings and the control connection is left open. This is identical to the state in which a user finds himself immediately after the control connection is opened. If you are going to log in afterwards, send a REIN command before sending a USER command.

Return Values (bold indicates success):

- 120 Service ready in nnn minutes
- **220 Service ready for new user**

- 421 Service not available, closing control connection

  This may be a reply to any command if the service knows it must shut down.

- 500 Syntax error, command unrecognized

  This may include errors such as command line too long.

- 502 Command not implemented

FTP Commands (REST)

Command: REST (Restart)

Description: Identifies the data point within the file from which the file transfer will resume.

Usage: REST <Marker> <CRLF>

Parameters: Marker represents the server marker at which file transfer is to be restarted.

Example:

```
SendData dsSocket1, "REST 244" & vbCrlf
```

Comments: REST does not cause the file transfer but skips over the file to the specified data checkpoint. REST is immediately followed by the appropriate FTP service command, which causes the file transfer to resume.

Return Values (bold indicates success):

- No response indicates success
- **350 Requested file action pending further information**
- 421 Service not available, closing control connection

  This may be a reply to any command if the service knows it must shut down.

- 500 Syntax error, command unrecognized

  This may include errors such as command line too long.

- 501 Syntax error in parameters or arguments
- 502 Command not implemented
- 530 Not logged in

FTP Commands (RETR)

Command: RETR (Retrieve)

Description: This command causes the server to transfer a copy of the file, specified in the pathname, to the client. The status and contents of the file at the server site are unaffected.

Usage: RETR <FileName> <CRLF>

Parameters: FileName is a fully qualified path and filename at the server site.

Example:

```
SendData dsSocket1, "RETR /pub/cgvb/misc/somefile.zip" & vbCrlf
```

Return Values (bold indicates success):

- 110 Restart marker reply

  In this case, the text is exact and not left to the particular implementation; it must read:

  MARK yyyy = mmmm

  where yyyy is User-process data stream marker, and mmmm server's equivalent marker (note the spaces between markers and "=").

- 125 Data connection already open; transfer starting
- 150 File status okay; about to open data connection
- **226 Closing data connection; the requested file action was successful**
- **250 Requested file action okay, completed**
- 421 Service not available, closing control connection

  This may be a reply to any command if the service knows it must shut down.

- 425 Can't open data connection
- 426 Connection closed; transfer aborted
- 450 Requested file action not taken; file unavailable (e.g., file busy)
- 451 Requested action aborted: local error in processing
- 500 Syntax error, command unrecognized

  This may include errors such as command line too long.

- 501 Syntax error in parameters or arguments

- 504 Command not implemented for that parameter
- 530 Not logged in
- 550 Requested action not taken; file unavailable (e.g., file not found, no access)

FTP Commands (RMD)

Command: RMD (Remove Directory)

Description: Causes the directory specified in the pathname to be removed as a directory (if the pathname is absolute) or as a subdirectory of the current working directory (if the pathname is relative).

Usage: RMD <Path> <CRLF>

Parameters: Path is a fully qualified path on the server side.

Example:

```
SendData dsSocket1, "RETR /users/johnsmith" & vbCrlf
```

Return Values (bold indicates success):

- **250 Requested file action okay, completed**
- 421 Service not available, closing control connection

  This may be a reply to any command if the service knows it must shut down.

- 500 Syntax error, command unrecognized

  This may include errors such as command line too long.

- 501 Syntax error in parameters or arguments
- 502 Command not implemented
- 530 Not logged in
- 550 Requested action not taken; file unavailable (e.g., file not found, no access)

FTP Commands (RNFR)

Command: RNFR (Rename From)

Description: The first half of the file renaming process. Specifies the old path and filename name of the file being renamed.

Usage: RNFR <FileName> <CRLF>

Parameters: FileName is a fully qualified path and filename at the server site.

Example:

```
SendData dsSocket1, "RNFR source.zip" & vbCrlf
```

RNFR must be immediately followed by a "rename to" command (RNTO) specifying the new path and filename.

Return Values (bold indicates success):

- No response indicates success
- **350 Requested file action pending further information**
- 421 Service not available, closing control connection

  This may be a reply to any command if the service knows it must shut down.
- 450 Requested file action not taken; file unavailable (e.g., file busy)
- 500 Syntax error, command unrecognized

  This may include errors such as command line too long.
- 501 Syntax error in parameters or arguments
- 502 Command not implemented
- 530 Not logged in
- 550 Requested action not taken; file unavailable (e.g., file not found, no access)

FTP Commands (RNTO)

Command: RNTO (Rename To)

Description: The second half of the file renaming process. Specifies the new path and filename of the file being renamed.

Usage: RNTO <FileName> <CRLF>

Parameters: FileName is a valid filename at the server site.

Example:

```
SendData dsSocket1, "RNTO destination.zip" & vbCrlf
```

Comments: RNTO must be preceded by a "rename from" command (RNFR). Together RNFR and RTNO rename a file on the server.

Return Values (bold indicates success):

- **250 Requested file action okay, completed**
- 421 Service not available, closing control connection

  This may be a reply to any command if the service knows it must shut down.
- 500 Syntax error, command unrecognized

  This may include errors such as command line too long.
- 501 Syntax error in parameters or arguments
- 502 Command not implemented
- 503 Bad sequence of commands
- 530 Not logged in
- 532 Need account for storing files
- 553 Requested action not taken; file name not allowed

FTP Commands (SITE)

Command: SITE (Site parameters)

Description: SITE is used by the server to provide services specific to the system that are essential to file transfer but not sufficiently universal to be included as commands in the protocol. The nature of these services and the specification of their syntax can be stated in a reply to the HELP SITE command.

Usage: SITE <String> <CRLF>

Parameters: String is any string argument.

Example:

```
SendData dsSocket1, "SITE chmod 646 myfile.zip" & vbCrlf
```

Comments: You could use SITE, for example, to change permission attributes of a file using the following syntax:

```
SITE CHMOD<Attribute><Filename>
```

Return Values (bold indicates success):

- **200 Command okay**

- 202 Command not implemented, superfluous at this site
- 500 Syntax error, command unrecognized

  This may include errors such as command line too long.
- 501 Syntax error in parameters or arguments
- 530 Not logged in

FTP Commands (SMNT)

Command: SMNT (Structure Mount)

Description: Allows the user to mount another file system data structure without altering login, accounting information, or transfer parameters.

Usage: SMNT <Path> <CRLF>

Parameters: Path is the path of another file data system.

Example:

```
SendData dsSocket1, "SMNT /users/johnsmith" & vbCrlf
```

Return Values (bold indicates success):

- 202 Command not implemented, superfluous at this site
- **250 Requested file action okay, completed**
- 421 Service not available, closing control connection

  This may be a reply to any command if the service knows it must shut down.
- 500 Syntax error, command unrecognized

  This may include errors such as command line too long.
- 501 Syntax error in parameters or arguments
- 502 Command not implemented
- 530 Not logged in
- 550 Requested action not taken; file unavailable (e.g., file not found, no access)

FTP Commands (STAT)

Command: STAT (Status)

Description: Causes a status response to be sent over the control connection in the form of a reply.

Usage: STAT [<PathName>] <CRLF>

Parameters: PathName is a valid path on the server.

Example:

```
SendData dsSocket1, "STAT /users/johnsmith/myfile" & vbCrlf
```

Comments: STAT may be sent during a file transfer (along with the Telnet IP and Synch signals—see the RFC 959 Section on FTP Commands) in which case the server will respond with the status of the operation in progress, or it may be sent between file transfers. In the latter case, the command may have an argument field. If a full pathname is specified, STAT is analogous to the LIST command except that data shall be transferred over the control connection. If a partial pathname is given, the server may respond with a list of file names or attributes associated with that specification. If no argument is given, the server should return general status information about the server FTP process. This should include current values of all transfer parameters and the status of connections.

Return Values (bold indicates success):

- **211 System status, or system help reply**
- **212 Directory status**
- **213 File status**
- 421 Service not available, closing control connection

  This may be a reply to any command if the service knows it must shut down.

- 450 Requested file action not taken; file unavailable (e.g., file busy)
- 500 Syntax error, command unrecognized

  This may include errors such as command line too long.

- 501 Syntax error in parameters or arguments
- 502 Command not implemented
- 530 Not Logged In

FTP Commands (STOR)

Command: STOR (Store)

Description: Prepares the server to receive a file via the data connection.

Usage: STOR <FileName> <CRLF>

Parameters: FileName is a fully qualified path and filename at the server site.

Example:

```
SendData dsSocket1, "STOR newfile.zip" & vbCrlf
```

Comments: The Store command causes the server to accept the data transferred via the data connection and to store the data as a file at the server site. If the file specified in the pathname exists at the server site, then its contents shall be replaced by the data being transferred. A new file is created at the server site if the file specified in the pathname does not already exist.

Return Values (bold indicates success):

- 110 Restart marker reply

  In this case, the text is exact and not left to the particular implementation; it must read:

  MARK yyyy = mmmm

  where yyyy is User-process data stream marker, and mmmm server's equivalent marker (note the spaces between markers and "=").

- 125 Data connection already open; transfer starting

- 150 File status okay; about to open data connection

- **226 Closing data connection; the requested file action was successful**

- **250 Requested file action okay, completed**

- 421 Service not available, closing control connection

  This may be a reply to any command if the service knows it must shut down.

- 425 Can't open data connection

- 426 Connection closed; transfer aborted

- 450 Requested file action not taken; file unavailable (e.g., file busy)

- 451 Requested action aborted; local error in processing
- 452 Requested action not taken; insufficient storage space in system
- 500 Syntax error, command unrecognized

  This may include errors such as command line too long.
- 501 Syntax error in parameters or arguments
- 504 Command not implemented for that parameter
- 530 Not logged in
- 532 Need account for storing files
- 550 Requested action not taken; file unavailable (e.g., file not found, no access)
- 551 Requested action aborted: page type unknown
- 552 Requested file action aborted

  Exceeded storage allocation (for current directory or dataset).
- 553 Requested action not taken; filename not allowed

FTP Commands (STOU)

Command: STOU (Store Unique)

Description: Prepares the server to receive a file and instructs the server to save the file with a unique name in the target directory.

Usage: STOU <CRLF>

Parameters: None.

Example:

```
SendData dsSocket1, "STOU " & vbCrlf
```

Comments: The Store Unique command works exactly like STOR except that the resultant file is to be created in the current directory under a name unique to that directory. The 250 Transfer Started response must include the name generated.

Return Values (bold indicates success):

- 110 Restart marker reply

  In this case, the text is exact and not left to the particular implementation; it must read:

MARK yyyy = mmmm

where yyyy is User-process data stream marker, and mmmm server's equivalent marker (note the spaces between markers and "=").

- 125 Data connection already open; transfer starting
- 150 File status okay; about to open data connection
- 226 Closing data connection; the requested file action was successful
- 250 Requested file action okay, completed (unique filename included on this line)
- 421 Service not available, closing control connection

   This may be a reply to any command if the service knows it must shut down.

- 425 Can't open data connection
- 426 Connection closed; transfer aborted
- 450 Requested file action not taken; file unavailable (e.g., file busy)
- 451 Requested action aborted; local error in processing
- 452 Requested action not taken; insufficient storage space in system
- 500 Syntax error, command unrecognized

   This may include errors such as command line too long.

- 501 Syntax error in parameters or arguments
- 504 Command not implemented for that parameter
- 530 Not logged in
- 532 Need account for storing files
- 550 Requested action not taken; file unavailable (e.g., file not found, no access)
- 551 Requested action aborted; page type unknown
- 552 Requested file action aborted; exceeded storage allocation (for current directory or dataset)
- 553 Requested action not taken; filename not allowed

FTP Commands (STRU)

Command: STRU (File Structure)

Description: Specifies the structure type of transmitted data.

Usage: STRU <StructureType> <CRLF>

Parameters: StructureType is one of the following ASCII characters:
F—File structure (default)
R—Record structure
P—Page structure
See RFC 959 for information on using nonfile structures.

Example:

```
SendData dsSocket1, "STRU R" & vbCrlf
```

Return Values (bold indicates success):

- **200 Command okay**
- 421 Service not available, closing control connection

  This may be a reply to any command if the service knows it must shut down.

- 500 Syntax error, command unrecognized

  This may include errors such as command line too long.

- 501 Syntax error in parameters or arguments
- 504 Command not implemented for that parameter
- 530 Not logged in

FTP Commands (SYST)

Command: SYST (System)

Description: SYST is used to find out the type of operating system at the server.

Usage: SYST <CRLF>

Parameters: None.

Example:

```
SendData dsSocket1, "SYST" & vbCrlf
```

Comments: Supposedly, the reply has as its first word one of the system names listed in the current version of the Assigned Numbers document [4]. However, I don't see this as being something you can count on. New systems are popping up all the time. The public documentation may or may not keep up with it.

Return Values (bold indicates success):

- **215 NAME system type**

  NAME is an official system name from the list in the Assigned Numbers document.

- 421 Service not available, closing control connection

  This may be a reply to any command if the service knows it must shut down.

- 500 Syntax error, command unrecognized

  This may include errors such as command line too long.

- 501 Syntax error in parameters or arguments

- 502 Command not implemented

FTP Commands (TYPE)

Command: TYPE (Representation Type)

Description: Determines how data will be transmitted.

Usage: TYPE <DataType Code> <CRLF>

Parameters: DataType Code is an ASCII character (or characters) that identifies a data representation type.

Example:

```
' -- Set binary mode
SendData dsSocket1, "TYPE I" & vbCrlf
```

Comments: Typically you will use the TYPE command to toggle ASCII or binary mode (Image). Use the image type when sending and receiving files of any kind. Use the ASCII type only when transmitting text.

Several types take a second parameter. The first parameter is denoted by a single ASCII character, as is the second Format parameter for ASCII and EBCDIC; the second parameter for local byte is a decimal integer to indicate Byte size. The parameters are separated by a <SP> (Space, ASCII code 32).

The following codes are assigned for type:

A—ASCII *

E—EBCDIC *

I—Image (use this for binary file transfers)

L <byte size>—Local byte Byte size

----

*—A and E types take any one of these three second Parameters:

N—Nonprint

T—Telnet format effectors

C—Carriage Control (ASA)

The default representation type is ASCII Nonprint. If the Format parameter is changed, and later just the first argument is changed, Format then returns to the Nonprint default.

Return Values (bold indicates success):

- **200 Command okay**
- 421 Service not available, closing control connection

  This may be a reply to any command if the service knows it must shut down.
- 500 Syntax error, command unrecognized

  This may include errors such as command line too long.
- 501 Syntax error in parameters or arguments
- 504 Command not implemented for that parameter
- 530 Not logged in

FTP Commands (USER)

Command: USER (User Name)

Description: Specifies the user's name on the remote system. Use with the PASS command to log in.

Usage: USER <UserName> <CRLF>

Parameters: UserName is the name of the registered user on the FTP system.

Example:

```
SendData dsSocket1, "USER johns" & vbCrlf
```

Comments: The USER command is sent immediately after connecting to an FTP server on port 21 after receiving a line that starts with the code 220, indicating that the server is ready for you to send it USER and PASS commands to log into the FTP server.

The PASS command should immediately follow the USER command.

If you have an account on the FTP server, you can specify your username and password. If you would like to log in anonymously, specify "anonymous" for the username and your e-mail address for the password.

You can send the USER and PASS commands at any time during the session to change control to a new user.

Return Values (bold indicates success):

- **230 User logged in**
- **331 Username okay, need password**
- 332 Need account for login
- 421 Service not available, closing control connection

  This may be a reply to any command if the service knows it must shut down.

- 500 Syntax error, command unrecognized

  This may include errors such as command line too long.

- 501 Syntax error in parameters or arguments
- 530 Not logged in

WHAT'S ON THE CD-ROM?

Sample Code

The sample code is installed in the default directory under the \Sample Code folder. All code will run in both Visual Basic 5.0 and 6.0, with the exception of the WebClasses folder, which contains a WebClass. WebClasses are only supported in Visual Basic 6.0.

If you have issues around the sample code, please check the web site (carl.franklins.net/vbip) before you send me email. You may find the answer there.

Dolphin Systems' dsSocket TCP/IP Control

This book includes the demo version 1.90 of Dolphin Systems' dsSocket control for Winsock communications. Although all of the sample code is written with dsSocket, the cfInternet objects (which provide complete functionality of FTP, SMTP, POP3, and NNTP) can use either dsSocket or the Microsoft Winsock control. See Chapter 9 for details.

Internet Protocol Documentation (RFC Database)

Just like in the VB 4.0 version of this book, I have included all the RFC (Request For Comments) documents up to January 24, 1999. The RFC documents are the blueprints of Internet Protocols. They describe how different protocols and utilities work. You can use these as a reference when programming code for any of the protocols on the Internet. For example, if you want to write a custom control for Internet Relay

Chat you can look up the RFC document that describes how IRC works, and formulate your code from the protocol laid out in the document.

The RFCFind program is installed in the default directory. It lets you search through all the RFC documents, which are stored in an MDB file (Microsoft Access).

Music

I had lots of fun with the last book. I put three songs on it that I had recorded and performed. In the same spirit I offer "Bye Bye Blackbird," my arrangement of the famous Henderson and Dixon standard. This was a 3:00 A.M. inspiration that I recorded in my home studio. It has only three instruments: bass guitar, rhythm guitar, and lead guitar. But, it really came out quite good. Enjoy!

INDEX

Type declarations, 202–204
TYPE FTP command, 407–408
Type Library, dsSocket, 16, 18
types, DSSOCK.BAS, 18

U

UDP (User Datagram Protocol),
    13–14, 48–50
UIDL POP3 command, 377
Universal Resource Locator. *See* URL
    addresses
Universal Time, accessing, 53–54
Unix-to-Unix Copy Protocol, 63
UNIX TRN newsreaders, 357
Unix wildcards, 166–168
UNLINK HTTP method, 178
update POP3 state, 117, 119
uploading
  data
      ASP form responses,
          265–266
      with cfSockClient, 293–299
      with dsSocket, 32–33
      to HTML forms, 188,
          245–246
  files
      with cfSockClient, 305–308
      FTP, 145, 155, 168–170, 230
URL addresses, 176–177
Usenet news
  articles
      archiving, 92
      information on, 83, 338–339,
          354–355
      listing, 76, 77, 219–220
      message numbers, 65, 89
      MessageIDs, 65, 221
      posting, 76, 78, 84–87, 221–222,
          350–351
      replying to, 86–87
      retrieving, 82–83, 218–221,
          349–350

selecting, 339–340
      text format of, 71–72
      viewing, 77, 78
      WILDMAT searches of, 68–69,
          88
      XPAT searches of, 90–91
  headers, article, 72, 79–82, 90–91,
      352–353, 356–357
  newsgroups, 63
      descriptions of, 88–89, 344–345,
          351–352
      listing, 87–88, 219, 340–347
      masking, 218
      retrieving, 348–349
      selecting, 66, 69, 218–219,
          337–338
  newsreaders, 76–98, 357
  overview of, 63–64
  programming techniques,
      73–76
  See also NNTP protocol
USER command
  FTP protocol, 408–409
  POP3 command, 115, 118, 124,
      377–378
User Datagram Protocol (UDP),
    48–50
usernames
  e-mail, 115, 118, 124, 377–378
  FTP protocol, 142, 380–381,
      408–409
UU encoding/decoding, 129–133
  sending files by SMTP, 134–136
  UUDecode routine, 134
  UUEncode routine, 133
UUCode.bas, 129, 133–134
UUCP, 63

V

versions, NNTP, 65–66
viewing Usenet articles, 77, 78
Visual Basic

wildcards, search
  Unix, 166–168
  WILDMAT, 68–69, 88
WILDMAT NNTP commands, 68–69, 88
Windows API, 201
Windows NT Server, 190. *See also* Internet Information Server (IIS)
Windows NT Workstation, 249, 267
Winsock API, 16
Winsock programming
  cfWinsock objects, 211–216
    cfWinsockDS, 211–215
    cfWinsockMS, 211, 214–215
    Control property of, 215–216
  dsSocket
    cfWinsockDS object, 211–215
    creating new objects in, 211–212
    data, receiving, 33–43
    data, sending, 32–33
    DSSOCK.BAS module, 18
    installation and loading, 16
    IsDotAddress function, 18
    multiple server connections, 28–31
    ParseString function, 19, 76
    shareware vs. registered, 15
    socket connection example, 20–27
    socket disconnection example, 27–28
    SocketConnect function, 18
    UDP support by, 48–50
    error handling, 32–33, 43–45
      command line options, 46
      Debug.Print error trapping, 47
      error codes, 44–45
      error logs, 47–48
      user notification of, 46–47
    Terminal program, 50–52
    usefulness of, 3–4
    WINSOCK.VBP project, 20
    See also specific protocols
WithEvents keyword, 212, 217–218, 316
World Wide Web
  HTML and, 174
  HTTP protocol for, 173–174
  as Internet access option, 1–2, 173
  URL addresses for, 176–177
  See also HTTP protocol; Internet; Web pages
WorldTRAIN Website, 275
WriteLogFile function, 155–157

X

XGTITLE NNTP command, 88, 351–352
XHDR NNTP command, 90, 352–353
XINDEX NNTP command, 353–354
XOVER NNTP command, 83, 354–355
XPAT NNTP command, 90–91, 356–357
XTHREAD NNTP command, 357

To use this CD-ROM, your system must meet the following requirements:

Platform/Processor/Operating System. IBM or compatible machine running Windows 95/NT. Visual Basic 6 must be running on your machine to take advantage of the sample code included.

Hard Drive Space. The sample code and other tools will take up 92 MB hard drive space

Peripherals. CD-ROM drive